DATE DUE

DEMCO 38-296

Since the beginning of the eighteenth century the philosophy of art has been engaged in the project of finding out what the fine arts might have in common, and thus how they might be defined. Peter Kivy's purpose in this very accessible and lucid book is to trace the history of that enterprise and then to argue that the definitional project has been unsuccessful, with absolute music as the continual stumbling block. He offers what he believes is a fruitful change of strategy: instead of undertaking an obsessive quest for sameness, let us explore the differences among the arts. He presents five case studies of such differences, three from literature, two from music.

With its combination of historical and analytic approaches this book will appeal to a wide range of readers in philosophy, literary studies, and music, as well as to nonacademic readers with an interest in the arts. Its vivid style requires no technical knowledge of music on the part of the reader.

Philosophies of Arts

Philosophies of Arts
An Essay in Differences

PETER KIVY

CAMBRIDGE
UNIVERSITY PRESS

≡ OF THE UNIVERSITY OF CAMBRIDGE
, Cambridge CB2 1RP, United Kingdom

NIVERSITY PRESS
The Edinburgh Building, Cambridge CB2 2RU, United Kingdom
40 West 20th Street, New York, NY 10011-4211, USA
10 Stamford Road, Oakleigh, Melbourne 3166, Australia

© Peter Kivy 1997

First published 1997

Printed in the United States of America

Typeset in Palatino

Library of Congress Cataloging-in-Publication Data
Kivy, Peter.
Philosophies of arts : an essay in differences / Peter Kivy.
p. cm.
Includes bibliographical references.
ISBN 0-521-59178-3 (hardback). – ISBN 0-521-59829-X (paperback)
1. Arts – Philosophy.   2. Aesthetics, Modern.   3. Arts – Philosophy –
History.   I. Title.
BH39.K575   1997
700'.1 – dc21   96-37698
                                                                  CIP

*A catalog record for this book is available from
the British Library.*

ISBN 0-521-59178-3 hardback
ISBN 0-521-59829-X paperback

For Frank Sibley,
who showed me the way

Now from hence may be seen, how these Arts *agree*, and how they *differ*.

James Harris (1744)

Contents

Preface

In the fall of 1992 I was privileged to deliver the Presidential Address to the American Society for Aesthetics on the occasion of its fiftieth anniversary. The event called, I thought, for some stock taking and perhaps something in the way of a suggestion, at least, of one direction the philosophy of art might take in the coming years. For I thought we were at a point where an alternative to the single-minded pursuit of art's "definition" was open, and beckoning.

I saw my task in that lecture as twofold: to try to show how we had come to the place we were at in Anglo-American aesthetics, which might well be called the period of Danto, without exaggerating that philosopher's importance to the discipline; and to try to mark out, by precept and example, another direction that some of us, at least, might take: the direction of "differences."

In the speaker's allotted fifty-minute hour I could present only a historical sketch and two minute "case studies" in "differences." But the project continued to possess me. The result is the present monograph: an attempt to trace in more detail the theoretical pathway that has led from the origination of the task of defining the work of art, in the eighteenth century, to the present state of affairs in which that task still seems to dominate discussion and, so it seems to me, to discourage philosophers from the equally interesting task of studying the arts in their particularity.

The organization of the volume is fairly straightforward. In the first two chapters I give an account of how I see the history of aesthetic theory from Hutcheson to Danto, in its attempt to

ix

define the "modern system of the arts," with absolute music as the litmus test of success or failure. Chapters 3 through 7 provide case studies in literature and music as an antidote to the obsessive search for what is common to the arts: they provide, that is, "differences," the "philosophies of arts," as opposed to the philosophy of art, that my title is supposed to suggest.

In no way am I urging, on philosophical grounds or any other, that the traditional task of defining the work of art is either impossible or exhausted as a philosophical enterprise. Nor am I recommending that it be given up for any other reason. What I am recommending, or gently suggesting, perhaps, is that at least some of us give it a rest and try to study the arts, *as philosophers*, in their differences rather than in their sameness: that alongside the philosophy of art we have philosophies of arts. Many of my colleagues in the profession may not be by nature or learning so inclined. Those who are I hope will join me in a task that is not so much new as new to these times. It is a task that deserves to be revived to the enrichment and diversification of the discipline.

I am indebted to a number of people who were immeasurably helpful to me in producing the final manuscript of this book. Stephen Davies and Richard Eldridge read the entire manuscript, and provided valuable and searching criticism. Professor Eldridge motivated me to include a whole new chapter on truth in fiction, which I had been working on as a lecture and an article. And I also tried to respond to his worries over my avoiding any discussion of the value component in the concept of poetry. I tried to answer a number of objections Professor Davies made with regard to my treatment of Jerrold Levinson on musical profundity, the theory of musical value sketched in the final chapter, and various other points.

But some of Eldridge's and Davies' comments and criticism I had to let alone, not because they were off the mark, but, to the contrary, because they raised such broad issues that they could not be treated in short responses. Rather, such issues will have to be addressed at length as the discussion develops (or I hope develops) after the publication of my book. In any event,

Messrs. Davies and Eldridge are responsible for numerous improvements in my text and, of course, for none of its remaining faults.

My colleague and friend Laurent Stern was kind enough to accede to my request to read, on very short notice, the new chapter (Chapter 5) on truth in fiction. I am most grateful for his help in that regard and absolve him from complicity in its remaining weaknesses.

I would also like to thank Terrence Moore of Cambridge University Press, who has, for the past few years, been a constant source of encouragement to me in my work. He has eased my manuscript through the intricate maze that leads from a gleam in the author's eye to a real book one can hold in one's hand. I greatly appreciate his help and support.

This book is dedicated to the late Frank Sibley. Alas, he died before he could know that I had done so. It is a pitifully inadequate tribute in comparison with the contribution he made to the profession, and to my work.

Chapter 1

How We Got Here, and Why

§1 The most widely and persistently pursued problem in aesthetics, or the philosophy of art, is the problem of stating what it is to be a "work of art," what it is to be "art." It is sometimes called the problem of *defining* "art."

This problem was bequeathed to philosophy by eighteenth-century philosophers and critical theorists. It is the result of certain crucial changes in our attitude toward what we now call "the fine arts" that occurred in the age of the Enlightenment. These changes are dealt with and explained in what might be called the "standard account" of the matter. It is an account generally accepted by philosophers of art and intellectual historians, including myself. I have not come to quarrel with the standard account. But I do have a quarrel with the major outcome of things, as the standard account understands them. I have a quarrel with the task that was bequeathed us, of stating what it is to be "art." But before I can quarrel I must first present the standard account – at least my version of it.

§2 Certain things transpired in the eighteenth century to alter, in very important ways, how we think about and experience works of the fine arts, some of them philosophical or in some other way theoretical, others "institutional" (for want of a better word). There is no particular order in which they ought to be listed, for they are not a chronological series of causes and effects. Rather, they must be thought of as an interrelated, reciprocal system of causes and effects, all operating simultaneously. The following are the philosophical, theoretical, and institutional

1

"happenings" I have in mind, listed in an almost completely arbitrary order:

1. The coming into being of the branch of philosophy known as "aesthetics"
2. The forming of what Paul O. Kristeller has denominated "the modern system of the arts"[1]
3. The evolution, in various forms, of what has come to be called, after Kant, the "aesthetic attitude," or the "attitude of aesthetic disinterestedness"[2]
4. The establishment of the fine arts museum, the concert hall, and the institution of the public concert
5. The rise of instrumental music into an equality with vocal music, both as an occupation for composers and as a focal point for audience interest

§3   When I took my first courses in philosophy, I was told in more than one of them that there were five branches of the discipline: logic, metaphysics, epistemology, ethics, and aesthetics. The division seemed to me etched in marble. But as most philosophers, and all philosophers of art, know, such a division of labor would have been unthinkable before the middle journey of the eighteenth century. In particular, there was nothing that was, or that could have been called, the autonomous philosophical discipline of aesthetics (or philosophy of art).

This is not to say, of course, that what we call the philosophy of art, or aesthetics, was not practiced until 1746. As is well known, Plato and Aristotle spoke eloquently, and with a philosophical voice, of poetry and painting and something we translate as "music." They raised clearly philosophical questions about these activities and obviously thought they were in some sense related to one another.

But even so cautious a statement about what Plato and Aristotle were doing as this one must be tempered with more than a grain of salt. For Plato, it is clear from the *Ion*, thought that poetry was radically different from both painting and sculpture, in an absolutely crucial way, since the whole point of the dialogue between Socrates and the rhapsode is that epic and lyric poetry, like divination, come from the god, not from "art," and two of the "arts" that can be mastered, and hence do not come from the god, are painting and sculpture, along with such other "arts" as generalship, navigation, and driving a chariot. Thus "there is an art of painting as a whole," but "all the good epic poets utter all those fine poems not from art but as inspired and possessed, and the good lyric poets likewise. . . ."[3] So even in acknowledging that Plato discussed some of the things philo-sophically that we call the fine arts, it is a mistake to think he was engaging in *the* philosophy of art as we think of it. He simply did not have the subject matter, namely our "modern system of the arts," to mark out the discipline and, indeed, did not even apparently think of our "arts" of poetry, painting, and sculpture as the same in all crucial respects, witness the sepa-ration of the former from the two latter vis-à-vis the sources of creation.

The same caution must be exercised in our reading of what Plato and Aristotle said about "music," since it is unclear what they were really talking about – certainly not "absolute music" in the nineteenth-century sense. And, indeed, the same caution must be expressed in regard to what philosophers (or any one else) said about music in the High Renaissance, where we do know what the music sounded like. For it was the "science" rather than (in our sense) the "art" of music that was the sub-ject.[4]

Again, it would be a mistake to think that philosophical ques-tions concerning the arts were not discussed in the Middle Ages and Renaissance. It is clear that Medieval "aesthetics" was not solely expressed in theological terms, as is sometimes thought, but "naturalistically" as well;[5] and although the Renaissance did not yet possess either the modern system or the discipline of "aesthetics" to go with it, it was the cauldron in which they both were brewing.[6] In both periods people were philosophizing about beauty and the "arts."

Without the modern system there could not be *the* philosophy of art – only philosophizing about things that were later to be seen as of a piece. Before they were seen as of a piece, however, there was nothing for *the* philosophy of art to be about, that is to say, *the* philosophy of all of *the* arts.

I am not, of course, saying that the arts of music, painting, literature, and the rest did not exist before the eighteenth century. What did not exist was the belief that they formed a separate class: that they belonged with each other. And it was that belief that made the discipline of aesthetics possible: that gave it its subject matter, *the* arts, all of them, and the task of saying why they were *they*.

§4 The evolution of what Kristeller called "the Modern System of the Arts" was "officially" completed just before midcentury. In Kristeller's words, "The decisive step towards a system of the fine arts was taken by the Abbé Batteux in his famous and influential treatise, *Les beaux arts réduit à un même principe* (1746)."[7] In Batteux's work, the system is fully in place and named: *les beaux arts*. Equally significant, Batteux gives, in his title, not only the system and its name but the philosophical project they imply: finding the *même principe*. The quest for the real definition of the fine arts was now in full swing and, except for a brief and by no means universally observed Wittgensteinian interlude, continues to the present moment.

Indeed, although Batteux dots the "i," a number of earlier writers were already engaged in the modern philosophical discipline of aesthetics. In England, Joseph Addison's "Pleasures of the Imagination" (1712) and Francis Hutcheson's *Inquiry Concerning Beauty, Order, Harmony, Design* (1725); in France, the Abbé DuBos's *Réflexions critiques sur la pöesie et sur la peinture* (1719); in Germany, Alexander Baumgarten's *Meditationes philosophicae de nonnullis ad poema partinentibus* (1735) – all can be seen as pioneering treatises in the new "science" of aesthetics: the first full-length works devoted solely to the subject, with Baumgarten giving us the name in something like its modern sense.

Thus by midcentury the discipline of aesthetics was a going concern, with its primary goal of a "definition" of the fine arts already set and, for most, seen as *achieved*, in the Platonic and Aristotelian theory of mimesis: the *même principe* of Batteux and various others.

4

That representation was the principle on which the first modern definitions of art were based is not surprising. It was a principle venerable with age and with the authority of classical antiquity – in particular, Plato and Aristotle. And the art world had no apparent counterexamples, except for pure instrumental music, which was at midcentury still a minor art, if an art at all, in the eyes of philosophers, literary theorists, and the general public.

Thus the confluence of the modern system of the arts and the autonomous discipline of aesthetics as a recognized department of philosophy laid upon philosophers the task of giving a real definition of art and produced the first modern examples of such a definition in a plethora of mimetic accounts.

Given the classical texts and the apparent nature of the case, it did not seem difficult to encompass all of the literary and dramatic arts as well as all of the visual arts under the umbrella of mimesis or representation. Of what Kristeller characterizes as "all the five major arts of painting, sculpture, architecture, music and poetry,"[8] only music and architecture would have been problematic. Architecture is, of course, a very special case, being both a fine and a useful art. But certainly there were attempts to make it out to be representational, at least in two ways: first, in the rather straightforward claim that its gross, manifest features were indeed representational, columns as trees and that sort of thing; second, in the far more sophisticated Pythagorean claim of Renaissance theorists that architectural proportions represent harmonic proportions of the universe, as was also claimed for the proportions of the division of the musical octave.[9] In any case, it is my impression that architecture was not at the center of the enterprise, and I will have nothing more to say about it.[10] It is the other problematic, music, that, I think, plays the pivotal role, and I will have a good deal to say about that.

§5 Why music? Noel Carroll has argued that what has motivated and driven new "definitions" of art in the twentieth century has been "the theoretical task of coming to terms with virtually continuous revolutions in artistic practice...." The "task has been to provide the theoretical means for establishing that the mutations issued from avant-garde practice belong to the family of art." In other words, "one might say that a great deal of modern philosophy of art is an attempt to come to a philosophical understanding of the productions of the avant-garde."[11]

That the twentieth century has, as Carroll puts it, produced "virtually continuous revolutions in artistic practice" makes the motivating force of the avant-garde on the task of defining the work of art palpably obvious during the period. But if Carroll is right, it suggests that we might look more closely at the eighteenth-century attempts to define the fine arts – the first such attempts in the modern era – to see if perhaps the same is true there.

Given that artistic revolutions can be slow as well as rapid, it does not seem inappropriate to interpret the rise of absolute music in the second half of the eighteenth century as an artistic revolution of impressive magnitude and, further, to see the new instrumental idiom as *the* avant-garde art of the age of Enlightenment. I have argued elsewhere that the obvious, prima facie difficulties in construing absolute music as a representational art made it the crucial case for any attempt to understand the nature of the fine arts in terms of mimesis, which was, at the time, the only game in town.[12] The *même principe* was representation of nature; and if absolute music could not be perceived as that, either the project must fail or absolute music, which was rapidly becoming at least the equal of vocal music in the eyes of composers, would have to be read out of the "modern system of the arts."

We can now see more clearly, with the help of Carroll's observations concerning the prominent role of the avant-garde in motivating definitions of art, why absolute music was a crux for the Enlightenment theorists. It is not as if pure instrumental music had been invented in eighteenth-century Mannheim and Vienna. Music for instruments alone had been performed at least since the Middle Ages. The point is that during a certain period in the history of art music, namely, the second half of the eighteenth century and the first years of the nineteenth, the writing of music for instruments alone rapidly moved from sideshow to center ring, from the relatively peripheral interest of the composer to at least equality with vocal music. Before this time the composer made his living in the service of the church, patron, and opera house. And the overwhelming majority of his works, even in the case of as devoted a composer of absolute music as Bach, were vocal. But in the period from the time of Bach's death to the flowering of Haydn, Mozart, and the early Beethoven, the tide was reversed, to the point that for Haydn the opposite was the case (although Haydn valued his vocal works above his instrumental ones). It is for musicologists to suggest which sociological and economic influences came to bear on this trend. It is for us to scrutinize its effect on the philosophical task of defining the fine arts.

Because there has always been instrumental music in the West, there has always been a potential threat to a mimetic theory of the arts that included music *tout court* in the system. But during the early period of theorizing, from DuBos (say) to Batteux, the relative unimportance of instrumental music made it impotent as a challenge to the representational theory of art. It could simply be ignored as a peripheral case, indeed ignored without mention or explanation.

What could not be ignored was vocal music, which is probably what most philosophers in the period meant by "music" anyway. But vocal music did not present the difficulties to theory that instrumental music was to do when it emerged fully fledged. Indeed, the groundwork for the acceptance of vocal music into the modern system had already been laid by the end of the sixteenth century.[13] How so?

The story is something like this. Vocal polyphony before the Council of Trent (pre-Tridentine polyphony) had evolved into an extremely complex musical fabric that might well be described as a "setting" for the text very much in the jeweler's sense of the word. The text, like a jewel, was placed in a structure so elaborate and alluring in its own right as to overpower it aesthetically: a great compliment to the text, indeed, to consider it a gem worthy of such a luxuriant setting but not a compliment to its *meaning*, which, as the clerics complained, was rendered completely unintelligible by the music. As is

7

well known, the abolition of polyphony was actually considered as a way of foregrounding the text. Polyphony prevailed, although in a different form. One might say that in the works of Palestrina it was curtailed. However, that is a needlessly negative and largely uninformative way of putting it. What really happened was that one aesthetic of text setting began giving way to another: the "jeweler's" way to the way of representation. For what, I suggest, Palestrina was attempting to do in his "curtailed" counterpoint was to represent in music human linguistic expression, on the hypothesis that since human linguistic expression can make a text intelligible, so too can the musical "representation" of it. Whether or not this is the way Palestrina and his contemporaries put it to themselves, it is a viable and rewarding way to read his (and their) works.

In any event, the representational aesthetic of text setting soon emerged in a quite explicit and theory-driven form, in the invention of the *stile rappresentativo* and in the opera, both heralded by theories and admonitions to the effect that the musical representation of passionate human speech is or ought to be at least one of the composer's major goals. Pietro de' Bardi described this new aesthetic of composition as "imitating familiar speech by using few sounds. . . ."[14] While Giulio Caccini, one of the first composers of *stile rappresentativo* and opera, said that ". . . I have endeavored in those my late compositions to bring in a kind of music by which men might, as it were, talk in harmony. . . ."[15] If Palestrina had this cat in the bag, it certainly was out now.

Thus more than one hundred years before Batteux et al. enunciated the "modern system" and brought it under the *même principe,* the groundwork for vocal music's induction into the fine arts club had already been laid. By the end of the sixteenth century, vocal music was consciously and explicitly, as well as intuitively and implicitly, being practiced as a representational project: the representation, broadly speaking, of human expression. It was ripe for the plucking, and at least as early as DuBos it was plucked.

We now understand something about the role of music in the

formation of the modern system and the mimetic theory that tied its members together in the first half of the eighteenth century. Neither vocal nor instrumental music posed a problem: the former because it was easily seen, and had been since the end of the sixteenth century, as representational of human expression; the latter because, compared with vocal music, it was simply inconsequential, at the center of neither the composer's nor his audience's concerns. Indeed, one gets the idea that in educated circles a "gentleman" who played a musical instrument was, far from being admired for it, considered something of an eccentric. It was his "hobby horse" or his addiction. Thus instrumental music was not one of the "liberal arts," but a kind of curiosity, and it could safely be ignored by the modern system or, if noticed at all, given fairly perfunctory treatment (as in DuBos).

But all of this changed as absolute music started coming to the fore. I want to be careful here about stating my hypothesis. I am certainly not saying that composers before this period were not deeply interested in pure instrumental music, did not lavish the whole arsenal of their compositional skills on it when the occasion arose, or that it did not sometimes form a substantial part of their output. The instrumental music of Bach alone would belie all of those claims (as would the instrumental music, earlier, of Frescobaldi and Giovanni Gabrieli). But even in a case like Bach's, vocal music was the center of professional life, the major source of income, and the spiritual core of the creative life. It was this that changed in the second half of the eighteenth century, when it became possible to make instrumental music one's profession, the spiritual core of one's creative life. For some major composers, instrumental music thus became at the same time the cutting edge, the "experimental" art of the century, the avant-garde among all the other arts. And in becoming all of these things, it became at the same time the major challenge to the representational theory of the modern system, the only apparent and important counterexample, the "Fountain" of its time. We must look at the attempt to meet this challenge now if we are to understand how we got from there to here.

§6   In the second half of the eighteenth century, two options
were open to philosophers for dealing with the growth of absolute music: to reject its bid to become one of the fine arts or
to find a way of making it, broadly speaking, a "representational" art. Both options were explored with a fair degree of
uncertainty reigning among all concerned, most notoriously
Kant, who for profound reasons could never quite make up his
mind. The obvious third option, a theory of art other than some
form of representationalism, was not yet in the offing, even in
Kant's third *Critique* (at least as I read that ever-problematical
text). And when alternatives to mimesis began to appear, again
I would suggest it was the avant-garde art of absolute music
that provided the major initiative.

To give some brief idea of the struggle with absolute music
in the latter half of the eighteenth century, one can do no better
than to adduce the example of Kant. The question for Kant was
not so simple as whether music was representational. And it
might be useful to weigh what he had to say in this regard
against his Scottish contemporary, Thomas Reid, with whom he
has been compared, in recent years, in more than one respect.

For Reid, there is no hesitation in construing music as one of
the fine arts on the basis of melody alone, with mimesis the
connecting thread. "To me it seems," he writes, "that every
strain in melody that is agreeable, is an imitation of the human
voice in the expression of some sentiment or passion, or an imitation of some other object in nature; and that music, as well
as poetry, is an imitative art."[16] Nor is there any doubt that
instrumental as well as vocal music is intended, for at the very
outset of the discussion Reid refers to both.[17]

The notion that even melodies played on instruments are representations of human vocal expression was old hat by Reid's
time; Francis Hutcheson, whose work in aesthetics Reid knew
well and referred to explicitly, had already expressed such sentiments, not new in 1725.[18] What is perhaps more original is
Reid's attempt to construe "harmony" as a representation of
human speech as well. Hutcheson had left harmony to the in-
nate sense of "original" beauty (in his terminology), as opposed
to the "relative" beauty of imitation: "Under *original beauty* we

may include *harmony*, or *beauty of sound*, if that expression be allowed, because harmony is not usually conceived as an imitation of anything else."[19] But Reid is bound and determined to make harmony as well a representational feature of music, and he tries to do so, furthermore, without appeal to any neo-Pythagorean notion of musical harmony as a reflection of the *harmonia mundi*.

As might be expected, the analogy drawn between harmony, which is to say, the simultaneous production of many sounds, and human linguistic behavior is not between sound and soliloquy but between sound and conversation. Reid begins: "As far as I can judge by my ear, when two or more persons, of a good voice and ear, converse together in amity and friendship, the tones of their different voices are concordant, but become discordant when they give vent to angry passions; so that, without hearing what is said, one may know by tones of the different voices, whether they quarrel or converse amiably."[20] The same contrast between harmony and discord in conversation is reflected, Reid continues, in what, though vaguely and naively described, we would call "functional harmony":

> When discord arises occasionally in conversation, but soon terminates in perfect amity, we receive more pleasure than from perfect unanimity. In like manner, in the harmony of music, discordant sounds are occasionally introduced, but it is always in order to give a relish to the most perfect concord that follows.[21]

Reid, like most philosophers of his age, was a self-proclaimed musical naif. Had it been otherwise, he might also have seen the possibility of extending his conversational analogy, along with the notion of conflict resolution, to the important larger musical forms of his day: the large-scale sonata movement, for one. In any case, Reid concludes on a tentative rather than confident note: "Whether these analogies, between the harmony of a piece of music, and harmony in the intercourse of minds, be merely fanciful, or have any real foundation in fact, I submit to those who have a nicer ear, and have applied it to observations of this kind."[22]

11

§7 If Reid showed some diffidence in applying the *même principe* to music, he showed no lack of confidence in construing music as a fine art, on the basis at least of melodic representation; and melody, after all, was agreed on all hands to be the "soul of music," its most essential element. With Kant, however, the question of music was never conclusively resolved. And it was Kant, not Thomas Reid, whose influence in this regard pervaded philosophical thought in the first half of the nineteenth century.[23] Saying that in the third *Critique* absolute music did not come to be seen, decisively, as one of the fine arts is tantamount to saying that for *philosophy*, for *aesthetics*, it did not – that is how important *that work* is to the philosophy of art, as the culmination of eighteenth-century aesthetic thought and the continuation of same in the first half of the century to come.

The question, for Kant, was not nearly as straightforward as it may appear from his rather confident statement in the *Anthropology* (1798) that "it is only because music serves as an instrument for poetry that it is *fine* (not merely pleasant) *art*."[24] For if this statement is to be credited, Kant *had* made up his mind to exclude absolute music from the modern system, and had done so merely on the basis of its lack of representational content. A poetic text could supply such content in the case of vocal music, and vocal music alone, then, was to be designated fine rather than agreeable art. But in the third *Critique* Kant is far from so simple a statement and has pushed the question of absolute music beyond merely the question of "representation" or "content" – indeed, to the question of "form."

Kant, let me hasten to add, is no "formalist," if by that is meant someone who thinks, as Clive Bell and Roger Fry seemed to have thought at certain points in their careers, that form is the only artistically relevant feature of artworks. The whole difficult doctrine of the "aesthetic ideas" in the third *Critique* demonstrates this beyond doubt. But he did think that the question of whether music – absolute music – is a fine art crucially involved form in two very distinct ways. And in regard to both, at least when they are put together, the answer is far from decisive for absolute music.

What is most familiar in the literature on the third *Critique* with regard to music is the question, in §14, as to whether single musical tones can be beautiful or, at best, merely agreeable. We might call this the first stage of Kant's argument, and it turns on whether individual musical tones are perceived as having form. For it is only through the conscious perception of form that the free play of the cognitive faculties, and hence pleasure in the beautiful, can arise.

The notorious passage in which Kant expresses his view on this matter is rendered as follows by Kant's early English translator, J. H. Bernard (1892): "If we assume with Euler that colors are isochronous vibrations (*pulsus*) of the ether, as sounds are of the air in a state of disturbance, and – what is more important – that the mind not only perceives by sense the effect of these in exciting the organ, but also perceives by reflection the regular play of impressions (and thus the form of the combination of different representations) – which I very much doubt – then colors and tone cannot be reckoned as mere sensations, but as the formal determination of the unity of a manifold of sensations, and thus as beauties."[25] The next English translator to attempt the third *Critique*, James Creed Meredith (1911), gives a very similar reading of this passage, except that the crucial phrase Bernard has as "which I very much doubt" is given by Meredith the opposite sense: "which I still, in no way doubt."[26] He is followed in this by the third *Critique*'s most recent English translator, Werner S. Pluhar, who renders it "and which, after all, I do not doubt at all."[27]

To doubt or not to doubt is the question, and it arises simply because of textual variation. The first and second editions of the *Critique of Judgment* have it Bernard's way, "gar sehr zweifle," the third edition Meredith's and Pluhar's, "gar nicht zweifle."[28] Is the third edition's version a correction or a misprint? The smart money, these days, seems to be on the former, and I will adopt that assumption, because for one thing, as Theodore E. Uehling has pointed out, it accords better with what Kant has to say later on.[29] So we may take it that Kant has decided, in the first stage of his argument about absolute music, that individual musical tones, since they have consciously perceivable form, as regular perturbations of a physical medium, can be beautiful. As yet, however, he has said nothing of their being *fine art*. That is to come.

A second stage of the argument can be discerned in §51, where Kant again frames the question of whether Euler's vibrations can be taken in as objects of perception present to consciousness or whether we merely register their effect. The details of Kant's argument need not detain us here. What does interest us is Kant's conclusion with regard to music. Of the two alternatives, Kant concludes:

> The difference which the one opinion or the other occasions in the estimate of the basis of music would, however, only give rise to this much change in the definition, that either it is to be interpreted, as we have done, as the *beautiful* play of sensations (through hearing), or else as one of *agreeable* sensations. According to the former interpretation, alone, would music be represented out and out as a *fine* art, whereas according to the latter it would be represented as (in part at least) an *agreeable* art.''[30]

Uehling has called attention to the significance in this passage of the phrase "as we have done," which implies that Kant has already, presumably in §14, treated music as the beautiful play of sensations, and thus implies as well that he has opted there, as here, for the view that Euler's vibrations are present to sensible representation.[31]

Of interest too is the phrase "in part at least," which suggests that, for Kant, the question of whether music (or anything else) is a fine art may not always have a categorical yes or no answer: that, in other words, something can be artlike or, rather, art in one respect but not in another. I shall return to this thought in a moment.

In any event, it appears that in §51 Kant has plumped for music as a fine art on the basis of his decision that individual tones have a perceivable form as Euler's vibrations. This brings us to the third stage of the argument.

It would be curious indeed if Kant, or anyone else in the eighteenth century, should let the question of whether music is a fine art turn merely on whether it has perceivable *form*. For the *même principe* that holds the fine arts together is representation, and Kant, for all his emphasis on form, has not rejected it. So although it may seem as if, in §51 Kant has let form do the whole job for him, that impression is quite dispelled in §53 and §54, as we now shall see.

What, then, is the "representational content" of music for Kant? He begins with a platitude of his time: the "representation" of the emotions through musical "representation" of passionate human speech. But to it Kant adds the distinctively Kantian notion of the "aesthetic ideas."[32] The complete thought is this:

> Its [music's] charm, which admits of such universal communication, appears to rest on the following facts. Every expression in language has an associated tone suited to its sense. This tone indicates, more or less, a mode in which the speaker is affected, and in turn evokes it in the hearer also, in whom conversely it then also excites the idea which in language is expressed with such a tone. Further, just as modulation is, as it were, a universal language of sensations intelligible to every man, so the art of tone wields the full force of this language wholly on its own account, namely, as a language of the affections, and in this way, according to the law of association, universally communicates the aesthetic ideas that are naturally combined therewith. But, further, inasmuch as those aesthetic ideas are not concepts or determinate thoughts, the form of the arrangement of these sensations (harmony and melody), taking the place of the form of a language, only serves the purpose of giving an expression to the aesthetic idea of an integral whole of an unutterable wealth of thought that fills the measure of a certain theme forming the dominant *affection* in the piece.[33]

It will not be necessary for present purposes to explicate fully the difficult notion of the aesthetic ideas. Suffice it to say that it is through the evocation of the aesthetic ideas that "representational content" becomes integrated into works of the fine arts in the way appropriate to them *qua* fine arts. They do not constitute a statable content – they are "unutterable." A statable content is what gives birth to them – but must not be confused with the aesthetic ideas that are the true, "unutterable" content of the fine arts as fine arts. It is the aesthetic ideas that for Kant satisfy the demands of the *même principe*.

But something else is necessary for the aesthetic ideas to constitute, on the "representation" side, a work as a work of fine art. The evocation of the aesthetic ideas is a necessary but not sufficient condition. In addition, the aesthetic ideas must provoke the free play of the cognitive faculties of imagination and understanding. And this, we learn in §54, the aesthetic ideas in music cannot do; in absolute music they ultimately have their payoff not in the free play of the cognitive faculties but merely in a physical feeling of bodily well-being. "In music the course of this play is from bodily sensations to aesthetic ideas (which are the Objects for the affections), and then from these back again, but with gathered strength to the body."[34] And the conclusion to be drawn from this failure of the aesthetic ideas in absolute music to engage the free play of the cognitive faculties is that, like "jest," music "deserves to be ranked rather as an agreeable than a fine art."[35]

We now have an apparent contradiction: in §51 Kant says that music is a fine art because sounds exhibit perceived form as Euler's vibrations, but in §54 he says that music is not a fine art but an agreeable art because its aesthetic ideas engage only the body and not the imagination and understanding in free play. But the proper response to this apparent contradiction, I suggest, is to recognize, as Kant seems to license us to do in §51, that the answer to "Is it fine art?" is not necessarily a categorical yes or no but quite possibly " 'Yes' in part, 'No' in part." The answer that Kant gives is that absolute music is artlike in one respect and not artlike in another. It is a fine art in respect of form but not in respect of representational content. And hence it is not fully a fine art. Furthermore, in seeing this we now understand his statement in the *Anthropology* that it is the addition of poetry that makes music a fine rather than an agreeable art. For the aesthetic ideas in poetry, unlike those in absolute music, can engage the imagination and the understanding in free play. This is the Kantian way of saying that poetry makes music fully a

16

fine art, and not just a fine art in respect of form, by giving it the representational content it lacks without a text.

Kant, then, was not so much indecisive in his view of absolute music as decisive in placing absolute music in an indecisive position: half fine art, half not; fine art in respect of form, agreeable art in respect of content; fine art–like but not fully fine art – not, in short, categorically one of the fine arts. And so large does the figure of Kant and the third *Critique* loom, retrospectively, over eighteenth-century philosophy of art, prophetically over that of the nineteenth, that from the philosopher's standpoint if Kant did not conclusively make absolute music a fine art, that must be taken as the judgment of his century as well. The making of the modern system of the arts was left philosophically unaccomplished, the failure of absolute music to be understood philosophically as a full-fledged member evidence of failure.

Nor was the problem of absolute music completely resolved in the work of the two greatest aestheticians of the nineteenth century, Schopenhauer and Hegel. For in this regard Schopenhauer played Reid to Hegel's Kant, and the philosophical vote on absolute music is again one for, one against. To this standoff we now must turn our attention.

§8   It has been said that music is *the* Romantic art. It was said by the Romantics. It cannot be a mistake (I am tempted to say *therefore*) to see music, in the first half of the nineteenth century, as maintaining its place as the avant-garde art form: the art form that challenged and motivated the continued attempt to give art its real definition.

Nowhere is this motivating force of music more apparent than in Schopenhauer's philosophy of art, where it occupies the highest rank among the arts. For Schopenhauer there was certainly no hesitation at all in classifying music as a fine art, and absolute music is unequivocally what he meant, first and foremost. That he played Reid to Hegel's Kant in this respect is reinforced by the fact that Schopenhauer's theory of the fine arts still retains the character of a representational theory, although the object of representation has changed from a psychological or behavioral to a metaphysical one.

There is little need to delve deeply into the intricacies of Schopenhauer's metaphysics. For present purposes we need only remind ourselves that for Schopenhauer "the object of art, the depiction of which is the aim of the artist, and the knowledge of which must consequently precede his work as its germ and source is an *Idea* in Plato's sense, and absolutely nothing else . . ."[36] and that the Platonic ideas are an expression of the ultimate reality, the Kantian thing in itself, which Schopenhauer characterizes as a metaphysical "will." Finally, it is the peculiar nature of music, alone among the fine arts, to represent the will, not indirectly by representing the Platonic ideas, as the other arts do, but by being a direct copy of the will itself:

> Thus music is as immediate objectivication and copy of the whole *will* as the world itself is, indeed as the Ideas are, the multiplied phenomenon of which constitutes the world of individual things. Therefore music is by no means like the other arts, namely a copy of the ideas, but a *copy of the will itself*, the objectivity of which are the Ideas."[37]

It should not go unnoticed that even though Schopenhauer puts absolute music squarely among the fine arts, and gives it pride of place in its direct relation to the will, this can also be seen as evidence of the difficulty absolute music still presented. For one cannot help feeling that it is just because absolute music is so difficult to construe representationally that Schopenhauer gives it as object of representation the very thing that we cannot directly experience at all, thus putting the success or failure of music to represent it beyond our powers to determine.

But furthermore Schopenhauer is very clear about its being absolute music with which he is concerned. For when he is through talking about music *sans phrase* and goes on to discuss music with text, he warns of the danger of the music following the text too closely and becoming its slave, thus losing its unique identity as music, the direct copy of the will. The words

> should never forsake that subordinate position in order to make themselves the chief thing, and the music a mere means of expressing the song. . . . Everywhere music expresses only

the quintessence of life and of its events, never these themselves, and therefore their differences do not always influence
it. . . . Therefore, if music tries to stick too closely to the words,
and to mould itself according to the events, it is endeavouring
to speak a language not its own.[38]

If Schopenhauer, then, fully enfranchised absolute music as a
fine art, independent of text, on fairly recognizable "representational" grounds, Hegel was still waffling on the question at
about the same time.[39] And to see how up in the air the question
still was, from the philosophical point of view, it is to Hegel's
Lectures on the Fine Arts that we now must turn.

§9 What is so infuriating about Hegel's remarks on music is
not merely their lack of clarity. As well, it is impossible to tell
what specific musical works he has in mind when he says what
he does about "music." He makes only one reference to a specific composer as a composer of absolute music, and none at all
to a particular work of absolute music. And as we shall see, this
makes any interpretation of what he believes about absolute music, *as we know it*, pure guesswork. In a word, we don't know
what Hegel was talking about, even if *he* did.

A certain irony emerges, I think, when one compares what
Schopenhauer did to advance absolute music's claim to the
status of fine art with what Hegel did. For although Schopenhauer was firm in his conviction that absolute music merited
such a status, and Hegel, as we shall see, equivocated, Schopenhauer supported his conviction with what can only be described
as the moribund theory of musical representation, while Hegel
was perhaps the first philosopher of the first rank to avoid "representation" talk altogether in this regard and construe music
purely in terms of "expression": *ausdrücken* and *Ausdruck* are
the verb and noun, respectively, that Hegel consistently used to
explicate the relation between music and its "content." And to
the extent that expression theory was the wave of the future in
the first quarter of the nineteenth century and representation
theory was, increasingly, an outmoded vestige of the past, and,
furthermore, to the extent that expression theory was to do for

music what representation theory never could – convince a philosophical community that absolute music deserved its place in
the Pantheon – Hegel's waffling did more for the future status
of music as a fine art than Schopenhauer's conviction.

For Hegel, then, music was expression: the expression of the
inner life. The theory is three-termed: the composer "expresses," the music is his "expression," and the listener is "expressed to" to the extent that she is deeply moved by the
musical experience. It is a self-expression theory in that the
composer must be deeply moved by what he expressed in his
music in order for the music to be a successful expression and,
therefore, for the listener to be expressed to, which is to say,
deeply moved by what is heard.

When "music" satisfies the threefold criterion of expression,
it is fine art. The question before us is, Over what real objects
does the term "music" range when they succeed in satisfying
this criterion, and over what real objects when they do not? In
particular, does absolute music satisfy the criterion in respect of
expressive content? For that is the crucial point over which Hegel
anguishes and which it is so difficult for us to get clear about
in anguishing over his text.

Perhaps the most suggestive statement that Hegel makes with
regard to the status of absolute music as a fine art is the following:

> [A]mongst all the arts music has the maximum possibility of
> freeing itself from any actual text as well as from the expres-
> sion of any specific subject-matter, with a view to finding sat-
> isfaction solely in a self-enclosed series of the conjunctions,
> changes, oppositions, and modulations falling within the
> purely musical sphere of sounds. But in that event music re-
> mains empty and meaningless, and because the one chief
> thing in all art, namely spiritual content and expression, is
> missing from it, it is not yet strictly to be called art. Only if
> music becomes a spiritually adequate expression in the sen-
> suous medium of sounds and their varied counterpoint does
> music rise to being a genuine art, no matter whether this con-
> tent has its more detailed significance independently ex-

pressed in a libretto or must be sensed more vaguely from the notes and their harmonic relations and melodic animation.[40]

We learn three important things from this passage: that absolute music without spiritual content is not fine art; that music can gain spiritual content, and thus possess the status of fine art, by being married to a text; and that at best some absolute music can have spiritual content, though "more vaguely" than texted music, and thus can possess the status of fine art. But what we do not learn is what specific examples are, and what are not, fine art. The reason we must know this is that if what we take to be paradigmatic instances of art music fail to be that for Hegel, then we would be loath to say that Hegel had succeeded, philosophically, in enfranchising absolute music, as we understand it, as a fine art.

One passage that does indeed strongly suggest Hegel's failure to enfranchise fully what we take to be art music is the following critical comment on the absolute music of his own day. "Especially in recent times," Hegel writes, "music has torn itself free from a content already clear on its own account and retreated in this way into its own medium; but for this reason it has lost its power over the whole inner life, all the more so as the pleasure it can give relates to only one side of the art, namely bare interest in the purely musical element in the composition and its skillfulness, a side of music which is for connoisseurs only and scarcely appeals to the general human interest in art."[41] The text leaves no doubt that the music under discussion fails to be fine art, in failing to appeal "to the general human interest in art." But whose music is this? One possible answer, all too obvious, is suggested by the recent translator, T. M. Knox, in a footnote to the passage: "Is this an allusion to, for instance, Schubert and Beethoven?"[42] That conclusion is hard to escape, and damaging enough, since if Beethoven's instrumental music fails on Hegel's account to qualify as fine art, we can reasonably question whether in Hegel absolute music itself has qualified.

Furthermore, "recent times," *neurer Zeit*, is far from precise in its extension. "Modern times" is another possible translation.[43] Would that include the instrumental music of Haydn and Mozart? Hegel does, in fact, give high praise to the symphonies of Mozart. Indeed, it is the only reference of a specific kind to absolute music in the whole section on music in Part 3 of the *Lectures*. Unfortunately, it is of no help whatever in answering our question, since Mozart is being praised only for his masterful orchestration, his use of instruments, which is the topic under discussion in that place.[44]

So we are left with the likely conclusion that Hegel did not think the instrumental music of Beethoven and Schubert qualified as fine art, and at least the possibility that he thought the late Haydn and Mozart may have failed to qualify as well. That Hegel's doubts about absolute music were wide-ranging rather than confined to the "contemporary" music of Beethoven and Schubert (which is denigrating enough to the status of absolute music as a fine art) is given support by a passage at the beginning of his discussion of poetry, which follows directly after the section on music. In his transition from music to poetry, Hegel tells us,

> music must, on account of its one-sidedness, call on the help of the more exact meaning of words and, in order to become more firmly conjoined with the detail and characteristic expression of the subject-matter, it demands a text which alone gives fuller content to the subjective life's outpouring in the notes. By means of this expression of ideas and feelings the abstract inwardness of music emerges into a clearer and firmer unfolding of them.[45]

It is indeed quite hard to square this passage with the position Hegel seems to start out with. For whereas in the beginning Hegel holds out the possibility of music as a fine art with or without a text to fix its content, here he says that music must – "so muss sich die Musik"[46] – seek the support of a text to gain its content and, one must assume, its status as a fine art. Knox, early on, takes this, rather than the more liberal view, to be Hegel's doctrine and sees in it the seeds of Hegel's failure to talk intelligibly about music without text:

22

He seems to think music ought to have a meaning but that this can only be detected when it is associated with words in opera and songs. This is perhaps why he may be at sea when he comes to deal with instrumental music.[47]

Without undertaking the imposing task of producing a complete, systematic account of Hegel on the fine arts, I can do little here but enumerate the positions Hegel might be taking, on first reflection, with regard to absolute music. On Knox's interpretation, he would seem to be denying that music without text can be fine art at all. On the most liberal interpretation, he must at least be denying that the instrumental works of two of the greatest practitioners of that art – one, indeed, arguably the greatest – have the status of fine art. And somewhere between would be the view that, according to Hegel, the whole body of "modern" instrumental music, back to and including the late instrumental masterpieces of Haydn and Mozart, fails to be inducted into the modern system, which would mean either that Hegel thought some music of the future might gain that status or, perhaps, that Hegel was more comfortable with baroque and preclassical instrumental style. (The latter, as a matter of fact, is not altogether without textual support: some of Hegel's descriptions of how absolute music might gain intelligible emotive content sound like descriptions of music where there is, in each movement, one *dominant affection* rather than the contrasting affections of "contemporary" sonata form.)

But even on the most liberal construction, we are driven to the conclusion that Hegel did not, any more than Kant, make a single-minded, philosophically persuasive case for absolute music as one of the fine arts: as an undisputed member of the modern system. The only thing that is certain and decisive is that Hegel thought music with a text qualified. In Hegel, absolute music, and therefore the modern system itself, still hung in the balance.

§10   From the rise of the instrumental idiom in the last thirty or so years of the eighteenth century, through Hegel as well as Kant, absolute music precipitated an extended crisis for the project of "defining" art. But absolute music did, of course, finally make it into the modern system, partly, as I have suggested, because of the "expression" theory that Hegel, among others, developed. Other causal factors, or perhaps symptoms (it is difficult to tell which), also played a role: in particular, the development of program music and the tone poem, and the increasing willingness of nineteenth-century writers to put literary or pictorial interpretations on such monuments of absolute music as the piano sonatas, string quartets, and symphonies of Beethoven, which became fair game for poets and poetizers and others of that ilk. It was, so to speak, a case of life imitating art or, in this instance, art imitating its philosophy.

With music firmly settled in the modern system, the next crisis, at least as I read the history of aesthetics, came from another quarter: the visual arts, with music this time providing the anchor rather than the tide. I refer to impressionism, postimpressionism, and the rise of formalism in the writings of Clive Bell and Roger Fry.

If we return to Noel Carroll's claim that it is the problematic works of the avant-garde that drive aesthetic theory to formulate new definitions of art, and ask ourselves whether this holds good for the rise of formalism, the answer is a resounding affirmative and the artworks precipitating the crisis are not far to seek. For beginning with impressionism, and accelerating with the postimpressionists, it was increasingly difficult to reconcile what was seen in these paintings with the accepted principles of realistic representation or competent draftsmanship. If rendering *la belle natur* was to be the standard of success, then Manet and Monet, Cézanne and Van Gogh, Seurat and Gauguin could not pass muster. Combine with this the fact that the camera, a "gadget," could now put the representation of nature within the grasp of anyone, child or adult, and you can easily surmise the motive behind Roger Fry's remark that "if imitation is the sole purpose of the graphic arts, it is surprising that the works of such arts are even looked upon as more than curiosities, or ingenious toys, are even taken seriously by grown-up people."[48]

The turn to form, "significant form," as Clive Bell famously put it,[49] as the sole defining property of the representational and contentful arts seems even more bizarre (to the present writer at any rate) than the turn to representation and content, previously, as the means of establishing absolute music in the modern system. For as Bell himself observed, the ability to maintain "formal" concentration at a concert is a hostage to fortune; and when concentration lapses, there is nothing more natural or easy than to slide into revery. "Tired or perplexed, I let slip my sense of form . . . and I begin weaving into the harmonies, that I cannot grasp, the ideas of life."[50]

Now leaving out Bell's obviously normative assumption that attention to pure form is the favored stance before absolute music, the having of "ideas of life" in response to it a "slide" or a "slip" from genuine aesthetic concentration, what his scenario of musical listening does remind us of is how easy it is for anyone, even a dyed-in-the-wool musical formalist, to have pictorial or narrative images occasioned by absolute music, or, in opposite terms, how difficult it is to keep this from happening, if one so desires. It's "natural," if one wants to put it that way, to respond to music with images; and that makes it all the easier, all the more plausible, to those so inclined to appeal to such images as the representational "content" of absolute music in order to capture it for representation and (by consequence) the modern system.

But the reverse procedure has just the reverse character. Indeed, it is far harder, nigh on to impossible, *not* to see even abstract visual designs "as" representational (cf. "seeing figures in clouds").[51] And reading a novel merely as a formal structure seems just about like the Zen problem of *not* thinking of crocodiles. You may say that I am caricaturing formalism. To the contrary, at least in its first gush of enthusiasm, when it was still *formalism,* that is exactly what Bell and Fry were asking us to do. Bell says, "The representative element in a work of art may or may not be harmful; always it is irrelevant."[52] But if at best representation is irrelevant, at worst irrelevant and harmful, what else are we being asked to do than frame it out: experience the work without it. That, indeed, is just what the musical model is meant to illustrate. For in ab-

25

solute music, when our concentration is unimpaired, pure
form is what we are perceiving:

> [W]hen I am feeling bright and clear and intent . . . I get from
> music that pure aesthetic emotion that I get from visual art.
> . . . [A]t moments I do appreciate music as pure musical form,
> as sounds combined according to the laws of a mysterious
> necessity, as pure art with a tremendous significance of its
> own and no relation whatever to the significance of life; and
> in those moments I lose myself in that infinitely sublime state
> of mind to which pure visual form transports me.[53]

Roger Fry, in *Transformations,* presented unequivocally the formalist creed for literature, as well as for the visual arts.[54] And if
you find it difficult to imagine experiencing Rembrandt as pure
form, abstracted from all representational content, how much
more difficult will you find the exercise when its object is *Pil-
grim's Progress.* Yet that is precisely what Fry demands of you:
"[T]he appearance of an esthetic structure is deliberately chosen
as a bate to lure the reader for an ulterior, non-esthetic end, but
it surely is a common experience that a reader can fully relish
the bait without so much of a scratch from Bunyan's hook."[55]
Nor is Fry loath to generalize the point in claiming that "the
purpose of literature is the creation of structures which have for
us the feeling of reality, and that these structures are self-
contained, self-sufficing, and not to be valued by their reference
to what lies outside."[56]

Bell says, "To appreciate a work of [visual] art we need bring
with us nothing but a sense of form and colour and a knowledge
of three-dimensional space."[57] I assume Fry must endorse its
equivalent for the literary arts. That anyone could actually believe this about literature – believe, that is, that its content is
irrelevant to its artistic merit or significance or to our aesthetic
experience – may be hard for us now to credit. But if any doubt
remains that this is what Bell and Fry were saying, even in light
of the above quotations, the following reminiscence of Bell's,
written at a time when he apparently had withdrawn some distance from his early extravagances, will convince even the most
ardent skeptic. Bell recalls

some gibberish Roger once wrote – for the benefit of intimate friends only – gibberish which did possess recognisable similarity of sound with [Milton's] *Ode on the Nativity* but did not possess what he firmly believed it to possess, i.e. all, or almost all, the merits of the original. The gibberish was, of course, deliberate gibberish – a collection of sounds so far as possible without meaning. It was highly ingenious, and I am bound to reckon the theory behind it pretty, seeing that it was much the same as one I had myself propounded years earlier as an explanation of visual art.[58]

It hardly seems necessary, considering what has gone before, to say anything further about what Roger Fry's exercise in gibberish was supposed to show or how obvious its utter failure to show it – obvious, in the event, even to Bell, from whence came its inspiration.

§11   I do not know of any case in the philosophical literature – at least in the literature of aesthetics – more prone than that of formalism, as a real definition of art, to the charge that, whatever its technical difficulties, vicious circles, and the like might be, it so violates our common sense as to constitute an obvious reductio ad absurdum of itself on that basis alone. And one way of putting the matter is to say that the formalists came a cropper by choosing exactly the wrong model – perversely wrong – for the visual and literary arts, namely, absolute music.

Absolute music, as we have seen, eventually achieved the status of fine art. After it had, through, I suggested, the Romantic "expression" theories of art, the willingness of so many nineteenth-century writers to give literary and pictorial interpretations of the absolute music canon and the rise of "literary" instrumental forms, it was still in no condition to provide a model for formalist aesthetics. Far from it, the "contentful" arts were the model for *it*.

But by midcentury, a profound change was being wrought in musical aesthetics, with which the name of Eduard Hanslick is closely associated. In 1854 Hanslick published his widely read monograph, *Vom Musikalisch-Schönen*, which went through no less than ten editions during the author's lifetime. It was Hanslick who first put before the world (in a readable, nontechnical prose) a palpably formalist account of absolute music. "The content of music is tonally moving forms," Hanslick happily put it.

> What kind of beauty is the beauty of a musical composition?
>
> It is a specifically musical kind of beauty. By this we understand a beauty that is self-contained and in no need of content from outside itself, that consists simply and solely of forms and their artistic combination.[59]

Hanslick's example was followed in England by Edmund Gurney, whose compendius *The Power of Sound* (1880) presented a systematic and detailed version of formalism in music based on what Gurney called "ideal motion," initially described by him as "the *oneness of form and motion* which constitutes the great peculiarity of melody and the faculty by which we appreciate it."[60] The resemblance of Gurney's "ideal motion" to Hanslick's "tonally moving forms" and to Bell's "significant form" is, I think, no illusion. In any case, by the time Bell came to write *Art* in 1916, music had, besides Hanslick and Gurney, numerous formalist interpreters, including the young Heinrich Schenker. And although the notion that music is a purely formal art was by no means universally subscribed to, absolute music had become, in many circles, *the* paradigm of aesthetic formalism: ready and waiting to serve as Bell's exemplar and so to partially verify Walter Pater's familiar and prophetic declaration that it is to music that all other arts aspire, just the reverse of a long history in which music aspired to the other arts.

But just as the contentful arts are the wrong model for absolute music, so absolute music is the wrong model for the contentful arts. And it seems to me at this point in the history of aesthetics that one might well have begun to doubt seriously whether a single theory, a single real definition, could lasso both the contentful arts and absolute music together in the same modern system. Furthermore, one might well have begun to suspect that if literature or painting was an inappropriate model for absolute music, and absolute music was an inappropriate model for painting and literature, there are as well other poor models deeply imbedded in the tradition, so old and undisputed as to be unnoticed. But there they may be, unperceived obstacles to our understanding of "the" arts.

Indeed, "wrong models" is the theme of this monograph. And Chapters 3 through 7 present case studies in the individual arts, meant to reveal the wrong models and, it is to be hoped, supply the right ones. But before we get to that, and to appreciate more fully the predicament we are in, we must first take cognizance of not just how we got here, but where, in fact, we presently are. I turn to that question now.

Chapter 2

Where We Are

§1 As I said at the close of the preceding chapter, one might well have begun to suspect, with the rather obvious failure of formalism to deal with the "representational" arts of painting and fiction, and with a long history of failures of representation and expression theory to deal with absolute music, that perhaps there was something deeply flawed in the whole enterprise of defining art itself. I said it, of course, with the benefit of nearly a century's worth of hindsight and am under no illusion that I would have been any more capable, then, of either diagnosing the disease or prescribing a cure. A lot of philosophy had to come and go before alternatives to the *traditional* "task of defining a work of art" could be seriously contemplated.[1]

The prevailing theory of art, from Croce to Collingwood, from Ducasse to Dewey, was expression theory, in a streamlined, twentieth-century model. Formalism was in the background, expression theory pretty much in center ring. There were, of course, alternatives: "aesthetic attitude" theory, to name one; but expression theory, for the most part, had a stranglehold on the philosophy of art.

This stranglehold and the lure of aesthetic attitude theory were both terminated not so much by technical objections to the theories themselves, which certainly were abroad, but rather, finally by the realization, from two separate quarters, that the enterprise itself, the task of defining a work of art, for which expression theory and aesthetic attitude theory were merely the current options, was suspect: seriously flawed in some philosophically deep way.

Two paths have been followed, in recent years, away from the traditional task of defining art. The first has led to a denial of the whole project. This is the path of the Wittgensteinians, who claim that the term "art" has a different "logic," different logical criteria of application from the "common property" criteria always assumed by the traditional task.

Another, and in my view more difficult, path has been taken by, most notably, Arthur Danto. Here the traditional task is not repudiated; rather, the concept of the *kind* of property we are looking for when we undertake the traditional task is profoundly changed.

One might well ask why I think the latter path more difficult (and, I should add, more fruitful and exciting). Isn't altering the task more radical than "merely" altering the property? I think not. It is far easier to throw out the baby with the bathwater than to perceive that you were mistaken about which was which. And it is a far more drastic perturbation of our conceptual scheme to take the baby for the bathwater than to start with an empty tub.

Be that as it may, it is important for understanding where we are in the traditional task, and where we might go, to canvass both alternatives. I begin with the earlier: the Wittgensteinian transformation.

§2 We derive the notion of what a "real definition" is supposed to do, of course, from Plato. And although the underlying ontology of the quest has been held to be different by different practitioners of the art, the generally stated goal has always been to find the "common property" with which "it" is, without which "it" isn't. For if there is no such property, then when we call all of the "its" by the same name, "we gibber," as Bell put it for the visual arts.[2]

The *locus classicus* for demurring from this traditional task of real definition is the discussion of "games" in Ludwig Wittgenstein's *Philosophical Investigations* (1953), the first, most familiar application of this discussion to the traditional task of defining "art" that of Morris Weitz.

That the common-property quest in defining art was compromised well before the entrance of the *Philosophical Investigations* on the philosophical scene is graphically illustrated by the opening pages of an article the American philosopher De Witt Parker published in 1939. Parker began: "The assumption underlying every philosophy of art is the existence of some common nature present in all the arts, despite their differences in form and content; something the same in painting and sculpture; in music and architecture."[3] He continued:

> The philosophy of art [which seeks some common nature in the arts] has however many things against it. The very possibility of a definition of art may be challenged on at least two grounds. In the first place it may be claimed that there is no significant nature common to all arts which could serve as a basis for a definition.[4]

If I were to read these sentences today to anyone in the philosophy of art who was unfamiliar with Parker or his essay, he or she would be convinced I was reading from Weitz or one of his followers. Clearly, the real definition of art, through the common-property route, was suspect long before Wittgensteinian aesthetics made its appearance in Anglo-American philosophy. But Parker's prescience ends here. For the alternative he offers for finding the common property of artworks is not some drastic Wittgensteinian change in the "logic" of concepts but merely the substitution of a three-property definition for a one-property one. The notion of a real definition is still very much in place, in terms of a common, albeit complex, "property."[5] As Weitz himself observed, "[I]nstead of inveighing against the attempt at definition of art itself, Parker insists that what is needed is a complex definition rather than a simple one."[6]

Weitz's own proposal, first put forward in his widely read essay, "The Role of Theory in Aesthetics" (1956), was that the real definition of art be given up as a hopeless, useless, and misdirected endeavor: hopeless because there is no common property, simple or complex; useless because we do not need such a common property to talk about works of art intelligibly or to give "meaning" to the general term "art"; misdirected because the project completely misconstrues the "logic" of the term. "Knowing what art is is not apprehending some manifest or latent essence but being able to recognize, describe, and explain those things we call 'art' in virtue of these similarities."[7]

Art then, on Weitz's view, is an "open" concept (following Wittgenstein's discussion of games in *Philosophical Investigations* 66 and 67).

> A concept is open if its conditions of application are emendable and corrigible; i.e., if a situation or case can be imagined or secured which would call for some sort of *decision* on our part to extend the use of the concept to cover this, or to close the concept and invent a new one to deal with the new case and its new property. If necessary and sufficient conditions for the application of a concept can be stated, the concept is a closed one.[8]

But the concept of "art" cannot be closed. For "the very expansive, adventurous character of art, its ever-present changes and novel creations, make it logically impossible to ensure any set of defining properties."[9] And so:

> "Art" itself is an open concept. New conditions (cases) have constantly arisen and will undoubtedly arise; new art forms, new movements will emerge, which will demand decisions on the part of those interested, usually professional critics, as to whether the concept should be extended or not.[10]

As became apparent in the years following the publication of his essay, Weitz failed to distinguish between two theses, an epistemic one and an ontological one. Weitz himself came to acknowledge this in later writings. For it might well be that we tell whether something is a work of art by noting family resemblances (the epistemic claim) even though, in fact, what makes it a work of art is some (unknown) property common to all artworks (the ontological claim). The analogy here is with natural kinds like "water," where we tell that something is water, in ordinary circumstances, by its resemblance to other samples of the stuff we have experienced in the past and have been doing so since time out of mind, even though (as we now know) all samples of water *do* in fact have a common "property" that makes them all water, namely, their molecular structure (i.e.,

H_2O). Similarly, it might well be that all works of art have a common (unknown) defining property (the ontological claim) even though we perforce tell which are and which are not works of art by noticing "strands of similarities."

Finally, there is what one might call a "meaning" question here, not always fully disentangled from the ontological and epistemic claims. For in saying that we do not need a common property to talk intelligibly about art, Weitz is answering Plato's claim, present so prominently in Bell but implicit in others as well, that it is through *reference* to a common property that the word "art" at least in part gets its meaning; that common-property reference is a necessary condition on the word "art" having meaning at all.

I shall put aside the meaning question altogether, although it is by no means a trivial one. My interest is in the ontological and epistemic claims: in particular, in what would follow for the future course of aesthetic inquiry if the Wittgensteinian account were true, either in its epistemic or in its ontological form or in both forms together. In his 1956 article Weitz argued that the end of aesthetic theory making has been to come to a real definition of "art." For Weitz the end of the quest for a real definition is ipso facto the end of theorizing. What then is left for us to do? Weitz says:

> The primary task of aesthetics is not to seek a theory but to elucidate the concept of art. Specifically, it is to describe the conditions under which we employ the concept correctly. Definition, reconstruction, patterns of analysis are out of place here since they distort and add nothing to our understanding of art.[11]

Suppose, now, you believe that the Wittgensteinian epistemic claim is correct but the ontological claim is false – in other words, you believe that we do generally tell whether something is a work of art by the method of family resemblance and the rest. If you believe this, then, presumably, there is no need for you to give up "theorizing" about art if that is your inclination. Since the Wittgensteinian claim is, for you, an epistemic, not an ontological, one, you can leave it to the "aesthetic epistemologists" to explicate and go on pretty much with business as usual, looking for that elusive common property.

If, on the other hand, you are a down-and-out ontological Wittgensteinian who believes that family resemblances are all there is out there, either epistemically or ontologically, you will of course, have to eschew "theorizing," at least as Weitz understands it, and stick to the task, as Weitz describes it, of elucidating the concept of art.

But at least as I understand matters, what you would be doing in elucidating the concept of art, once the Wittgensteinian "logic" itself was elucidated, which in the main it has been, at least for present purposes (or else you wouldn't be at the stage you are, of accepting it), would be examining problematic cases and trying to determine whether or how they might be works of art. And you would do so by noting family resemblances to paradigm cases. In other words, you would look for similarities and differences, tote them up, and either declare them in or declare them out and, in the process, sometimes alter the "concept" of art by so doing. You would be right back in the "sameness" business. The search for sameness might not be as obsessive for the Wittgensteinian as it must be for the traditional theorist. Nonetheless, it would have to be firmly in place, or else the problematic cases, the works of the avant-garde that were putting pressure on the concept, cluster concept thought it be, would be too frequently put down as nonart or borderline cases, and that would be simply to give up the game. The Wittgensteinian's central concept is, after all, family *resemblance.* It is resemblance that makes the thing work.

My advice to the Wittgensteinian, then, would be the same as to the traditional theorist: give resemblance (and your project) a rest. My theme is *differences.* But I still have a way to go before I can be more specific.

§3 The Wittgensteinian move in the philosophy of art was never a popular one, and at the present time it is not a going concern. The traditional task of defining the work of art is back in fashion, with a vengeance, if indeed it ever really was absent.

Many developments in the philosophy of language have taken

place since 1953; and the Wittgensteinian model, in general, does not seem so attractive an alternative to a supposedly bankrupt tradition, although analysis by necessary and sufficient condition is not in high repute these days either. The fact is that there are alternatives to cluster concepts or business as usual, à la Plato. But I must leave these questions to those who know better than I how to deal with them.

There is a simpler, less philosophically expansive reason why I reject the Wittgensteinian model for art. It is simply that the only argument for its being a proper model is a bad argument. Here it is, in Weitz's words: "[W]hat I am arguing, then, is that the very expansive, adventurous character of art, its ever-present changes and novel creations, make it logically impossible to ensure any set of defining properties." Any traditional definition "forecloses on the very conditions of creativity in the arts."[12] It is no exaggeration to say that Weitz places almost the full weight of his argument that "art" *must* be an open concept on the claim that this and only this is consistent with the "creativity" of art, that a traditional definition "forecloses" on artistic "creativity."

But it is not at all clear just what the cash value of "creativity" is in Weitz's original claim. Even if (say) representation were a necessary condition for an art, it could hardly foreclose on "originality" or "creativity," since both (and I assume they are not synonymous) can be exhibited within the constraints of representation and, as far as I can tell, can continue to be exhibited in infinitum: there are infinite changes to be rung on the theme of "representation."

What Weitz has in mind for "creativity" and "originality" must be something other than this. What it is becomes more apparent in his writing after the essay of 1956; and that his argument is exactly the same except for the absence of the word "creativity" is, as I shall argue, highly significant. Here is Weitz's argument as restated in *The Opening Mind* (1977): "For my argument against theories of art was (and is) that they attempt to state definitive criteria for a concept whose use has depended on and continues to depend, not on its having such a set, but rather on its being able, for its correct use, to accommodate new criteria that are derived, or derivable, from new art forms whose features demand emendation, rejection, or expansion of extant criteria."[13]

This is the same argument, exactly, that we had in "The Role of Theory in Aesthetics," except for the palpable absence of the word "creativity," notably present in the earlier argument. Why the absence? I think it is because Weitz has simply made the term synonymous with the terms of his own (Wittgensteinian) logical model, redefined it in a way that does indeed make it impossible for there to be creativity in art unless "art" is understood in the Wittgensteinian manner.

Here is what has happened. Creativity, at least of a certain kind, call it "radical creativity," has simply come to mean by definition, in Weitz's account, adding new criteria to the cluster concept of art or deleting established criteria. Radical creativity is what we see happening in artistic revolutions, where something startling, even outrageously new, is achieved in the art world, where the thing produced is so different from previous things we recognized as artworks as to lead us to doubt whether the thing could be an artwork at all. And in the passage just quoted this has become, by stipulation, the process of Wittgensteinian criterion making and criterion breaking. So of course it now turns out that the only logical model that can accommodate radical creativity in the arts is the Wittgensteinian model, because radical creativity has been implicitly defined in terms of the model. Furthermore, this was already the case in Weitz's earlier statement, where the term "creativity" was still in place.

Now we have already seen that nonradical creativity is perfectly compatible with real definitions of art. There is no limit to novelty within (say) representational painting or, to take another example, tonal music. Weitz's argument must be taken to be, then, that the open-concept model has to be the correct one for the concept of "art" because it is the only model consistent with radical creativity in the arts. But now we see directly that there is no argument. Weitz has not shown that the open-concept model alone can accommodate radical creativity. He has made it the only possible model by defining radical creativity in terms of that model. And since, as Weitz himself asserts, the creativity "argument" is the one on which he bases his Wittgensteinian analysis of "art," the only reason for accepting the analysis has gone down the tubes. That radical creativity can be accommodated only by the Wittgensteinian model is in need of an argument, which Weitz never gives.

Can radical creativity be accommodated by the traditional, common-property necessary-and-sufficient-condition model? Weitz has not, as I have just argued, given us any reason to think it cannot. And, as a matter of fact, the most powerful analysis of radical creativity in our time, that of Arthur Danto, is based on that very model. We cannot know where we are in the philosophy of art, or where we might go, without taking the measure of Danto's work in the field.

§4 The "crisis" in aesthetics reflected by the Wittgensteinian move is precipitated by the acute awareness that the traditional task of defining the work of art by common property, necessary and sufficient conditions, genus and difference has so far been a failure, and a failure that began with Plato – with, in other words, the beginning of philosophy itself, as we understand and practice it. Weitz sees in this failure the persistent application of the wrong logical model to the concept of art. But there are those, beginning with Maurice Mandelbaum and, later, George Dickie, who diagnose the failure rather as the persistent search for the wrong kind of "common property." Among these I place Danto – but not, as others do, among the defenders of the so-called institutional theory of art, at least narrowly construed.

Danto's most systematic exposition of his view can be found in *The Transfiguration of the Commonplace* (1981). In that work he offers the seemingly old-fashioned, indeed antique, proposal that the common property of all works of art, their genus in the Aristotelian scheme of definition, is *representationality*. All artworks are representations.

To see how Danto's proposal represents a new beginning as well as a return to a tradition – "neorepresentationalism" might be the appropriate name for it – we must briefly examine Danto's favorite example: a pair of visually indistinguishable objects, one an artwork, the other just a real thing; or its augmented version, a trio of visually indistinguishable objects, one an artwork, the second a different artwork, the third just a real thing.

So much has been written in recent years about this aspect of Danto's aesthetic theory that it scarcely seems necessary for me to add my voice to the chorus. Suffice it to say that because such objects as urinals, bicycle wheels, snow shovels, Brillo boxes, beds, and blank canvases have been exhibited, and apparently accepted, as works of art, it becomes a pressing philosophical problem to explain how these artworks are distinguished from their counterparts outside the museum and in their workaday worlds and, in addition, how two visually identical objects, two blue canvases, for example, might be two different works of art with two distinctive subjects (or no subjects at all).

Danto's now-famous response to this philosophical puzzle was to claim that identifiable features can indeed be found to distinguish artworks from their real-world counterparts and artworks from their perceptually identical artwork twins, but features "the eye cannot decry – an atmosphere of artistic theory, a knowledge of the history of art: an artworld."[14] It was this claim that separated Danto at once from Wittgensteinian antiessentialism on the one hand and traditional essentialism on the other, while still enabling him to produce an essentialist definition of art.

Specifically, Danto maintained in *The Transfiguration of the Commonplace* that works of art are distinguished from the real things with which they might now be confused, in the present state of things, in that "the former are about something (or the question of what they are about may legitimately arise)."[15] And, by consequence, perceptually indistinguishable artworks can be told apart by what, in particular, they are about.

However, "aboutness" can be only the genus of "artwork," not its full essence, for clearly things other than artworks belong to it. So to the genus must be appended its difference. "The thesis is that works of art, in categorical contrast with mere representations, use the means of representation in a way that is not exhaustively specified when one has exhaustively specified what is being represented."[16] To put the point another way, a work of art, in contrast to a mere representation, not only possesses a content but *"expresses* something about that content."[17]

The genus of artworks – what might be called the "aboutness" criterion – has, it is apparent, been quite circumspectly formulated to ward off counterexamples. Not all visual works of art, let alone works of absolute music, are about anything. It is always open to the artist or critic to correctly claim that a work of art possesses no content whatever, yet remains a work of art for all that. But all the aboutness criterion requires is that it *make sense* to ask what the work of art is about, not that it actually be about something, as it wouldn't, for example, to ask what a bicycle or a fish is about. So the aboutness criterion can exclude the bicycle or the fish while embracing the contentless canvas.

The problem of the aboutness criterion concerns, it hardly needs pointing out, the parenthetical escape clause: *"or the question of what they are about *may legitimately arise."* What legitimizes the question of aboutness? How do we determine, if not merely by intuition, that it can be legitimately asked of a blank canvas in a museum of contemporary art but not of a bicycle in a department store or a fish in a net? And can it be legitimately asked of a piano sonata or a string quartet?

If we are going to decide the question merely by intuition – decide, perhaps, how the question "What is it about?" sounds to the ordinary language ear in any given case – then many, like myself, will find it as odd to ask what most pieces of absolute music mean as to ask what any piece of decoration or pure design means or, for that matter, what a bicycle or a fish means. It might be replied that absolute music is art, that is, "fine art," and neither decorative art nor a bicycle or fish is *that.* Now thus baldly put, the response seems clearly question-begging. For it is just the status of absolute music as a fine art that is being tested by asking whether the question of aboutness can be legitimately raised with regard to it, and one can't very well invoke its status as a fine art to prove that very thing.

There is, however, a less obviously question-begging way of responding to the question of whether aboutness can at least sensibly be asked of absolute music. Absolute music, after all, has at least a history since the eighteenth century of being classed by some (though not all) with the fine arts. So that should make it at least a possible candidate for aboutness or content of some kind. Bicycles and fish have no such history, and so no even prima facie case to be made for their being about anything. Easel painting has a long history of aboutness, in other words, of representation. So when one sees a blank canvas exhibited in an art gallery as (ostensibly) a work of art, it seems altogether plausible to ask, no doubt perplexedly, "What is it about?" even though the answer might well be, "It isn't about anything." Now absolute music has no such history of (undisputed) representation. But because it has, since the late eighteenth century, been customarily classified, at least in some circles, with the representational fine arts, absolute music has gained, so to say, a representational history "by association." Although it has no such history as absolute music, it does as a "generally accepted candidate for fine art membership." The answer to the question "What is it about?" may, in the case of absolute music, *always* be, "It isn't about anything." Nonetheless, the question is legitimate because of the association of absolute music with the representational arts since the Enlightenment. Bicycles and fish have no such association and hence lack even prima facie candidacy for aboutness. To ask what they are about is to ask an obviously illegitimate, not to say absurd, question.

But this response will impress only someone who is not initially skeptical about the very process by which absolute music is supposed to have been gathered into the fold of the fine arts. As we have seen, however, that process was far from decisive and did not run its course until one hundred years after Kristeller's "Modern System of the Arts" is assumed to have been in place. Thus the historical tradition of absolute music as a fine art is both recent and tentative. It can well be questioned, therefore, whether absolute music is a fine art at all, on the basis of the very tradition being appealed to by those who might claim that the "traditional" association of absolute music with the fine arts legitimates the raising of the aboutness question in regard to it. It is just not clear whether the question "What is it about?" can legitimately be asked of absolute music, and so it is at least arguable that absolute music does not even satisfy the most minimal condition, on Danto's view, for something's being art.

There may yet, however, be ways to bring absolute music within the ambit of Danto's theory: kinds of "aboutness" for absolute music beyond the minimal criterion. Here are three candidates: (a) Absolute music may be "about emotions." (b) Absolute music may be "about fictional worlds" of some kind that it generates (the way a novel is). (c) Absolute music may be "about itself." None of these alternatives will work. But each deserves a run for the money.

§5 The first alternative, call it the theory of "emotive aboutness," is at least mentioned in passing by Danto himself:

> Music is not generally regarded as an imitative art, though both Aristotle and Plato regarded it that way, and there have been those who supposed that if it did not merely express the emotions, it in some way mimed them. But from the perspective of the concept of medium, the intermediary substance and avenue of transmission from subject to spectator, music shares crucial features with painting and sculpture and drama.[18]

It is not clear whether Danto is suggesting here that he might endorse some version of "emotive aboutness" for absolute music or is merely calling our attention to its existence.[19] Is the fact that Plato, Aristotle, and others have found such a view attractive being used, if not as an argument from authority, or a vox populi, at least as a hint that the view is not altogether implausible?

In any case, Danto lets the matter drop and (as a substitute?) goes on to argue that music shares other "crucial features with painting and sculpture and drama." There is no need for us to canvass these other shared features. *They* cannot bring absolute music into Danto's account, for aboutness is the necessary (though not sufficient) condition. What these (purported) features can show, which no one doubts, is that music is at least like the fine arts in certain nontrivial ways.

But whether or not Danto has entertained an "emotive aboutness" theory for absolute music, we certainly can do it for him.
First, what, briefly, would such a theory look like?

A very large number of those who theorize about such matters
(including myself), as well as (I venture to say) all lay listeners
to music, believe that, in some sense or other, music possesses
expressive properties: that is to say, it is sometimes sad, sometimes joyful, sometimes angry, and so on. Accounts of what is
meant by music's being sad or joyful or angry or whatever differ
widely. But at least some suggest or imply that if a piece of
music is (say) sad in one section, then sadness is its "content"
there; in that place, the music might be said to be "about sadness." Indeed, one might even want to say that we can specify
more fully what is conveyed about the sadness. Jerrold Levinson, for example, writes: "Granted, musical works typically lack
a representational content. . . . However, musical works have
other sorts of content, in particular *expressive* content."[20] Furthermore, this expressive content may be articulated beyond the
bare statement that such and such a passage is melancholy or
joyful or whatever. Thus, on Levinson's view, some passages in
Brahms's Sonata for Violin and Piano in D Minor "express violent passion, and thus . . . express passion as violent."[21]

Now once we have gotten to the point of saying that passages
in a work of absolute music have expressive "content," that that
expressive content is violent passion, and that the passages express the passion *as* violent, we have quite enough, one would
think, to satisfy Danto's aboutness requirement. And as a great
deal of Western art music since the sixteenth century has such
recognizable expressive features where an emotion is expressed
as so-and-so, we have a firm historical tradition in place that
validates the question "What is it about?" for *any* passage of
music in the tradition, even though the answer in many cases
will be "It's not about anything," since a great deal of music is
not expressive of any particular emotion at all. Danto, then,
seems to have his desired conclusion in Levinson's analysis.[22]

But does he? The crucial question is whether agreeing that
sadness, joy, and so forth – what I like to call the "garden-
variety emotions" – are properly "perceived in" music commits

43

one to anything like Levinson's conclusion. Specifically, does it commit one to ascribing any semantic or representational property to music? Does it commit one to musical aboutness? It is common to characterize a musical passage as "calm" or "turbulent" or "vigorous." Surely it makes no sense to claim that that, ipso facto, commits one to saying that the music represents those things, or is about them, or that those things are its "content" in a semantic sense of the word. They are merely its "content" in that they are "in" the music, as the colors are "in" the painting: they are part of its "musical content." Why should it not be the same with "sad," "joyful," "angry," or any of the other garden-variety emotions as ascribed to music?

Clearly, one compelling motive behind the move from "sad" to "about sadness" might be prior commitment to Danto's analysis of art. If one were convinced that Danto (or a Danto-like theory) were right, one would have a big stake in having it the case that absolute music, a potential counterexample, is *about* the garden-variety emotions when expressive of them. But one cannot, after all, take up that view merely on systematic grounds. It would be a nice outcome for Danto's position if music's being expressive of the garden-variety emotions, which it often is, meant ipso facto that it were also about them. It remains, however, to be proved that that is the case. That calm music is not, ipso fact, about calmness, or turbulent music about turbulence, makes that abundantly clear.

But, it may be objected, if we are not attributing at least minimal semantic content to absolute music by ascribing the ordinary emotions to it, what are we doing? My view is that we are ascribing perceptual qualities to the music, perhaps emergent or supervenient ones, just as we are apparently doing when we call it calm or turbulent. I have spelled out some of the details and consequences of that elsewhere, and will not discuss them here.

§6 That absolute music could be about fictional worlds might seem a bizarre thing to claim at this point in the history of aesthetics, and more appropriate to late Romanticism than to the present state of aesthetic and musical analysis. Nevertheless, such a claim has recently been made by a philosopher of extraordinarily keen insight and intelligence, far from a wild ecstatic. And if he is right, then a conclusion about absolute music compatible with Danto's analysis of the visual arts will have been made in a completely unexpected way.

In an intriguing article called "Listening with Imagination: Is Music Representational?" Kendall Walton adduces numerous examples of what he describes as absolute music generating at least fragmentary "fictional worlds."[23] The general purpose of his article is to bring absolute music into the ambit of his own theory of representation as "make-believe."[24] That purpose is not directly relevant to my concerns here, although I shall come back to it briefly in a moment. Nor is it necessary for us to canvass all of Walton's ingenious examples and their ramifications. What I shall do is examine one of his illustrations of musical fiction, which will give us enough of an idea of what he is about to see how, if Walton is right, absolute music can be secured for Danto. In the event, I will argue that the case has not been satisfactorily made.

Consider the opening eight bars (piano solo) of the Adagio of Mozart's Piano Concerto in A, K. 488. Walton writes:

> The upper voice is *late* in coming to the A in bar 8. There are precedents for this tardiness earlier in the passage. The upper voice was late in getting to the A (and F#) at the beginning of bar 3; in bar 4 it participates in a suspension; in bar 6 it is late getting to the C#. In the first two cases the bass waits "patiently" for the soprano to arrive. But in the second phrase, the bass can't wait. It is locked into a (near) sequence, which allows no delay. In bar 6, as in bar 8, the bass has moved on, changing the harmony, by the time the soprano arrives.[25]

Walton sees in this description of the music the implication of a musical fiction – a kind of "story" in the opening of Mozart's Adagio. The musical story may not have characters with names and personalities, events with fully fleshed-out fictional details. "But why shouldn't it count as fictional anyway, as representing instances of lateness, fortuitousness, etc.?" He goes on:

It would be inadequate to think of the music as merely indi-
cating or expressing the *property* of lateness; it portrays a particular (fictitious) instance of something's being late on a
particular occasion. Listeners imagine something's being late
on a particular occasion; they do not merely contemplate the
quality of lateness.[26]

The lateness of Mozart's theme is, of course, but one among
many, indeed a multitude of, such "fictions" in absolute music.
So the ultimate conclusion to be drawn from this example, and
ones like it, which Walton is not reluctant to draw, is that the
works of so-called pure instrumental music are fictional to their
very core:

It looks as though they may have worlds teeming with life,
just under the surface at least – like swamp water seen
through a microscope. If we follow through on our purist in-
clinations to reject stories or images or meanings attached to
music as unmusical, if not childish or silly, we must begin to
wonder how much of what we love about music will be left.[27]

Walton, a trained musician, is well aware of the dangerous
implications of what he is saying for the understanding of the
music he and we most cherish for its "purity." "Our experiences
of music seem shot through with imaginings," he writes, "yet
I, at least, continue to resist the idea that Bach's *Brandenburg
Concerti* and Brahms's symphonies have fictional worlds, as
Crime and Punishment and *Hamlet* do."[28] A good deal of Walton's
article is devoted to how he can save our experience of the "purity" of absolute music while still seeing it as a veritable zoo of
"fictions." I shall have something more to say about the "content" of music when I discuss, later on, my own views on absolute music, which are at the very heart of the thesis of this
book – the thesis of "differences." But our present task is to see
if the initial premise of "fictions" in absolute music, in Walton's
sense of that term, is initially plausible, convincing enough to
save absolute music for Danto's account of art.

I begin by extracting from Walton's account what I take to be
an implicit argument something to this effect: (a) Listening suc-

cessfully to music requires listening to it with "imagination" – "imaginatively." (b) Listening to music "imaginatively," with "imagination," implies imparting fictions to it, hearing fictions in it. (c) Therefore, music contains fictions, is fictional, at least in some minimal sense of those words.

I think this argument is totally wrongheaded because although the first premise is certainly true, the second is just as certainly false. And whether or not Walton ever intended that his article express such an argument, it is an argument worth refuting, for the process of refuting it will be a convenient way of revealing what in his "fictional" way of listening to music is troubling and implausible.

I believe the argument in question gains its footing on the confusion between or the ignoring of two different roles the imagination can be seen to play in our lives or, perhaps, the failure to recognize two different faculties we possess that have both been called "imagination." This bipartite division of the faculty of imagination (if "faculty" is the right term for it) has been recognized at least since Kant's first *Critique*, if not before. I shall call these two parts or functions or "imaginations" "fictional imagination" and "constructive imagination."

The fictional imagination is familiar enough and seems to have been what seventeenth- and early-eighteenth-century thinkers had exclusively in mind, as, for example, in Francis Bacon (1605): "[T]he Imagination, which beeing not tyed to the Lawes of Matter, may at pleasure ioyne what Nature hath seured, and seuer that which Nature hath Ioyned, and so make vnlawfull Matches and diuorses of things...."[29] In this sense of "imagination," it is axiomatic that to listen to music "with imagination" is to listen to music "fictionally" – to impute fictions to music or hear fictions in it.

But surely it is not that kind of imagination that is necessary for musical listening; rather it is the kind of imagination we have become familiar with from the *Critique of Pure Reason* – the kind that synthesizes raw data into our perceptual/conceptual world. It is perfectly true that listening "without imagination" would impoverish our musical understanding. Indeed, that is a gross understatement: more accurately, it would make listening to *music* impossible; it would not be music that we heard.

Let me try to clarify this point with a simple illustration that, by degrees, can be worked up to any complexity one wishes, including Walton's musical fictions. Without the functioning of what I called the "constructive imagination," a listener would not hear melodies but merely individual tones occurring seriatim. Hearing individual tones melodically, as "joined together," when, after all, they are not is an "imaginative" task.[30] But this hardly makes melodies "fictions": it is not fictionally true that the individual tones of "Là ci darem la Mano" are a melody; it is literally true.

But just as one hears individual tones as connected, as a melody, with the operation of the constructive imagination, one hears a melody as having a certain character as well with the constructive imagination's cooperation. One hears a calm melody or an agitated melody and so on. And again, it is not fictionally true that the melody is calm or agitated; it is literally true.

We can now return to Walton's example of the delayed melody and see directly that it is no more fictionally true that it is delayed than that it is a melody or that it is tranquil. Nothing is represented as delayed: the melody *is* (nonfictionally) delayed, although it requires imaginative listening to hear the delay, just as it does to hear the melody; it requires, in other words, the constructive imagination.

Now to this it might be replied that, after all, it does no harm to talk about the melody as fictionally delayed, and such talk has the advantage of bringing absolute music into the ambit of Danto's theory of aboutness or Walton's own theory of make-believe. But for someone like myself, who has no such prior theoretical commitments, neither consideration carries any weight. Furthermore, it is not a harmless *façon de parler* at all. Rather, it leads to conceptual troubles of its own.

Music does sometimes "represent"; it does sometimes generate (or help to generate) fictions; and we want, indeed *have,* a way of talking about this. A melody that delays reaching a musical goal, like the one Walton talks about, can be used, for just that reason, to represent fictionally a character's delay in an opera (say) or a programmatic symphony. The melody of "Là ci darem la mano," we want to say, "represents" Don Giovanni's expression of feigned love to Zerlina by its melodic sweetness, seductiveness, and beauty. The melody is the medium, not the message; the fact, not the fiction. We want to say that a few dabs of yellow represent a flower, make it fictionally true perhaps that the flower is there, in front of the apple. What we do not want to say is that the *yellow dabs* are represented. *They* are what is doing the representing. What we do not want to say is that the melody is fictionally delayed; its literal, musical delay is what is making it fictionally true that some character in an opera or a programmatic symphony is fictionally delaying.

Perhaps someone can find another intelligible way of talking about these things. But the way we now talk about them, as above, seems all right to me: it is natural, conforms to the way we talk with regard, for example, to representational painting, and is firmly in place. That being the case, I have no reason to change my way of talking about such things, and see awkwardness or even unintelligibility lurking in the prospect. To conclude, I find no help for a Danto-like theory of musical aboutness from Walton's direction. His notion of how absolute music might generate fictional worlds, and what these worlds might be like, avoids many of the pitfalls of the familiar Romantic effusions, with their overly detailed, largely irresponsible "readings" of the musical literature. However, it fails to convince me of either its plausibility or its utility as an account of what we appreciate and enjoy in music. (More about the latter is to come.) Only the third alternative remains: that music may be internally representational, that, in other words, it may refer to and be "about" *itself*.

§7 A number of years ago, before Danto's full account appeared in *The Transfiguration of the Commonplace* and existed only in some sketches in the periodical literature, Richard Kuhns quite presciently saw a possible direction a Danto-like theory of absolute music might take. This is not to say that that was the stated purpose of Kuhns's brief article. Rather, Kuhns aimed at refuting Roger Scruton's claim that music cannot be representational,[31] by showing that Danto's theory (in the form it then was in) allowed a kind of musical representation in its own terms. Nevertheless, the result of Kuhns's exercise, if he is correct, is to establish a way in which music can fulfill Danto's aboutness criterion.

Kuhns enumerates three ways in which music might be seen to be self-referential and hence about itself:

> Music quotes music. Bach quotes Vivaldi. Bach quotes Bach. . . .
>
> Tones in music represent other tones. A modulation from major to minor refers as it moves, and establishes referring relationships as it sounds. . . . Tones both sound and refer as they sound. . . . This mode of representation is one of music's most powerful representational capacities.
>
> Music is built on repetitions, repeats, themes and variations, modulations, twelve-tone rows – all of these means are representational because each heard phrase or section leads the listener to hear other phrases and sections.[32]

Of course, all of the phenomena Kuhns cites are genuine phenomena of musical listening and appreciation. The question is, Should they be interpreted *semantically* – that is to say, in terms of "reference" and "representation"? Again one might argue "from above." Having already accepted Danto's analysis of art, a semantic interpretation of the phenomena is a theoretical desideratum or imperative. But viewed in the absence of such a theoretical commitment, what are we to say? We do surely experience these musical features. Is our experience semantical or representational? With that question in mind, let us go through them one by one.

In absolute music, musical "quotations" (that many of us put them in scare quotes is indicative of our skepticism) are of two general kinds. First is the kind where someone else's theme is taken by a composer for his own composition; for example, someone else's theme is used as the subject for a fugue or as the theme in a theme and variations. Second is the kind where a composer at some point weaves another composer's theme into

his composition, as in the twenty-second of the Diabelli Variations, Op. 120, where Beethoven introduces a theme from *Don
Giovanni*, Leporello's "Notte e giorno faticar," just as if it were
a "natural" part of its structure. (It is the latter kind that we are
most prone, I think, to call "quotation.")

Of course, to call such things "quotations" in the first place
is to beg the question in favor of a semantic interpretation of
them. We usually mean to assert propositions thereby when we
"quote" other authors' words in our own writings. And because
of that, the term "quotation" is frequently put in scare quotes
when used to refer to these musical cases, obviously evidence
of many people's reluctance to give the term its literal, semantic
sense in the musical cases.

If musical "quotations" are really *quotations,* then their use
must be, at least in some of the standard cases, to *assert* things.
But what do they assert? What did Beethoven (or his work)
assert when he incorporated Mozart's theme in the twenty-
second of the Diabelli Variations? What did he (or his work)
assert when he used Diabelli's waltz for his variations in the
first place? The desperate will say that he (or it) asserted: "It is
possible to get from Diabelli's theme to Leporello's aria with
musical coherence," or "It is possible to get all of these variations out of Diabelli's waltz." Is that what we want to say? Is
that how wide we want to make the concepts of quotation, assertion, and the rest? On such a construal, a pot would make an
"assertion": "It is possible to be a pot of this shape, of this material, of this size, etc." Therein madness (and semiology?) lies.
There is more to quoting, on my view, than absolute music has
to give, which is why music only "quotes." (That is not music's
shortcoming, but its nature; not its curse, but its blessing.)

Kuhns's other two examples rely heavily on the idea of intra-
opus reference: that is to say, features of a work "referring" to
other features of it, either predictively, where a passage "refers"
to another that is to come, or retrospectively, where a passage
"refers" to or "recollects" a passage that has gone before. In the
former instance, one might want to say that the "referring" passage leads you to expect what is to come, in the latter to remember what has taken place; and in both cases, the "referring"

passage "suggests" to you, brings to mind, what you have heard or will hear but are not now hearing.

The question again is whether there is enough of the right stuff here to compel us to construe these musical phenomena as even vaguely or remotely "semantic." It is *not* enough simply because a passage "suggests," raises in your mind, another passage that was, or is to come to describe the passage as "referring," the relationships as, even broadly speaking, "semantic," even though that suggestion was intended by the composer and reliably occurs in the qualified listener. Plenty of artifacts, after all, are designed with the intention of parts suggesting other parts without our wanting to impute semantic properties to them. And nature abounds with cases of "suggestion" as well. (Clouds are a "sign" of rain, and unless one is a Bishop Berkeley, one hardly wants to remove the scare quotes.) Such intention to suggest, and success in suggesting, may indeed be necessary conditions for meaning, but they are certainly not sufficient.[33]

To be sure, music is a complicated artifact involving in its creation, its study, and its performance many complex symbol systems, musical notation being the most obvious and complex among them. But I speak here only of absolute music as a heard and aurally appreciated object of aesthetic attention. And Kuhns, I think, has provided no convincing argument that that "object" of aesthetic attention and appreciation exhibits semantic, referential, or representational features of the kinds he discusses. I see no promise in this direction of musical self-reference for the gathering up of absolute music into Danto's theory of art. And although I cannot claim to have canvassed all other possibilities to that end, I am at least persuaded that so far the prospects are bleak. So until I am confronted with more favorable prospects, I will consider the case against an "aboutness" account of absolute music closed.

§8 I have been arguing that the history of aesthetic theory, from its modern beginnings in the eighteenth century to its present, flourishing state, has been almost a single-purpose quest for the "common property," with absolute music as the perennial *experimentum crucis* (except in formalism, where it is the paradigm case). And as things presently stand, that quest remains the major activity of philosophers of art, with no settled-on solution in hand.

This is not to say that differences in the arts have not, historically, been recognized as an object of philosophical concern. In the eighteenth century, how the arts differ, and what their rank order of value is, was a central question for the young discipline of aesthetics. This question persisted well into the nineteenth century. In general, the eighteenth-century answer was that the arts differ in medium, the nineteenth-century answer (Schopenhauer, for example) that they differ in kind of object of representation. And it is perhaps in the work of Hegel and Schopenhauer that the quest for differences produced its most interesting philosophical results.

However that may be, the overriding concern was, and continues to be, the search for sameness; and that search has blinded the philosophical community to a bevy of questions of more than trivial importance, involving the arts not in their sameness but in their particularity. Furthermore, the near hegemony of representation, or, to use Danto's more inclusive concept, "aboutness," as the defining theoretical concept has determined the way we perceive, misperceive, or fail to perceive the individual arts in various pernicious ways.

I am not for a moment suggesting that the search for definition, for sameness, is either fruitless or necessarily doomed to failure. Nor am I even suggesting that as a philosophical enterprise it be held in abeyance until the times are more propitious. It will always, in the nature of the case, have a firm hold on the philosophical consciousness of many, if not most. To recommend that it be abandoned, even temporarily, would be to no useful purpose whatever.

Rather, what I am urging, by both precept and example, is that the project of philosophically scrutinizing the individual arts – both "high" and "low" – and their distinctive differences be taken off the back burner and put up front. There is no reason we cannot keep two kettles boiling at once. Such is my precept.

My example, which follows, consists of "case studies" in the

53

pursuit of differences in the arts. With the long historical narrative of how we got to the present point in aesthetics behind us, we now turn to artistic differences, at least some of them, as I presently perceive them. It is the first step in a project that others besides myself have already undertaken and that, I hope, more will be enticed to explore.

Chapter 3
Reading and Representation

§1 Most philosophers of art would agree, I thank, that if any-thing is an established fact in their discipline, it is that literature is largely, and in an important way, a "representational" art. There are, indeed, some isolated dissenters from this orthodoxy. A vigorous and insightful argument against the representational status of poetry was indeed run by Edmund Burke in Part 5 of his highly influential *Philosophical Enquiry into the Origin of Our Ideas of the Sublime and Beautiful,* where he concluded "that po-etry, taken in its most general sense, cannot with strict propriety be called an art of imitation."[1] But it seems to have gotten lost in the flap over the sublime. Clive Bell and Roger Fry, as well as other formalist critics, have made a brave attempt to discredit this generally accepted "fact." And there is a school of literary theory today that, by implication, denies it, since according to its members, texts are about texts, not about "the world out there," whereas believers in literature as representation surely believe that what literature represents is precisely "the world out there" (and, of course, the bodies and minds that inhabit it). On the whole, however, the "fact" of literature as a represen-tational art remains intact.

Furthermore, if literature being representational in essence is an almost universally accepted fact among philosophers of art, it is also one of the most venerable, having been established, most would say, in the earliest "philosophy of art" we possess: Plato's, as laid out in *Republic* 3 and 10.

This old and established "fact" I wish to question seriously. For although Plato certainly believed that certain kinds of what we would consider literature, and certain parts thereof, are representational, he did not, as readers of the *Republic* well know, believe that "literature" *tout court* is mimetic (for which read "representational"). I suspect that a general tendency, throughout the history of thought on the subject, to ignore this important aspect of Plato's doctrine has helped lead to the general complaisance with regard to the received opinion that *all* literature is quintessentially a representational art.

But before we get to Plato and the historical roots of our problem, we must deal with two preliminary matters. First, we must have some idea of how we are construing the troublesome concept of "representation." Second, I must give at least an initially plausible reason for challenging such a well-entrenched view as that literature, the oldest, most established of the arts in the modern system, is paradigmatically a representational art. So (for some perverse reason) second things first.

§2   If any art is paradigmatically representational it surely must be the art of painting (with the exception of pure decoration) as it has been practiced from antiquity to the twentieth century. And surely the first (but by no means the only) genre that would come to the contemporary mind at the mention of "literature" would be the novel, which has an unbroken tradition going back at least to the eighteenth century. So deeply is the former art "representational" and the latter "literature" that I can make the following two claims about each, respectively, with great confidence. No philosophy of painting worthy of the name could be considered successful if it could not give an account of how representation functions as an integral artistic part of what we call "representational" paintings. And no philosophy of literature worthy of the name could be considered successful if it could not give an account of how we experience and appreciate novels. I do not argue for these claims. I simply assume them. If you cannot share these assumptions, follow me no further.

To continue: if an argument is to be made for "literature," *tout court*, as a representational art, then the argument must certainly be made for the special case of the novel. There may be peripheral cases of literature – nonsense verse, for example –

that we would allow to elude the net of representationality without seriously compromising the representation theory of literature. But if such a central case as that of the novel should elude the net, we would justly consider the claim that literature is essentially representational thereby refuted outright. This is not to say, of course, that we could not continue to maintain, quite correctly, that some genres of literature, or some aspects of some genres, are indeed representational. Nonetheless, we would surely have to give up the familiar and comfortable notion that the representationality of "literature" is an old and established "fact." The case of the novel would mock such a notion.

But that is just what I want to claim: that novels cannot be construed as representational works of art at all, at least not in the sense of "representation" traditionally taken for granted.

Take the typical case of representation in the arts. I gaze at a Cézanne landscape and see a mountain. Well, a pedantic German professor is supposed to have corrected his young pupils in a similar situation: "No, you do not see a mountain; you see a picture." But we all know what we are talking about, at least for present purposes. We see a picture. We see a mountain. We see oil paint. We see a mountain "in" the picture, we "see in," to use Richard Wollheim's way of putting such things. All of these "seeings" and more make up our experience of the representation. And at this point we need be no more precise than that.

But it seems clear, to begin with, that we do not see things represented in novels. Indeed, novels are not perceptual objects at all. Of course we see pages and words and so forth. No one, however, thinks that *that* is seeing novels in an aesthetic or artistic sense. And we hardly "see in" novels their characters and settings, the way we see the mountain in Cézanne's painting or in any other analogous way.

It might be responded that we see in the imagination, in the mind's eye, what we read when enjoying a novel; and although that is not literally "seeing," it is close enough to save the notion that the art of the novel is representational. On this view, my reading a novel produces in my imagination, in my mind's eye, a kind of mental cinema, and my experience of the novel lies in the "perception" of that inner narrative motion picture. A novel, then, is a movie of the mind.

I believe that many people who are not in the business of making theories but read novels for whatever rewards and satisfaction that activity affords have something like the "cinema" idea of the thing in the backs of their minds. Furthermore, such an idea was widely held in the eighteenth century, minus, of course, the cinema analogy, when the modern system of the arts was in the process of being established and mimesis was the cement that was to bind the arts together. This picture was fully supported, it is important to note, by the then-reigning (though not completely unchallenged) account of language: John Locke's, as laid out, most fully, in Book 3 of the *Essay Concerning Human Understanding*.

According to the well-known Lockean view of language, words (with perhaps the exception of syncategorimatic terms) refer to "ideas" in the writer's or speaker's mind. When these words are uttered or written, they have the effect, if communication is successful, of arousing tokens of the types of those self-same ideas in the auditor or reader, respectively. Communication consists in the successful "transference" of ideas from writer or speaker to reader or auditor. And understanding a spoken or written message just is having tokens of the types of the speaker's or reader's ideas so aroused.

There are, I think, at least two good reasons for rejecting the cinematic account of novel reading. The first and more informal reason is that, judging from my own experience, it is quite out of step with the way I – and presumably others like me – read novels and, when you think about it, is quite repugnant to common sense. Second, to the extent that it relies on the Lockean model of language and communication, or something like it, it relies on a discredited model – not a real option for us at this time.

If I read, or hear recited, the immortal "Jack and Jill," I really do think that I sometimes visualize in my mind's eye a little girl in a dirndl and a little boy in lederhosen (don't ask me why), going up that hill to their tragic denouement. But, by contrast,

Fred Strickler Presents

A One-Hour Working Meditation
on Making Rhythm Dance

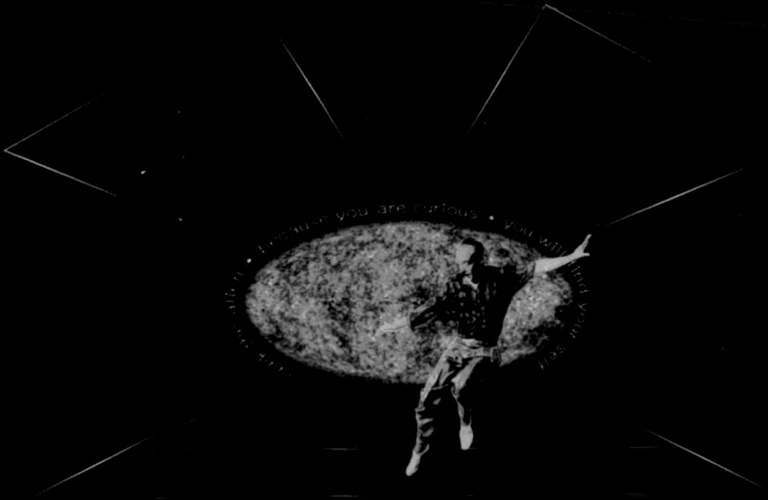

WHERE I LIVE

Virtuoso tap dancer & choreographer
Fred Strickler welcomes you to his home
in Riverside, California
for an intimate dinner al fresco and a show.

with guest artists:

Denise Donovan
&
Ray McNamara

Also included in the price of admission:
a spectacular view of the universe!

Fred Strickler Studio, Riverside CA

$40 per Person

Includes Dinner, Show, and Wine

Twelve Seats per Show

Buy Tickets Online

Dinner at 7:00
Show at 8:00
Wine at 9:00

Plan to arrive at 6:30pm for hors d'oeuvres and wine
(Please see reverse side for dates)

Fred Strickler Presents:

WHERE I LIVE

A One-Hour Working Meditation
on Making Rhythm Dance

Dinner at 7:00
Show at 8:00
Wine at 9:00

Please plan to arrive at 6:30pm
for hors d'oeuvres and wine

Friday	April	6th
Friday	April	13th
Saturday	April	14th
Saturday	April	21st
Friday	April	27th
Saturday	April	28th
Friday	May	4th
Saturday	May	5th
Friday	May	11th
Friday	June	1st
Saturday	June	2nd

www.fredstrickler.com

Buy Tickets Online

"What a pleasure it was to be in the audience Friday night to witness your World Premiere performance! I think you locked onto something very special in creating the level of intimacy you did for the event. The themes of your show resonated throughout the evening, particularly in a world where we often feel a great sense of inadequacy in its magnitude. Your beaming life and vitality however made us remember the significance of the personal touch in all human endeavors. Thank you for being you and the class act that you are."

Mark Broomfield 4/14/2007

when I read *Howards End,* at adult speed, it hardly does, or can, raise such images in my mind's eye as a running commentary, so to speak, on the text. This is not to say that no images at all are aroused. And I suspect that different parts of a novel will be arousal-effective for different readers, for all sorts of personal reasons, although some parts, perhaps because of their importance in the narrative, the vividness of the writing, or impressiveness of the event, are likely to be arousal-effective for everyone. I doubt, for example, that any competent reader fails to carry away from *Crime and Punishment* an image etched in memory of the murder scene.

Thus, in denying that the cinematic model is a plausible one for the experience of adult novel reading, I am certainly not denying that mature readers sometimes visualize in their imaginations, while reading, certain scenes or characters or whatever. What I am denying is that the arousal of such images can possibly be the whole ball of wax, or even a large part thereof. Vast stretches of novels are not *visualized* but *comprehended.* And that leads me to my second objection to the cinematic model of novel reading. For it is the main thrust of the Lockean account of language, as I understand it, that to comprehend just is to "visualize." And if it is the Lockean account that allowed various eighteenth-century writers to maintain the cinematic model of read literature as a way of saving literature for the representational theory of art, that salvage operation fails because the Lockean account fails.

That the Lockean account of language will not pass muster need hardly be belabored, I would think, at this point in time. It can come as no surprise to any of us that language comprehension cannot be a matter of images of dogs or donkeys popping into the reader's or listener's head as these words are read or heard. Surely that may happen, but that it must would make reading, speaking, and comprehension, at least as we know them, impossible. The meanings of words do not accrue by virtue of their reference to "images" or Lockean "ideas," and to so claim is, among other things, to fall afoul of Wittgenstein's private language argument. When we comprehend words and sentences, whether in a treatise on metaphysics or a three-volume

59

novel, we do not do so by having a running commentary of images present before the imagination.

Perhaps at this point the defender of the cinematic model will make the following suggestion. You grant that *sometimes* words cause images to pop into our heads, and that to *that* extent at least some vestige of Locke's linguistic model remains intact. We need not say that even where images are raised, the meanings of words lie in their reference to those images. All we need do is recognize that in certain circumstances words have that power of arousal. In what circumstances? Precisely in *literary* circumstances, of course. For it is precisely the nature of literary language to evoke images. Naturally, reading the *Critique of Pure Reason* or a mathematical treatise will not give rise to images in the mind's eye, because such books are written in prosaic or technical, in a word nonliterary, language. But it is just the genius of an E. M. Forster or a Jane Austen to maximize the image-provoking powers of language that we recognize as "literary."

I am willing to go a certain distance with this response. I think it is true that certain kinds of literary language, or, better, certain literary uses of language, are notable for their image-arousing powers. Furthermore, in certain literary genres – lyric poetry, for one – such language predominates and "imagining" is a major part of the exercise. When, for example, I read Goethe's *Das Veilchen* or listen to Mozart's setting of the poem, I do indeed have a rather vivid image – can hardly help having one – of the violet and the girl who mindlessly tramples it underfoot; and I am sure that is an important part of the artistic experience the poet intended.

But when the work is a three-volume novel or a long narrative poem, something very different is going on through protracted segments: certainly comprehension, but without visualization. And these protracted segments, both descriptive and narrative, are, I want to claim, not representational – neither as a picture is representational, nor even as an image-arousing part of a description or narrative might be. To a large extent, then, literary works such as novels and narrative poems are not representational arts.

Of course, there is a quite genuine, uncontroversial sense in which many literary narratives – one might even want to argue *all* – are "representational," the sense in which, for example, the "letter novels" of the eighteenth century consist in representations of letters through which the story is told. One might call this "textual representation," because a text is being represented by another text.

Letter novels are by no means the only examples of textual representation. Novels that present themselves to the reader as diaries, journals, and ship's logs are examples of textual representation. And even where the manner of textual representation is not made explicit, one might, if one had reason to do so, argue that textual representation of some kind or other is always "implied," as is, some have argued, a fictional narrator. The opening of *Moby Dick,* for example, is an unlikely candidate. "Call me Ishmael" sounds, without textual evidence to the contrary, like the opening of a conversation rather than a diary or other non-literary text. But even if that is how we construe it, we are not, after all, literally listening to a speaker. We are reading a text. And someone, it might be argued, had to have written this text – not, of course, Herman Melville; rather, some implied fictional writer. And so, it might be argued further, when the fictional writer is not made explicit, as in *Pamela* or *Gulliver's Travels*, we are to imagine one and, along with the imagined writer, an imagined text that the book in our hands represents. Perhaps we imagine Ishmael telling his story to one listener, while another, overhearing it, writes it down, like a court recorder; or perhaps the listener himself writes it down (as it is being told or afterward?).

But however far you want to carry this idea, and however doubtful carrying it this far, to imagined scribes and implied texts, may be, it is uncontroversial that some novels and other forms of literary narrative are textual representations. Nonetheless, this does not make even those uncontroversially textual representations counterexamples to the argument I am running here against the notion of literary representation. For it is the representation of the world by the literary work, whether that work consists in a textual representation or not, that is being denied. And a letter novel, no less than a fictional work that does not in any obvious way function through textual representation, is claimed to "represent" the world by those who think of read fiction in representational terms. It is *Pamela*'s "representation" of Pamela's world, not *Pamela*'s representation of Pamela's letters, that is here being denied. *Pamela* is not a "picture" of the world, even in the sense of a running series of mental images in the reader's mind.

Here, however, we reach a crucial juncture. It is now high time to state, at least approximately, how the concept of representation is to be taken. For it is bound to be pointed out by the defender of literature as a representational art that the way pictures represent hardly exhausts the resources of the concept. In particular, philosophers of mind talk about consciousness representing the world to us, and even talk about the "language of thought," without meaning to suggest that consciousness and thinking must be a matter of mental pictures. It seems sufficient reason to attribute representation to conscious thought that it possesses semantic content. And since literature certainly possesses *that*, it is "representational" in what has now become a perfectly canonical sense of the word. This riposte requires some careful attention, which brings us to the first (and so far evaded) question: How are we to construe the troublesome and difficult concept of "representation"?

§3 That the term "representation" is currently used in the way just described by philosophers of mind is not to be taken lightly or dismissed out of hand. Indeed, I do not intend to dismiss it at all.

As I understand this use, a system is representational if it possess not only syntax but semantic properties as well: a content. Using "representation" in this way properly distinguishes literature from, for example, absolute music (at least as many people, including myself, construe it). I have no desire to legislate this use of the representational concept out of existence, and couldn't if I wanted to. It is a valuable use and, as far as I can see, a canonical one.

But recognizing and applying this semantic, "content" sense of "representation" does not cut through the present thicket. We have not, at a stroke, made a case for literature in general or the novel in particular as a "representational" art. We have simply changed the subject. To put it another way, we have not solved a territorial dispute one way or the other, but simply redrawn boundaries.

The traditional question of whether something or other is a representational art is not, as I construe it, the same as the question of whether something or other has content. It is not as if the latter is an irrelevant or unimportant question. It *is* an important artistic fact that novels and plays have semantic content and string quartets do not. This matters greatly in how we appreciate these kinds of works. And there is nothing wrong with – indeed, there is much that is right about – framing such a distinction as between the representational and the nonrepresentational, as long as we know exactly what we are talking about. For before this use of the representational–nonrepresentational distinction, people were saying something very different when they said, for example, that literature is representational and absolute music is not. And what they were saying is simply not captured by the idea that the one possesses content and the other not.

What were they saying? It is not easy to answer that question exactly. But this much is apparent. The experience of (say) enjoying, artistically, a Cézanne still life or a seventeenth-century Dutch landscape painting has something intrinsically to do with the root meaning of "representation," that is to say, *representation* (as has been often enough observed). Something is *presented* to us that we experience *as,* in some "phenomenological" way, the thing represented. And it is in phenomenologically experiencing this that we gain some large part of our artistic enjoyment of these artworks.

I am well aware that this is an extremely vague way of putting things. But for present purposes there is no need to make them more precise. All I require from the reader, to get on with my agenda, is the admission that the subjective experience of content in a text is, from the artistic, aesthetic point of view, very different from the subjective experience of phenomenological presentation in a *re*-presentation.

63

"Representation" is a term currently in use for two very different kinds of things: the semantic properties of consciousness, or text, and the "phenomenological" properties of "presentation" in various of the visual arts (and elsewhere). It is in its latter use that I say we are mistaken in seeing the novel as a representational art. And it is no use to say the novel clearly is representational as that word is currently employed by philosophers of mind. For the way they use it does not capture what the term was meant to capture in its other, "phenomenological" use. It is the latter use, and what it picks out, that I am denying to the novel.

Perhaps it might be objected here that if "representation" in its semantic use and "representation" in its "phenomenological" use do not capture something common to both, there is no proper explanation of why the term has come to be used semantically. Well, there is no need to get stuck on this. Of course, there is something (perhaps more than one thing) that these uses have in common. They both pick out *content*, intentional objects *of* "representation." With both landscape paintings and novels we can verbalize what is "in" them, what they are about. This we cannot do for most string quartets, which are "just music." But even though in the case of artworks such as novels and landscapes, we can identify a content and thus call them semantically "representational," this does not make the former representational in the way the concept has been used since Plato. And it is in this traditional, vaguely "phenomenological" use that I am denying that the novel and some other literary genres are "representational."

§4   I suggested, at the outset of this chapter, that the subsuming of literature, *tout court*, under the umbrella of "the representational arts" has been thought by many to have taken place as early as *Republic* 3 and 10. That seems to be a part of aesthetic folk wisdom. In fact, it is false in an interesting way.

To be sure, Plato did construe literature, *as he knew it*, as a representational, which is to say *mimetic*, art. But literature as he knew it, let me suggest, was basically a performing art: its aes-

thetic or artistic payoff was not for a reader but for a spectator/
auditor.

It is obvious, of course, in the case of tragic and comic drama
that Plato has performance in mind. But I think it is important
to remember that this is true also of epic poetry, Homer in particular, as well as other poetical genres. Thus, when Plato addresses those who experience poetry, that of Homer in
particular, but apparently "the poets" in general, he describes
them as "spectators" who "behold" the poets' "performances."[2]

What these "performances" of epic poetry were like we can
only conjecture. We do know, from Plato's *Ion*, that the rhap-
sodes not only recited poetry to a "musical" accompaniment but
also commented on it as well (as "critics" or "interpreters" perhaps?). And we know also, from *Republic* 3, that these "perform-
ers" were not only reciters and commentators but frequently
"acted" and even provided vocal "sound effects." Thus Plato
describes (with outspoken disapproval) the performer who

> will be inclined to omit nothing in his narration, and to think
> nothing too low for him, so that he will attempt, seriously and
> in the presence of many hearers, to imitate everything without
> exception, . . . claps of thunder and the noise of wind and hail,
> and of wheels and pulleys, and the sounds of trumpets and
> flutes and pipes and all manner of instruments; nay even the
> barking of dogs, the bleating of sheep, and the notes of birds;
> and his style will either consist wholly of the imitation of
> sounds and forms, or will comprise but a small modicum of
> narration.[3]

Such "performances" were "representational" with a vengeance.

Of course the Greek playwrights, like modern ones, intended
their plays to be experienced as performances, as "representations" in the phenomenological sense. But apparently this was
true, if Plato is to be credited as a chronicler of his times, of epic
poets as well. So that even after the Homeric corpus ceased to
be an oral tradition (where clearly performance was the only
payoff) and became solidified into the texts we read, it continued to be a performance art, at least during Plato's lifetime.

Thus it is not Plato's account of "literature" I am opposing when I argue against the notion that literature is a representational art. I think Plato was correct in characterizing literature *as he knew it* as mimetic. And I, of course, am characterizing literature as I know it, and as it has been known since modern times, as nonrepresentational. The difference is that Plato's literature was a spectator art and literature in modern times is significantly a reader's art. (It is no accident, then, that the novel is a modern phenomenon – being the most reader-oriented of all literary forms.)

However, it is surely an overstatement to claim that literature as I know it, literature across the board, is a nonrepresentational art, just as it is an overstatement to characterize Plato as claiming that literature as he knew it, literature across the board, is a representational art. The reason it is an overstatement for me is obvious. Drama is a literary art form and is clearly representational: its aesthetic payoff is meant to be in a performance, where characters, actions, speaking, and setting are represented before our eyes and ears. The reason it is an overstatement to describe Plato's account of literature as representational, *sans phrase,* is far more interesting for what is to come and merits a separate hearing.

§5   In Plato's description of the mimetic performer, quoted in the preceding section, he ends by saying that "his style will either consist wholly of the imitation of sounds and forms, or will comprise a modicum of narration." Those familiar with this part of the *Republic* will recognize here an allusion to the well-known distinction, which Plato has made shortly before, among three "branches" of poetry:

> [O]ne branch of poetry and legend-writing consists wholly of imitation, that is, as you say, tragedy and comedy; another branch employs the simple recital of the poet in his own person, and is chiefly to be found, I imagine, in dithyrambic poetry; while a third employs both recital and imitation, as is seen in the construction of epic poems, and in many other instances, if I make you understand me.[4]

Plato's point here, easy to let slip away in the great to-do over the immorality of representation, is that *pure* narration, where we have only "the simple recital of the poet in his own person," where, in other words, the poet does not speak in the voices of his characters, but *tells* us what they said and did, we do not have representation at all. And this is invariant with whether or not the narration is recited; for a recited narrative of events and speeches is no more a phenomenological representation of them than is a read one. It says, rather than shows, how things went and what was uttered.

This is no minor concession to nonrepresentation in literature. The *Iliad,* for example, is a mixed mode (remember that we are talking about a performance, not a reading to oneself): it contains both "imitation" and "the simple recital of the poet in his own person," which is to say, narration and depiction. But when one considers how much of the *Iliad* is "the simple recital of the poet in his own person," it becomes evident that, far from thinking that literature *tout court* was mimetic, Plato thought that a large segment of it was not.

Furthermore, because Plato was working with a concept of literature, *all* literature (as he knew it), as a performing art, his theory, at least stated in this coarse-grained way, is not by any means unreasonable. For Greek drama, a performing art, it is obviously true – or as obviously true as for Shakespeare's or Ibsen's or Arthur Miller's drama. And since epic poems like the *Iliad* and *Odyssey* were not for Plato's contemporaries something to read, but something to see and hear, a play, as it were, a one-man show, they were also representational in much the same sense as the tragedies and comedies, except where it was "the simple recital of the poet in his own person."

§6 I do not think I am alone in seeing that Plato's is not a representational theory of literature but a representational theory of a part of literature. And certainly I cannot be alone in seeing that, for Plato and his contemporaries, literature was a performing art, not a reading art, its devotees spectators and auditors at a "representation," whether it was Euripides, with actors and a chorus, or Homer, with a "one-man band." I have, however, never read anything that gave the latter kind of performance its due, that recognized the significance of poetic recitation in understanding what Plato said when he said that literature was a mimetic art.

Where, then, does the notion of read literature as a representational art have its origin, if not (and it does not) in *Republic* 3 and 10? One can conjecture that the corner is turned, if not fully negotiated, in Aristotle's *Poetics*.

Paul Thom, in his book on the performing arts, calls attention to the place in *Poetics* 1450b where Aristotle says of the parts of a tragedy: "Spectacle is something enthralling, but is very artless and least particular to the art of poetic composition. The potential tragedy exists even without a performance and actors. . . ."[5] Of this passage Thom writes, in part, that Aristotle "thinks . . . staging is a dispensable accessory to tragedy: for if the tragedy is the poem, then staging is indeed incidental to it. The tragic effect is possible without staging: that is, the reader of the poem can be moved to pity and fear."[6]

Aristotle himself says nothing about *reading* tragedies in the passage Thom quotes. But if he is talking here about experiencing such works as the plays of Aeschylus, Sophocles, and Euripides without the "spectacle," the most obvious construction one can put on this passage is the one Thom does put on it: that Aristotle is envisaging the reading of such works.

There is, however, a problem in construing what Aristotle says in 1450b as a denial that spectacle is an essential part of tragic plays. Indeed, there would seem to be a blatant contradiction between such a denial and the famous definition of tragedy in 1449b, which says: "Tragedy is a representation of a serious, complete action which has magnitude, in embellished speech, with each of its elements [used] separately in the [various] parts [of the play]; [represented] by people acting and not by narration; accomplishing by means of pity and terror the catharsis of such emotions."[7] For if it is part of the definition of a tragic play that it is represented by people acting and not by narration, and if that is taken to mean people acting on the stage, not merely in the text, then "spectacle" must be an essential part of the tragic play, since people acting on the stage are a part of the spectacle and also a part of the definition of the tragic play.

However, there is no contradiction here. For note carefully what Aristotle says in 1550b: "[T]he potential for tragedy exists even without a performance and actors...," which I take to mean not that you can have the tragedy of *Antigone* in its complete form without a full performance, but that you can have tragedy in genres other than tragic plays; that, in other words, the class of tragedy is larger than the class of tragic plays. Not only does this interpretation avoid any contradiction between 1449b and 1450b; it avoids attributing to Aristotle the counterintuitive notion that the art of Aeschylus, Sophocles, and Euripides is not, essentially, a performing art.

What genre, then, was Aristotle referring to that has the potential for tragedy without performance? It seems likely to me that he was thinking of epic poetry, and in particular Homer, which comports well with *Republic* 10, where Plato refers to Homer as the chief among the tragedians.[8] Furthermore, if it is epic poetry that Aristotle is saying can be tragic "even without a performance and actors," then he is merely denying that "spectacle" – that is, a full dramatic production – is necessary for the appreciation of epic poetry, for epic poetry to have its tragic effect, and not that performance of the kind Plato describes, performance by the rhapsode, is unnecessary. So Aristotle is not saying anything new; in particular, he is not saying that epic poetry requires no performance at all and is, essentially, a reading art.

But although the passage under discussion does not yield the result of either tragic drama or tragic epic as a reading art, Aristotle does, in fact, make mention of "reading" in two places at the end of the *Poetics* (as we have it) where he compares tragic drama to epic poetry. He writes that "tragedy can produce its own [effect] even without movement, as epic does. For it is obvious from reading it what sort [of tragedy] it is." And again: tragedy "has vividness in reading as well as in performance."[9] It is not of minor significance, as we shall shortly see, that one translator renders the first of these passages in a slightly different way, to wit: "[T]ragedy fulfills its function even without acting, just as much as epic, and its quality can be gauged by *reading aloud.*"[10]

The first of these passages asserts that a tragic play need not be acted, as the second translator makes clear. Furthermore, the second translator makes "reading" out to be "reading aloud," which may well mean, then, being "read to" by the rhapsode; and in that case it would seem that Aristotle means by "reading" a tragic play simply experiencing the kind of one-person performance characteristic of epic poetry. And the second passage is ambiguous between being read to and reading to oneself; so there may be nothing new here beyond the assertion that tragic plays do not need the entire spectacle of a theatrical performance, but can be recited or performed by a rhapsode, like epic poetry, and still have the tragic effect. But "performance" it remains.

However, even if Aristotle really had in mind reading a tragic play to oneself, the second translation of the first passage calls our attention to the fact that when the ancients read "to themselves," they read *aloud.* Silent reading was a much later accomplishment.[11] So even where Aristotle speaks of a tragedy or epic being "read" rather than acted, he is talking about a minimal "performance": you are reading aloud to yourself. We are still not concerned with the modern experience of curling up with a good book.

In sum, then, we may say that Aristotle at most pushed literature in the direction of a reading art, as well as a representational one, by perhaps leaving his text open to that interpretation, in the following respect. He may have been suggesting that the tragic effect of plays can be experienced in reading the plays to oneself (which does not contradict his "definition" of tragic drama as including "spectacle," since what he is saying is that one can experience "catharsis" without spectacle, not that one is experiencing thereby tragic drama *as defined*). In Aristotle's world this "reading" meant reading aloud to oneself, in which case the reading remained a minimal performance: you performing the play to yourself. But as silent reading became the rule, there would be a strong inclination to understand Aristotle as referring to silent reading when he referred to reading *simpliciter.*

Out of this arises a possible source of a representational theory of literature *tout court,* including literature as a read art, not just a performed one, as in *Republic* 3 and 10. The argument can be summed up in the following statements. (a) The *Poetics* presents a quintessentially representational theory of tragedy, until the modern era one of the prominent, if not the most prominent, of the literary genres. (b) Aristotle's theory of representation is extended to the reading as well as the performing arts, although reading aloud, still a minimal performance, is what he is talking about. (c) In the period in which modern aesthetics was incubating, namely, the High Renaissance and seventeenth century, far and away the most influential aesthetic text was the *Poetics.* By the High Renaissance no one thought of epic poetry as an oral, performing art, and that Plato had so thought of it was either ignored or forgotten in the midst of the Aristotelian hegemony. This, I suggest, is how literature, *all* literature, read and performed, became thought of as a representational art and how Plato came to be seen as the source of the doctrine.

But this is a book about differences. And one difference that I mean to explore is that between read literature and the representational art of performed literature. Aristotle, if my reading of the history of aesthetics is to be credited, helped us, perhaps unintentionally, to take the wrong turn when he defined the tragic drama as mimetic and then denied that the tragic, for its cathartic effect, required spectacle. For that suggested, to a different age, that read tragedy, *silently read tragedy,* hence read literature, *silently read literature,* was a representational art.

The attraction of a theory that could encompass both performed and read literature under a single principle need hardly be dilated upon now, considering what has gone before in the preceding chapters. And in a period when reading was not widespread, the attractions of such a theory for literature far outweighed its perceived defects. But it will hardly pass muster in an age in which the most widely cultivated and consumed literary genre is the novel, the paradigm of reading art. It is high time for an alternative to be offered.

§7   What is literature, then? It is, in part, a representational art. Drama has its aesthetic payoff in production, where characters, speeches, actions, and scenes are "represented." Drama is a major part of literature, and it is representational.

But what is the novel? If it is in part representational, it is so only where distinct mental images are evoked in some "canonical" way (not, that is, as idiosyncratic images); and that would be "representation," at best, in a rather attenuated sense of the word. Attenuated though it is, I will grant that to representationalism.

What of the rest, though? What is the nature of that large part of the novel, as a read experience, that cannot for reasons given at the outset of this chapter be construed as representational even in the sense of image-evoking? I will not even attempt an answer to that question. For the novel is not one thing, and to track down all of the things it is would require an entire book, not merely a chapter in one. What I shall do, rather, is to try to say what, in part, one of the things in the novel is. That is a modest enough undertaking. But perhaps one of the precepts to be gleaned from this book is that modest undertakings, rather than grand designs, are the order of the day.

What I would like to talk about, oddly enough, are *descriptions:* those places where time is taken in the course of a narrative to introduce and describe to the reader some person, place, or object. I say "oddly enough" because it might be thought that descriptions in novels are just the parts that evoke images of the persons, scenes, or things described and, therefore, just the parts one should call "representational" in the attenuated sense. But I am of a different mind. And if I can convince you that descriptions, which seem a bad case for a nonrepresentational theory, are indeed not to be understood as "representational," even in the attenuated sense, I will have done a lot for my cause.

§8   Let me begin with a restricted generalization, full of exceptions. A very large proportion of the novels written since (and including) the eighteenth century take the form of a narrative stream, broken intermittently by pauses for fairly elaborate descriptions of persons, places, or things of later importance to the narration (notable departures from this scheme being the letter novels of the eighteenth century and self-conscious efforts to break narrative structure, as in such cases as Stern, Joyce, Faulkner, and Virginia Woolf). "Islands in the stream" is, I suppose, a good metaphorical first approximation, although frequently the stream will *begin* with an island, which is to say that frequently a novel will open with an elaborate description of a major character or important setting. (I will offer an aesthetically more enlightening model later on.)

Let us look at an example:

> When Flem Snopes came to clerk in her father's store, Eula Varner was not quite thirteen. She was the last of the sixteen children, the baby, though she had overtaken and passed her mother in height in her tenth year. Now, though not quite thirteen years old, she was already bigger than most grown women and even her breasts were no longer the little, hard, fiercely-pointed cones of puberty or even maidenhood. On the contrary, her entire appearance suggested some symbology out of the old Dionyon times – honey in sunlight and bursting grapes, the writhen bleeding of the crushed fecundated vine beneath the hard rapacious trampling goat-hoof. She seemed to be not a living integer of her contemporary scene, but rather to exist in a teeming vacuum in which her days followed one another as though behind sound-proof glass, where she seemed to listen in sullen bemusement, with a weary wisdom heired of all mammalian maturity, to the enlarging of her own organs.[12]

The most obvious point to be made about this description (from William Faulkner's *The Hamlet*) is that it hardly evokes an "image" of Eula at all. The prose is convoluted and rich. There are numerous allusions of a fairly intellectual kind. The passage is a veritable feast for the aesthetic taste in the beauties of language: indeed, we would not be far wrong in describing it as a kind of prose poem.

What, then, are the functions of this description, if not image evocation? We have flagged one already: it provides sheer, unadulterated aesthetic enjoyment of the American language at its highest literary level. But of course that cannot be the whole of it. For the description is part of a narrative, and functions within that narrative *qua* description. And if it does not evoke an image of Eula, what function *qua* description does it perform? Clearly, I think, it shares a function with artistic visual representations: it conveys information. What it does not share with them is the capacity to give one a phenomenological re-presentation. We learn from this description that Eula is a prematurely voluptuous young woman, dripping with sexuality. And this information is vital for the narrative that follows. An image of Eula, however, we do not have. That is not the point of this description, nor within its capability to provide.

Let me begin to fill out this account of literary description by first dealing with the following objection. Granted, the defender of the image model might say, the description of Eula does not, by itself, arouse a mental picture of her. But it does give us the material out of which *we* construct mental images through the mutual interaction of our imaginations, personal experiences, and fantasies. We know from Faulkner's description that Eula is a voluptuous, prematurely sexual girl. The rest we fill in, in a mental image based on young girls we have seen and known, and perhaps on our own sexual fantasies.

I imagine some of this kind of thing does go on in people's reading experiences. How much must vary with the individual. But if you believe, as I do, that reading a novel is an experience that should be under the control of the author to some large degree, then you cannot allow "free fantasy" to take charge. A writer on the subject of our emotional reaction to fiction has said, "It should seem quite extraordinary that so many philosophers should seek to make our responses to Anna's suicide or Desdemona's fate more intelligible by relating these masterpieces to our own banal fantasies."[13] A fortiori it can make little sense to say that what Faulkner's description "represents" – what it is meant to evoke – is my or your banal fantasy of overripe adolescence. The blurb on the back cover of my copy of *The Hamlet* says, "The Snopes family . . . is one of William Faulkner's most notable fictional creations. . . ." Just so: Eula is the creation

74

of Faulkner's extraordinary, fecund literary imagination, not my my feeble, paltry one.[14]

But at this juncture I can imagine another objection taking form. It is to the effect that I have carefully chosen, in Faulkner's description of Eula, a favorable case for what I am arguing: a case where the language is "intellectual" rather than cast in visual terms, so, naturally, not a case of image evocation. It will be objected that I have stacked the deck.

There is some truth in this allegation. I chose this case carefully, with an eye to supporting my position – but the ease with which I found the appropriate one suggests in itself how many such there are. I pursued this strategy to claim a quick victory. What I think I have established is that there are obviously many descriptions of the kind Faulkner gives of Eula that are neither intended to (I assume) nor capable of evoking a *controlled* mental image. Information vital to the narrative is provided in plenty, and artistic satisfaction in the beauty, richness, and structure of the language no less so. But even in the attenuated sense in which the linguistic evocation of images might be "representational," Faulkner's description of Eula, and others like it, are not examples of a representational art.

But what about descriptions that are more straightforwardly visual than conceptual? Those are the ones that seem to favor the representationalist's objections and to be recalcitrant to my own position. To the contrary, I want to argue that even straightforward visual descriptions – "He was tall, dark, and handsome," and the like – are not, in many of the interesting cases, image-evoking at all, but serve the same basic functions as the conceptual ones, of conveying information and affording aesthetic satisfaction. To make this case requires filling out more fully my own conception of the role of descriptions in narrative.

§9 "Winnie Verloc was a young woman with a full bust, in a tight bodice, and with broad hips. Her hair was very tidy. Steady-eyed like her husband, she preserved an air of unfathomable indifference behind the rampart of the counter." "Winnie's mother was a stout, wheezy woman, with a large brown face. She wore a black wig under a white cap. Her swollen legs rendered her inactive."[15]

Here are two brief, pithy descriptions (from Joseph Conrad's *The Secret Agent*) as straightforward and visually oriented as one could wish. Yet I ask the reader to say in all candor that she formed a mental picture of Winnie Verloc and her mother by attending to these lines by a master of English prose. For starters, the "pictures" are woefully underdetermined. Winnie Verloc has a full bust, broad hips, and tidy hair. But what color is her hair? And what does "tidy" hair look like, anyway? How tall is Winnie? What does she look like? All we have are hips, a bust, and tidy hair. These are body parts, not the appearance of a human being. Nor are we better off with Winnie's mother. She has a brown face and swollen legs. What's in between? How can I form a mental picture of a face when all I know is that it is brown? (I don't even know what shade of brown.)

Furthermore, descriptions come, so to speak, in the heat of battle, particularly "quick sketches" like these. If I am an adult reader, reading a page-turner at adult speed, a description can no more paint a picture than can a fleeting glimpse from the window of a train fix an image of the passing scene. This is not to say that reading at speed is the only way of reading. Certainly the reader, particularly the serious reader with a serious novel, may pause at a particularly arresting passage to savor, analyze, and, in the process reread. If the passage in question is a description and if the description is, upon such scrutiny, capable of evoking a mental picture, then so be it. I will not argue that point. *My* point is that there is a very common, indeed a paradigmatic, way of reading novels, in which the reader is engrossed in the narrative and reads accordingly, eager, if not breathless (depending on the novel), for the events to unfold. Descriptions go by, like the rest of the story, at a fair clip. In such a reading there is no time for images to form, even if the descriptions are not underdetermined. This I know from common sense and from my own experience, and I presume neither is eccentric.

If, then, it is not in evoking mental images that the purpose of a description lies, what is its purpose within a literary narrative? I have suggested two: to convey information relevant to the narrative and to provide, like the rest of the narrative, aesthetic appreciation in the linguistic medium. (I take it that enjoyment of the narrative is also a form of aesthetic appreciation.) But to say this much is not to say nearly enough. For what we want to know is not merely how literary descriptions resemble the rest of the narrative but how they differ: what makes them special. A former answer might have been: they are peculiarly "representational" in the sense of peculiarly suited to evoking mental pictures. Having rejected that answer, it is incumbent upon me to come up with another. That is the next task.

§10   I characterized literary descriptions earlier as islands in the stream of the narrative. We can begin to fill out this rather banal metaphor by remarking that it suggests the stationary versus the mobile: pauses in the narrative train of fictional events – not, it should be emphasized, pauses in the activity of reading.

Furthermore, descriptions present themselves as "set pieces" (at least that is the way they present themselves to me). They thrust out of the narrative to be appreciated as a separate literary genre, as it were, within the genre of the modern novelistic narrative. Two analogies suggest themselves: Shakespearean monologue and operatic aria. The latter is the one I shall explore.

What is known as "number" opera is made up of separate movements or "numbers," arias, duets, ensembles, choruses, and so forth, separated by a connecting tissue of "recitative." In its most paradigmatic form, in the eighteenth century, the recitative is for the most part "secco," a rapid parlando accompanied solely by a keyboard instrument. The secco recitative has essentially no musical interest in itself, but serves merely to advance the plot through a minimal musical conversation and monologue.[16] At certain crucial points in the drama, this narrative train is halted and a character "steps forward" to sing an aria. The arias are "concerted" pieces. The simple keyboard accompaniment gives way to a full-blown orchestral one; and each such "number" is a complete, self-contained musical composition that can be (and frequently is) lifted from the larger work of which it is a part and performed separately in a concert or recital.

In listening to an aria as part of a number opera (and I speak now from my own experience), one is listening to an utterance (usually of a heightened emotional kind) in a musical drama. But one is also listening to a musical composition, in a particular style, of a particular genre: the "rage" aria, the "patter song," da capo aria, cabaletta, cavatina, in Mozartian style, Handelian style, and so on. For opera is, among other things (as Edward Dent described it), a concert in costume.[17] And just as in all other examples of high art, we appreciate operatic arias under those descriptions whether or not we can call them by name or describe them in the accepted terms, or merely know them, half-consciously, "by acquaintance."

Let me suggest, now, that full-blown, extended literary descriptions are very much like the kinds of operatic arias I have been discussing in the way we experience and enjoy them aesthetically. Like operatic arias, many of them have a self-contained form. They represent a pause in the narrative flow out of which they thrust themselves. They are "set pieces" – "concerted" pieces, as it were – and like operatic arias are frequently "virtuosic," displaying, as in Faulkner's description of Eula, the writer's "musical" gifts. They fall into types; they have styles (compare Faulkner's descriptions with Fielding's). They are genres within genres.

In one respect, however, the relation of descriptions to their narrative frames differs in an important way from that of operatic arias to theirs. Whereas in the latter case the artistic value of the narrative structure, that is, the secco recitative, is usually nil, the artistic value of literary narrative is certainly equal to that of literary description. But this difference, marked though it is, does not affect the present argument in any way.

Furthermore, the development of operatic aria and recitative into the nineteenth century expands the description–aria analogy in an interesting way. Secco recitative disappeared in the Romantic era, in favor of a more continuous musical fabric in which, if the distinction between concerted number and recitative is maintained (as it tends not to be in Wagnerian music drama), there is nevertheless not a sharp discontinuity between them, the one flowing into the other, and there is even a "dialogue" between the two (something that Handel had already tried in his opera seria). Variations on the same theme of separation versus continuity are apparent in literary descriptions as well. For against the "standard" cases of pause in the narrative stream for descriptive set pieces there is also the interpenetration of the one with the other in a continuous narrative fabric.

What I have in mind is beautifully illustrated by the following passage (from George Eliot's *Scenes of Clerical Life*):

> Look at him as he winds through the little churchyard! The silver light that falls aslant on church and tomb, enables you to see his slim black figure, made all the slimmer by tight pantalouns, as it flits past the pale gravestones. He walks with a quick step, and is now rapping with sharp decision at the vicarage door. It is opened without delay by the nurse, cook, housemaid, all at once – that is to say, by the robust maid-of-all-work, Nanny; and as Mr. Barton hangs up his hat in the passage, you see that a narrow face of no particular complexion – even the small-pox that has attacked it seems to have been of a marginal, indefinite kind – with features of no particular shape, and an eye of no particular expression, is surmounted by a slope of baldness gently rising from brow to crown. You judge him, rightly, to be about forty. The house is quiet, for it is half-past ten, and the children have long been gone to bed. He opens the sitting-room door, but instead of seeing his wife, as he expected, stitching with the nimblest of fingers by the light of one candle, he finds her dispensing with the light of a candle altogether. She is softly pacing up and down by the red firelight, holding in her arms little Walter, the year-old baby, who looks over her shoulder with large wide-open eyes, while the patient mother pats his back with her soft hand, and glances with a sigh at the heap of large and small stockings lying unmended on the table.[18]

If we want to call this long passage by its appropriate name, I think it would be "A Description of Amos Barton"; "Description of a Character" is the genre. The main function of the paragraph (which I have quoted in full) is to convey information about Barton: he is slim, narrow-faced, pockmarked, bald, of no particular complexion or expression, about forty years old, walks briskly, acts with decision. But instead of laying that out in the standard set piece, Eliot presents us with a nonstandard layout in which fragments of character description are interspersed with narrative fragments, as well as with fragments of mise-en-scène. She thus gets across the description without impeding the narrative flow – indeed, gets it across in the very midst of the action (simple though that action may be).

Thus I suggest that part of our aesthetic appreciation of this passage lies in apprehending it as a different "solution" to the "description problem": as in the genre "Description of a Character," but in nonstandard form. Nor need we do this in a self-conscious way; for we can be perfectly well aware that we are enjoying this in the way I have described without being able to put it in just these terms. Furthermore, it is apparent not only that Eliot herself was well aware of doing what I have described, namely, giving a nonstandard character description, but that she purposely underlined this intention, thus forcing the reader to experience the passage in the very way I have described. For the fragmented, nonstandard description of Amos Barton segues, in the end, into the introduction of Mrs. Barton; and the very next paragraph turns out to be an absolutely standard, set-piece description of her, beginning in the most straightforward manner: "She was a lovely woman – Mrs. Amos Barton; a large, fair, gentle Madonna, with thick, close, chestnut curls beside her well-rounded cheeks, and with large, tender, short-sighted eyes," and continuing in kind.[19]

To summarize this part of the argument, I am claiming that character descriptions in novels, short stories, and other novelistic works are not examples of representational art, even in the attenuated sense of evoking "mental pictures," but do share both the capacity and the sometime function of representation, namely, to convey information. *Narratively*, that is their function. But what marks them out, aesthetically, from the general flow of the narrative – which also, after all, conveys information in the form of the "story" – is that character descriptions present themselves as a kind of separate, self-contained form-within-a-form and are appreciated as such. They are set pieces, "concerted numbers" in operatic lingo, that interrupt the narrative flow much as operatic arias interrupt the conversational flow of recitative. And the same argument, I would urge, can be made for descriptions of scenes and objects, although the orientation of the novel and related genres is so much toward people that character descriptions quite naturally have pride of place, high visibility, a more clearly discernible form and tradition.

So I have argued that just where one might expect read literature to be a representational art, if it is one at all – in the descriptions of characters in visual terms, how they look, how they behave – literature is not representational at all. The Horatian dictum of "Ut pictura poesis erit" is then a dangerously false analogy, and we should look elsewhere than pictorial or "phenomenological" representation for a proper aesthetic understanding of it.

"But what of the narrative train itself?" an objector might respond. "Surely it is goring the wrong ox to argue that description is not representational. The far more important question is whether or not pure narrative is, and that question you have not undertaken at all."

Well, of course, the main objections to why character descriptions are not representational in even the attenuated sense of image-evoking apply, pari passu, to read narrative. And the information-conveying function that character descriptions share with pictorial representations they share with narrative as well. What remains to be done for the narrative train, which I have done in small part for character description, is to provide a positive account of its aesthetic appeal. Many literary critics and theorists have undertaken bits and pieces of this task. But this is not the place for me to add my voice. For my main purpose is now complete, which was to at least cast serious doubt on the age-old and seemingly impregnable thesis that literature – *read* literature – is a representational art.

§11 Perhaps, though, it will be objected in the end by readers who have come with me all this way that I am just beating a dead horse. For I did say early on that the cinematic, mental-image concept of read literature flourished in the eighteenth century and received a devastating critique – indeed, what should have been its death blow – in Burke's *Sublime and Beautiful*. But such skeptical readers can assure themselves that the death of this horse has been greatly exaggerated by picking up almost any modern edition of a classic novel and reading the editor's introduction or afterword to the contemporary reader.

Here, for example, is Geoffrey Tillotson's characterization of the genius of Dickens in his afterword to a recent paperback edition of *Bleak House:* "With words he makes us see and hear his fifty men and women with the clarity of a talking film." There then follows a quotation of Dickens's description of a dog, on which Tillotson's comment is: "Do we not feel we know that dog – we can see him!"[20]

No: this horse is very much alive and kicking, and I have felt justified in going out to get him. Whether I have succeeded the future will determine. What remains is to show how what has transpired here fits into the general theme of this book.

§12 My theme is artistic differences. What I argued in the first chapters is that the general thrust of aesthetic theory, from the first formulation of the discipline itself in the age of Enlightenment, through the most recent contemporary examples, is toward unification: finding the commonalty that makes the modern system of the arts a system. We have been eager to find sameness, at the expense of difference.

I am not proposing total abandonment, or even a temporary moratorium, to the makers of theory, as some Wittgensteinians have done. What I am proposing is that there is another way to engage in philosophy of art, for those who may share my tastes and skills, and that is to pursue not the samenesses but the differences. Such an undertaking will have two beneficial results. It will tell us more about the individual arts. But, further, it will test our theories and keep them honest by, I believe, discovering to us old and unexamined assumptions about commonalties among the arts, which, on closer scrutiny, will turn out to be false.

Such, I believe, has been the result of my first "case study" in differences. No assumption has seemed so venerably secure as that literature is a representational art. Yet if my arguments here are good, a very large part of literature, including the modern novel, is not representational. And this certainly demands recognition by the makers of theories.

In my next "case study," I will continue my examination of literature, this time from the side of formalism (of a certain kind). Just as pictorial representation, so I have argued, is not a proper model for read literature, neither is formalism, even in the moderate form in which I am now going to discuss it. To think so would be going from Scylla to Charybdis. Another firmly entrenched assumption, although not nearly as antique as the representationality of literature, will in the process fall away.

Chapter 4

On the Unity of Form and Content

§1 In the preceding chapter I suggested that the earliest conclusion in aesthetics, still generally accepted, may be that literature is a representational art, like painting, sculpture, and (for
both Plato and Aristotle) music. I argued, furthermore, that that
conclusion is, for *read* literature, seriously mistaken. The point
was that in the overarching quest for unity, for sameness, in the
arts, a fairly obvious disanalogy between read literature and the
visual arts has been continually overlooked, or plastered over
with a patchwork of philosophical cosmetics. In the age of Plato
and Aristotle, when literature, which is to say, poetry, was entirely a performed art, the representational theory of literature
made a good deal of sense. But with the advent of such reading
arts as the novel and short story, the notion that literature, *all*
literature, is representational becomes quite untenable. Only the
obstinate quest for sameness has kept us from acknowledging
the fact; and the first fruits of the quest for differences form at
least the beginnings of a new approach to read literature that is
more faithful to its peculiar genius.

My second plea for differences is again directed at the art of
literature. But this time the literary shibboleth in my sights is
not an ancient one; it is, rather, of fairly recent coinage, though
no less obstinate and pervasive among "literary types" for its
youth. It is the thesis that literary form and literary content are
inseparable; or, put another way, that they are indistinguishable,
the one from the other. Its main proponent and, I think, the
source of the doctrine in its twentieth-century form is A. C.
Bradley. In his formulation, Bradley spoke of it as a defining
characteristic, not of literature in general but of poetry in par-

ticular. Yet, for a reason that will soon become apparent, I think it is inherent in Bradley's formulation of the doctrine, and certainly the case with others who have subscribed to it, that it must apply to the whole art of literature, as opposed to the nonliterary uses of language. And I shall so construe it here in this wider application.

Why, though, it may be asked, should a critique aimed at the doctrine of form–content inseparability be appropriate to the theme of my study: differences in the arts? For, after all, the unity of form and content in poetry is meant, is it not, to *distinguish* poetry from other things. Well, that is very true. But the things it was *not* meant to distinguish poetry from were the other fine arts. Quite the opposite: that is very clear in Bradley's highly influential statement of the doctrine, where he writes: "Poetry in this matter is not, as good critics of painting often affirm, different from the other arts; in all of them the content is one thing with the form."[1] And again: "And this identity of content and form, you will say, is no accident; it is of the essence of poetry in so far as it is poetry, and of all art in so far as it is art."[2]

We can now see straightaway why it would be queer to ascribe to Bradley the view that the inseparability of form and content applies to poetry but not to other forms of literature. For Bradley explicitly says that it applies to all of the arts. So if it applies to poetry and not to the novel (say), then Bradley would be committed to the absurd position that the novel is not art. I take it, therefore, that Bradley did not intend to distinguish poetry from prose artworks with the thesis of form–content identity, but meant to apply the thesis to all of the fine arts and, at least in part, to distinguish them from other modes of expression thereby.

So I see Bradley's claim that, in poetry, form and content are indissoluble as being deeply motivated by the same quest for commonality in the arts as the claim that read literature (and music, for that matter) is representational. From now on, therefore, I will take the thesis of the indissolubility of form and content to be a thesis about the fine arts *tout court:* it is the thesis that at least one thing all of the arts have in common, and separates them from other modes of expression, is the total fusion of form with content. I shall argue that this thesis, at least as far as I understand it, and am able to make it intelligible to myself, is false. It is false with respect to literature and the visual arts because form can frequently be distinguished from content in them. It is false with respect to absolute music because absolute music has no content at all, and hence it makes no sense to claim that *its* content is indissoluble from its form.

But before I go on to criticize the thesis of form–content identity, we must have some notion of where it came from and what precisely its philosophical attractions are. For if it is a thesis without attractions, there is little point in bothering with it, much less taking the trouble to refute it.

§2   The *fons et origo* for all twentieth-century versions of the form–content identity thesis is, I imagine, A. C. Bradley's lecture "Poetry for Poetry's Sake," in the *Oxford Lectures on Poetry* (1909). That statement of the view will provide both my basic understanding of the doctrine and the main target of my criticism. But, as we shall see, it is not likely to yield a single understanding of the claim that form and content are inseparable. Rather, a number of claims seems to fall under that description, not necessarily either equivalent or implied by one another. However, one claim stands out from the rest, both by precept and by example. I shall call it the "no-paraphrase" claim and use it as my first stab at understanding the form–content unity thesis, mainly because it has, I believe, an easily identifiable origin in modern philosophy.

I shall say a great deal here about poetry, because that is what Bradley does. But the reader must bear in mind that the doctrine in question is meant by him to apply to all of the fine arts. The "no-paraphrase" claim, then, with regard to poetry is that any attempt to state the content of a poem in any words other than those of the poem itself will not accurately paraphrase its content. So if we think of the words of the poem as its form, and what the poem says as its content, it turns out that they cannot be prised apart. The content can be stated only by those words, just that form, and just that form, hence, just is that content. If that were not the case – if the words, the form, were one thing and what the words said another – then, according to Bradley and his followers, what the poem says could be said in other words, its content could be put in another form. However, such is not the case. The poem cannot be paraphrased. Therefore, its content and form, what it says and how it says it, are one and inseparable. In short, in Bradley's words, "What that meaning is *I* cannot say: Virgil has said it."[3]

What could the attraction of such a doctrine be? It is, after all, on the face of it, pretty implausible. Isn't it the case that one of the very things literary critics are supposed to do, and what Bradley did, with no little distinction, is to help us understand what poems are saying by paraphrasing them for us in what is sometimes a very sophisticated critical language?

One way, I think, that we can help make clear to ourselves what the attraction of the claim might be that, in poetry, form and content are one, is to place it in historical perspective. And to do so I shall indulge in some slightly a priori history, which, I hope, is not too far from the facts.

I shall begin by asking what sense the classical world, either Greek or Roman, would have made of Bradley's claim. I think the answer is that it would have found the claim very puzzling indeed and rejected it out of hand. We can see why by recalling one very prominent role poetry played in the intellectual lives of the Greeks and Romans.

Recall that among the more famous and impressive poetic performances of the ancient world were not merely such narrative epics as the *Iliad*, *Odyssey*, and *Aeneid*, but Lucretius's *De rerum natura* and Parmenides' *Way of Truth* (lost to us, of course, except for some puzzling fragments). We can gather immediately, from the existence of these latter, didactic works, that for the Greeks and Romans it was as natural to convey philosophical and "scientific" results at the cutting edge in poetry as it is natural for us to convey the former in learned journals and the latter in mathematics.

We know, too, that narrative poems, though "fiction," were not treated in the classical world merely as "literary entertainment" (whatever that might really mean). They were themselves taken to be the sources of both practical and theoretical knowledge, their authors seers and wise men. Indeed, that epistemic claim was one of the objects of Plato's devastating critique of poetry in the *Republic* and elsewhere. In the event, in a way, Plato's critique prevailed. (More of that later.)

Thus it was natural for the Greeks and Romans to think of poetry as having a content with a vengeance. The content was not some out-of-the-way, esoteric, scare-quotes "content," but the rich, deep, full-blooded content of science, cosmology, and philosophy as they were then known and practiced.

How odd it would have seemed, then, to Lucretius, to instance the most obvious case in point, to read that somehow the content of his great poem was some ineffable thing, somehow inseparable from his mode of expressing it. On the contrary, Lucretius saw his poem as one of the ways of transmitting a cosmology, a science and a moral doctrine that certainly could be expressed nonpoetically and, in part, had been so expressed by his great Greek predecessors.

I am assuming here, I should add, that Lucretius's poem is not merely a compilation of other men's work – it is that, partly, of course – but a contribution to the atomists' "research" agenda, original both in its bold systematization of previous discoveries and in its contribution, I am conjecturing, of new thoughts and observations. The reader who cannot follow me in this assumption may substitute Parmenides' *Way of Truth* or the fragmentary poem of Empedocles' as an instance. I choose Lucretius's poem because my readers will be more or less familiar with it and because, in fact, Lucretius had a clear concept of what he was doing, shared by his contemporaries, that was generalizable to at least a large part of the poetic enterprise and might justly be termed the "sugar-coated-pill" theory.

As Lucretius would have it, poetic expression is the honey that makes palatable the medicine of content, be it philosophical, moral, or "scientific." On this view, the content of a poem is no more inseparable from its form, or mode of expression, than is the medicine inseparable from the honey. In this regard, I cannot resist quoting the great poet himself:

88

[B]ut as with children, when physicians try to administer rank wormwood, they first touch the rim about the cups with the sweet yellow fluid of honey, that unthinking childhood be deluded as far as the lips, and meanwhile may drink up the bitter juice of wormwood, and though beguiled be not betrayed, but rather by such means be restored and regain health, so now do I: since this doctrine commonly seems harsh to those who have not used it, and the people shrink back from it, I have chosen to set forth my doctrine to you in sweet-speaking Pierian song, and as it were to touch it with the Muses' delicious honey, if by chance in such a way I might engage your mind in my verses, while you are learning to see in what shape is framed the whole nature of things.[4]

Now I do not say that this is a good theory of poetry. But nor, by the way, am I convinced that it is a terrible or silly, or absolutely false theory, of at least *some* kinds of poetry. All I am saying right now is that this theory, and theories like it, which countenanced, indeed insisted upon, the precept that form or mode of expression in a poem is one thing, content, or what is expressed, another, were abroad in the ancient world, and indeed beyond it. For such a theory, it is no more plausible that what a poem says can be said only by that poem than that what a philosophical treatise says can be said only by that treatise.

When, then, and why did the notion that the content of a poem is ineffable in any other vehicle but the poem itself come to seem plausible? What need motivated the collapsing of poetic form into poetic content?

I have neither the time nor the expertise to trace the history of poetic theory from Plato to Bradley. But I venture the conjecture that by the time the eighteenth century rolled around, poetry as the source and conveyor of scientific, philosophical, or any other categorizable kind of human knowledge was a dead issue. The scientific revolution, the growth of specialization and professionalism in all forms of knowledge, practical as well as theoretical and humanistic, put an end to the epistemic claims of the ancient poets that Plato so deplored. It would have seemed almost as absurd in the Enlightenment to assert that the poem was a vehicle for the expression of scientific or philosophical knowledge at the cutting edge as it seemed sensible and commonplace in the ages of Parmenides, Plato, and Lucretius. Poetry, it would seem, had lost pretensions to knowledge, and Plato at last was vindicated.

§3 Perhaps a good place to begin to take the measure of the collapse of poetry as a purveyor of knowledge at the cutting edge in the Enlightenment is Pope's famous phrase: "what oft was thought, but ne'er so well expressed."[5] In a way, it might seem much like Lucretius's sugar-coated pill in early modern dress. But there is an obvious and crucial difference. For Pope, the poet is no longer a "seer," a discoverer of truths, but the purveyor of other people's truths. This is not the sugar-coated-pill theory of Lucretius. It is the old-wine-in-new-bottles theory. The distinction between form and content remains in place; and the form and content may both be splendid things. There is, however, no kudos for the poet as far as the content is concerned. The poet has merely selected it; it is the discovery of others.

Thus Pope's epigram does not save the poet's epistemic status. In order for that to be done we must secure for the poet a kind of knowledge that only he can command. What kind of knowledge can that be?

Well one thing the poet is in sole command of is poetic form or expression. If he were not in command of that, he would not be a poet. But if the form or expression *were* the content, then the poet would be in sole command of that content.

Put another way, if the content of the poem is ineffable, if, that is, only the poem can say what it says, then what the poem says, which only it can say, is an expression of content that only the poet can have "discovered." The poet is the world's greatest expert, the world's only expert, on the kind of knowledge his poem expresses, because it is the *only* example of that kind: it is sui generis content.

What I am suggesting, then, is that what makes the thesis of form–content identity in poetry attractive is its seeming power to regain for poetry its ancient epistemic status, lost in the wake of the scientific revolution and the specialization of the "knowing game." If the content of the poem could be paraphrased, then that paraphrase would inevitably fall into one of the categories of human knowledge populated by resident authorities who perforce would outrank the poet in expertise. (That, after all, is the substance of Plato's argument against the poets.) The poet would be thereby reduced to Pope's purveyor of platitudes. The ineffability thesis assures the poet his expertise. The poem just *is* its subject matter, and there can be no expert on the poem, no creator of that poem, no discoverer of that subject matter other than the poet. He cannot be outranked.

If I am right that it is this desire to rescue the poet's epistemic status by making him sovereign over a special, unpoachable knowledge reserve that drives the ineffability thesis, it should come, I think, as no surprise that the first powerful statement of that thesis comes in the final flowering of the Enlightenment, with the modern system of science and scholarship more or less in place. It comes, I suggest, in Kant's *Critique of Judgment,* also, significantly, the cradle of modern formalism (with Kant perhaps the unwilling father). So at least I shall now argue.

§4   In §49 of the third *Critique,* Kant introduces the both obscure and fascinating notion of the "aesthetic ideas," which we discussed briefly in the first chapter in regard to music. They are, Kant says, a counterpart of the "rational ideas" of the first *Critique,* in that both are concepts "to which no intuition (presentation of the imagination) can be adequate."[6]

In §49 Kant speaks primarily of the role of the aesthetic ideas in poetry, although he makes it clear that they function in painting and sculpture too.[7] And, as we have already seen, they figure as well in music, although they fail there in their ultimate aesthetic payoff of engaging the free play of the cognitive faculties.

It is the power to arouse the aesthetic ideas that imparts to works of the fine arts what Kant calls "spirit" (*Geist*).[8] And it is the sole privilege of *genius* to be able to make works of art in which this power resides.[9]

It is clear from the outset, even before Kant ascribes the ability to impart the aesthetic ideas to genius, that the possession of spirit, which is the ability to arouse the aesthetic ideas, is an important artistic value. Kant writes:

> Of certain products that are expected to reveal themselves at least to be fine art, we say that they have no *spirit*, even though we find nothing to censure in them as far as taste is concerned. A poem may be quite nice and elegant and yet have no spirit.[10]

It is worth noting that Kant says something can be "in part" a work of art without possessing spirit, which is to say, the power of arousing aesthetic ideas. This leads us to believe that spirit is not merely a value of artworks, but a necessary condition for being *entirely* art as well. As we shall see later on, there is a similar waffling in Bradley between the thesis that the unity of form and content is a necessary condition for being good poetry and the thesis that it is a necessary condition for being poetry at all. Kant, I think, is clearer about what he is claiming, as we have already seen in Chapter 1, that being fine art is a matter of degree or, to put it another way, that something can be fine art in one respect and not in another. In any case, I will not bother here about whether spirit is for Kant a defining property of poetry *qua* fine art or merely a good-making property. My sole interest is the nature of the aesthetic ideas themselves in Kant's scheme, which, I am claiming, is the first clear statement of what was later to become the form–content identity thesis. So I return now to the aesthetic ideas.

Kant's most detailed example – indeed, the only detailed example – of the workings of the aesthetic ideas is a poem by Frederick the Great. And when we recall that the imparting of the power to arouse aesthetic ideas is the province of genius alone, the choice of that example seems puzzling, to say the least. Did Kant really think Frederick the Great a poetic genius?

Part of the problem here may be that Kant is not yet quite comfortable with the modern sense of "genius," meaning an extraordinary creative gift, which, I believe, he himself gave its first philosophically deep formulation. For a good part of the eighteenth century the word "genius" referred to a faculty of mind that perfectly ordinary people could have in varying degrees: the faculty of generating ideas, mediocre or more than that, depending upon how much "genius" one possessed. According to this meaning of the term, anyone capable of producing a poem at all must have some degree of "genius," including the Great King.

But although this consideration may somewhat ease our puzzlement over Kant's choice of an example, it cannot entirely dispel it. For Kant does make it clear, in introducing and developing the concept of genius, that he is indeed formulating something like the modern notion of genius as the highest form of artistic creativity: Homer and Wieland are his examples. So we cannot entirely let Kant off the hook here in choosing a poem by Frederick the Great as an illustration of the power of genius to generate aesthetic ideas. There it is, and there is no getting around it. So after smiting our brows sufficiently, we can get on with the business at hand.

Kant says that "by an aesthetic idea I mean a presentation of the imagination which prompts much thought, but to which no determinate thought whatsoever, i.e. no [determinate] *concept*, can be adequate, so that no language can express it completely and allow us to grasp it."[11] And here is how Kant characterizes the working of the aesthetic ideas specifically in Frederick's poem: "The king is here animating his rational idea of a cosmopolitan attitude, even at the end of life, by means of an attribute which the imagination (in remembering all the pleasures of a completed beautiful summer day, which a serene evening calls to mind) conjoins with that presentation, and which arouses a multitude of sensations and supplementary presentations for which no expression can be found."[12]

We might characterize Kant as saying something to the effect that there are two levels of "content" in the king's poem: a statable, manifest content and an ineffable "sub-text," which is constituted by the huge range of "aesthetic ideas" the poem arouses in the reader. And it is the aesthetic ideas that constitute the true aesthetic content of the poem.

What might drive one to such a position? I suggest it is the following, in part mistaken chain of reasoning. The poem surely has a "content": it is not, in Kant's terminology, a "free beauty," like wallpaper or flowers. But this content cannot be the easily stated, manifest content of the poem, which would be nothing specially poetic and more properly the province of a scientific, philosophical, or practical discipline. And *any* statable content underlying the manifest content would suffer the same fate: for example, the statable allegory beneath the manifest content of an allegorical poem. So the true, poetic content of the poem must, by nature, be completely ineffable. This is Kant's doctrine, as expressed in the thesis of the aesthetic ideas; and it is the source, I suggest, in modern philosophy, both of the problem of how artworks can possess a content all their own, possible for them alone, immune to the inroads of the special sciences and practical disciplines, and of the first attempt at a powerful solution.

Furthermore, although Kant is certainly not a formalist with regard to the fine arts in general, nor with regard to the thesis of content ineffability, the constant companion of form–content identification, he forges a strong link between his own brand of formalism and his own concept of poetic content, and so sets a kind of precedent that later leads from the idea of a link between formalism and ineffability to the idea of their coalescence.

§5   The link that I speak of – between formalism in the Analytic of the Beautiful, and Kant's account of the content of art, in particular the aesthetic ideas, in the Deduction of Pure Aesthetic Judgments – is forged through the concept of the cognitive faculties' free play. That is to say, the free play of the cognitive faculties is the common source of our pleasure in the beauty of form, free beauty, as outlined in the Analytic of the Beautiful, and our pleasure in the true content of art, the aesthetic ideas, as outlined in the Deduction.

There is, to be sure, a subtle change in Kant's way of describing the "free play" from the Analytic to the Deduction. In the former place, we have such familiar descriptions as "the cognitive powers brought into play by this presentation are in free play" or "a free play of the presentational powers directed to cognition in general"[13] and so forth. By contrast, in the latter we get clearly similar but nevertheless interestingly distinctive char-acterizations. Here is one: "Hence it [the aesthetic idea] is a pres-entation that makes us add to a concept the thoughts of much that is ineffable, but the feeling of which quickens our cognitive powers and connects language, which would otherwise be mere letters, with spirit." And here another: "But the understanding employs this material not so much objectively, for cognition, as subjectively, namely, to quicken the cognitive powers, though indirectly this does serve cognition too."[14]

If I am right that, both in the Analytic of the Beautiful and in the Deduction, Kant is laying the satisfaction of free beauty and the aesthetic ideas to the same source, namely, the same state of the cognitive faculties, usually denominated their "free play," there is nevertheless a distinctive though subtle contrast in em-phasis. If I am not mistaken, the formulations in the Analytic of the Beautiful suggest a kind of pure, hedonistic satisfaction in the mere act of perceiving, those in the Deduction a satisfaction that is somehow spiritually uplifting and mind-expanding. This mind-enhancing propensity of the aesthetic ideas is made even more apparent in §53, Comparison of the Aesthetic Value of the Fine Arts, where Kant writes of poetry, which, among "all the arts . . . holds the first rank": "It expands the mind; for it sets the imagination free, and offers us, from among the unlimited variety of possible forms that harmonize with a given concept, though within the concept's limits, that form which links the exhibition of the concept with a wealth of thought to which no linguistic expression is completely adequate, and so poetry rises aesthetically to ideas."[15]

Now this distinction, between a kind of pure, perceptual plea-sure on the one hand and a quickening, mind-enhancing satis-faction on the other, is just what one might expect, given the contrasting objects of the two experiences. Both free beauty and the aesthetic ideas are alike in that they pleasure us without a concept: without a concept, *sans phrase*, in the former case, with-out a *definite, framable* concept in the latter. But the pleasure of free beauty is a pleasure in form, the pleasure of the aesthetic ideas a pleasure in "content," ineffable as that content might be. And it seems altogether appropriate that the pleasure in content

95

should have a profound effect on our cognitive powers where the pleasure in form should not. At least so it seems to me.

But notwithstanding this altogether plausible difference in effect, given the Kantian aesthetic, between the perception of free beauty and the cognition of the aesthetic ideas, it is the sameness of effect that is crucial, I want to argue, in the evolution of the form–content identity thesis. Whether one reads Kant, mistakenly, as a formalist in regard to the fine arts, as some have done, or, correctly, as a formalist in regard to free beauty but certainly not in regard to the fine arts, Kant has forged a link between content in the fine arts and formal beauty by subsuming them both under the play of the cognitive faculties. And it is this link that I see as the first stage in the process that culminates in Bradley's conflation of form with content in the *Oxford Lectures on Poetry*.

Kant himself should by no means be implicated in the conflation of form with content. He maintained, it seems to me, a clear distinction between them. What he did do, I suggest, was, perhaps for the first time, address the problem of their relation and resolve it to his own satisfaction, if not to ours, in a way that led others to complete the process of conflating the two – a result completely unintended by Kant, I am certain, and, as I shall argue shortly, completely wrongheaded as a solution to the problem it is supposed to address.[16]

Many, I have no doubt, will be skeptical about my belief that Kant's aesthetic ideas are to be seen as the first (or any) historical step in the aesthetic conflation of form with content that was completed by Bradley. But two further steps, as I see it, intervene between Kant and Bradley in this regard. And these steps, I think, are obvious enough to be beyond controversy. I want to turn to an examination of them now.

§6 As so often has been the case in our previous reflections, we find again that music plays a decisive role in the historical proceedings. For it well may be that the notion of conflating form with content finds its first, or at least its first influential statement in Hanslick's musical formalism. And after Hanslick, music exercises its influence once again, in Walter Pater's well-known and, as it turns out, decisive discussion of form and content in his essay "The School of Giorgione."

Hanslick was not so much a systematic philosopher as a maker of philosophically pregnant phrases, the most well known of them being "The content of music is tonally moving forms."[17] I emphasize that Hanslick was a phrase maker rather than a philosopher so that the conflation of musical form with musical content expressed in his famous epigram not be made too much of – in particular, that it not be taken as ascribing to music some esoteric meaning that can be expressed only in terms of its form. This is not a new and subtle account of how music expresses ideas. It is not an account of musical content at all. Hanslick's *bon mot* is, on the contrary, a catchy way of saying, not that music has a content peculiar in that it is inseparable from its form, but that *music has no content at all.*

However, now that I have cautioned the reader not to make too much of Hanslick's intriguing phrase as an early formulation of the form–content identity thesis, I had better caution against making too little of it either: that is, we should not make too little of its *historical* significance, just because his contemporaries and later readers *did* make too much of its philosophical importance vis-à-vis the *content* side of the equation. It is Hanslick's phrase, transmogrified into a metaphysical insight concerning the mysterious fusion of a real artistic form with a *real artistic content,* that, I think, provided the impetus for the doctrine of form–content fusion in poetry (and the other arts).

But the most proximate step to Bradley's doctrine is undoubtedly Walter Pater, whom Bradley mentions by name and whose "authority" he invokes in the *Oxford Lectures.*[18] There is, as far as I know, no evidence of a direct link between Hanslick and Pater. However, that music plays the leading part in Pater's attempt to integrate form with content (without, I should emphasize, totally obliterating the distinction) suggests the evident power of Hanslick's phrase and of his musical formalism, either direct or indirect as the case may be, over Victorian aesthetics. (Pater, after all, read German.)

§7 Pater was also no philosopher; and, like Hanslick, his greatest contribution to the form–content identity thesis (and to the philosophy of art) was a phrase – indeed, one that is far more familiar than any Hanslick ever coined. Pater famously said in "The School of Giorgione" (1877), "*All art constantly aspires towards the condition of music.*"[19] In fact, he liked the phrase so much that he said it four more times in the same essay.[20]

Pater is not the well-known and admired thinker that he is because of his philosophical views on art or any theory of criticism. So there is no point in trying to extract a sophisticated view from "The School of Giorgione." What we *can* get are some "tendencies."

Pater begins the essay by suggesting that it is differences in the arts, rather than what they have in common, that are most important to him. "Each art . . . having its own peculiar and untranslatable sensuous charm, has its own special mode of reaching the imagination, its own special responsibilities to its material." Thinking otherwise Pater calls "the mistake of much popular criticism."[21]

But as things develop, it becomes clear that Pater is only yet another seeker after the common demominator. Indeed, his famous motto is an expression of that very thing: that which all the arts share.

What, then, is the "condition" of music toward which all of the other arts strive? Pater leaves no doubt that it is the very identification of form and content that Hanslick had enunciated before him. And when we see Pater's celebrated phrase in its context, this becomes quite unmistakable:

> *All art constantly aspires towards the condition of music.* For while in all other kinds of art it is possible to distinguish the matter from the form, and the understanding can always make this distinction, yet it is the constant effort of art to obliterate it.[22]

Pater suggests at one point that in "the ideal examples of poetry and painting . . . form and matter, in their union or identity, present one single effect to the 'imaginative reason'. . . ." But it would seem to be his basic idea that the other arts may approach the condition of music – its form–content identity – while never truly attaining it, because their very essence is otherwise:

> It is the art of music which most completely realises this artistic ideal, this perfect identification of matter and form. . . . Therefore, although each [other than music] has its incommunicable element, its untranslatable order of impressions, . . . yet the arts may be represented as continually struggling after the law or principle of music, to a condition which music alone completely realises.[23]

One might venture to say, then, that Pater's theory, if we may so call it, aspires to the condition of formalism. But Pater is far too sensible to let its aspirations be fully realized. He no doubt perceived that formalism, among other things, was not consistent with his own practical criticism. It remained for Bradley, a far more "philosophical" critic, and a Hegelian one at that, at least as an interpreter of Shakespeare, to close the gap entirely between music and the other arts, although insisting that his was not thereby "a doctrine of form for form's sake."[24]

§8   I think it not too wide of the mark to characterize Bradley as wanting his cake and eating it too, for he wants all of the advantages of formalism without having to pay the price of a doctrine that, as he says, "empties poetry of its meaning. . . ."[25] But it is terribly hard, as we shall see, to determine what sort of thing, on Bradley's view, that "meaning" is that is left to him.

Before we can get to the main point of interest for us in Bradley's lecture, namely, the form–content identity thesis, some extraneous matters, at least from a contemporary perspective, must be cleared up.

To begin with, it appears that one of Bradley's major goals in "Poetry for Poetry's Sake," perhaps even the whole purpose of the thing, is to adjudicate between "the two contentions that the poetic value lies wholly or mainly in the substance, and that it lies wholly or mainly in the form."[26] We are likely, I think, to find this disjunction somewhat nonsensical and to give it short shrift: as to "wholly," a resounding "no" to either disjunct, and as to "mainly," an obvious "it all depends on the poem." Brad-

ley, however, took it very seriously indeed, and the whole theoretical apparatus of the lecture is martialed to reach our same
conclusion. The alternatives

> imply that there are in a poem two parts, factors, or compo-
> nents, a substance and a form. . . . But really in a poem, apart
> from defects, there are no such factors or components; and
> therefore it is strictly nonsense to ask in which of them the
> value lies.[27]

This aspect of Bradley's lecture I think we can safely ignore.
What is important is the theoretical apparatus itself, not the specific question that seems to have motivated it.

Second, Bradley has left it very unclear whether he is saying
that the fusion of form with content is the defining property of
poetry, whether it is the defining property of *good* poetry,
whether the goodness of poetry varies in degree with the degree
of fusion, or whether the degree to which something is poetic
varies with the degree to which it has fusion of form with content. Most generally Bradley seems to be hung up between giving a definition of what it is to be a poem and an analysis of
what it is to be a good poem.

In response to my reading of Bradley, here, as failing to distinguish clearly between the question of whether something is
a poem and whether it is a good poem, it might be replied that
this is no confusion at all, because the word "poem" is an *evaluative* word, the concept of poetry an *evaluative* concept. But
this response is, I think, itself a confusion, a failure to distinguish
among (at least?) three value issues. It will be useful to clear
this matter up before proceeding.

The word "poem," like the word "art" and many other such
words, is, indeed, both descriptive and evaluative. And it is evaluative in at least two ways, which I can best explain through
examples.

If I ask you whether the speech you heard last night was a
good speech, and you reply, "Good? It was *poetry!*" you are
using "poetry" in what might be called the "rhetorically evaluative way." You do not mean that the speech was really a
poem, but that it was a very good speech. You are playing on

the fact that we tend to think of poetry as the highest form of linguistic expression and using the sentence "It was *poetry*" rhetorically, to say that the speech was a very good one.

But there is a second way in which the words "poem" and "poetry" are evaluative. For *because* we think poetry is the highest form of linguistic expression, when we judge something (literally) to be a poem we are putting it in a more prestigious class of linguistic things than if we withheld that judgment from it, just as we do when we promote a soldier from major to general or give him the Legion of Honor.

Now the rhetorical use of "poem" and "poetry" to evaluate is, it seems to me, completely irrelevant to the confusion between the questions of whether something is a poem and whether it is a good poem. In their rhetorically evaluative use, the words "poem" and "poetry" are employed not to evaluate poems, but to evaluate other things. That's just the point of the rhetorical use.

It must be, then, the other way in which "poem" and "poetry" are evaluative – the bestowal of rank or prestige – that people have in mind when they aver that there is no distinction, and hence can't be any confusion, between the "factual" question of whether something is a poem and the evaluative question of whether a poem is a good one. For the so-called factual question isn't a nonevaluative question at all, since deciding that something is a poem is to bestow honor, prestige, value upon it, as when one promotes a soldier to higher rank.

However, it by no means follows that because "poem" and "poetry" are evaluative terms in the sense of bestowing rank, there is no distinction between the question of whether something is a poem and whether it is a good poem. To elevate something to the rank of "poem" is to place *some* value on it, to be sure. But that hardly renders meaningless the question of whether it is a good poem, except in the trivial sense that every poem has whatever minimum worth something must have to be elevated to that status at all. Surely, though, it would be pedantic in the extreme to point out that the answer to the question "Is it a good poem?" must always be yes, because every poem has that minimal good, hence is, in that respect, a "good" poem. The minimal is assumed, and the question is about something beyond that. Moreover there is the question of *comparative* goodness, which is not affected at all by the evaluative use of "poem" and "poetry" now under discussion. Some poems are better than other poems, regardless of the fact that "poem" and "poetry" are evaluative as well as descriptive words, and every poem has (some) value.

Thus the current notion, among some, that art words are evaluative by no means erases the fact that a clear distinction has to be made between the decision as to whether something is a poem or a symphony or an artwork, for that matter, and the other decision as to whether it is a good poem or good symphony or good artwork. And with regard to poems, it is that distinction that Bradley, so I believe, has failed to make clear to himself or to us.

Bradley himself must have been more than dimly aware of this ambiguity in his project, for he addressed it specifically in a note he later appended to the lecture. But even here the ambiguity never seems to get totally sorted out. So I shall simply assume that he is offering a definition of poetry, and generally of art, the closest he comes to saying as much being, "[T]his identity of content and form . . . is of the essence of poetry in so far as it is poetry, and of all art in so far as it is art."[28]

Contemporary analytic philosophy of art is comfortable with the notion that to define art is one project, to say what makes a work of art good or bad quite another. Bradley was not. Nor was Collingwood much indebted, I think, to this lecture of Bradley's, but very clear about what he was doing in conflating the definition question with the question of value, and in possession of a carefully worked out conceptual scheme to cover our contemporary intuitions, which want to keep those things distinct. Writing from a contemporary perspective, however, I have no compunction about seeing the question of defining poetry (or art) as a question apart from the question of poetic (or artistic) value. And thus shall I construe Bradley's thesis.

§9 With these preliminary matters disposed of, we can get down to our real business of determining what exactly the cash value *is* of the thesis that, in poetry, form and content are one, and evaluating that thesis as we go along.

The claim most central to Bradley's thesis, reiterated throughout his lecture, is that we can verify the form–content identity of any poem by simply trying and perforce failing to reexpress the content of that poem in different words. "Hence in true poetry," Bradley writes, "it is, in strictness, impossible to express the meaning in any but its own words, or to change the words without changing the meaning."[29]

This is not to say that we cannot state in our own words what a poem is "about," in some reasonable sense of the word. We can state what Bradley calls a poem's "subject." For example, "The subject of *Paradise Lost* would be the story of the Fall as that story exists in the general imagination of a Bible-reading public." But "the subject, in this sense (and I intend to use the word in no other), is not as such inside the poem, but outside it."[30] However, the identity thesis does not apply to the subject of the poem; that isn't even part of the poem: it is "outside it." It applies, rather, to something else called the "substance" or "content":

> Those figures, scenes, events, that form part of the subject called the Fall of Man, are not the substance of *Paradise Lost*; but in *Paradise Lost* there are figures, scenes, and events resembling them in some degree. These, with much more of the same kind, may be described as its substance, and they may be contrasted with the measured language of the poem, which will be called its form.

Unlike the subject, "substance is within the poem, and its opposite, form, is also within the poem.[31]

It is substance, or content, then, not subject, that the identity thesis is about. It is *this* that is inseparable from form in virtue of being unsayable in any form of language other than that of the poem itself. "A translation of such poetry is not really the old meaning in a fresh dress; it is a new product, something like the poem, if one chooses to say so, more like it in the aspect of meaning than in the aspect of form."[32]

§10 We have now reached the first vantage point from which we can look back and take stock. How plausible is the thesis that we cannot successfully say in words other than those of the poem what the poem is expressing?

In order to answer this question, we need to know what the criterion or criteria would be for a successful reexpression of a poem's content. How would we know whether it was possible unless we could evaluate our attempts and know when we had failed?

When we frame the question this way, two suspicions immediately creep in. One is that Bradley has made the criterion of success so stringent that we are bound to fail in the task of reexpression. The other is that this criterion might not just be unreasonably, excessively stringent but amount to a conventionalist sulk: making the nontranslatability thesis true by stipulative definition.

Of the latter possibility, we have evidence in such statements as "Meaning they have, but *what* meaning can be said in no language but their own . . .";[33] and "[I]f we insist on asking for the meaning of such a poem, we can only be answered 'It means itself' ";[34] and, finally, and I think most conclusively, "[I]t is, in strictness, impossible to express the meaning in any but its own words. . . ."[35] But if the failure of paraphrase is ensured merely by changing the words in any way, then, by definition, paraphrase is doomed to failure, because it just is the process of reexpressing one sequence of words with a different sequence of words. On this criterion of success for paraphrase, no linguistic expression, poetic or otherwise, would be susceptible of paraphrase.

But if we are generous and willing to acquit Bradley of the charge of conventionalist sulk, what can we substitute as a criterion of success in paraphrase? We get a good idea of what that might be in another way Bradley has of putting his argument for the impossibility of poetic paraphrase. "When poetry answers to its idea and is purely or almost purely poetic, we find the identity of form and content; and the degree of purity attained may be tested by the degree in which we feel it hopeless to convey the effect of a poem or passage in any form but its own."[36] The eye falls here naturally on the word "effect," which seems to be doing duty for "content" or "substance" or "meaning." For where it sounds profoundly wrong to claim that you can't ever convey the *meaning* of a poem through a paraphrase, it surely sounds altogether plausible to claim that you can't ever convey its *effect*. The *experience* of reading *Paradise Lost* cannot be got by doing anything but reading *Paradise Lost* – a fortiori, certainly not by reading a paraphrase or interpretation of the meaning of *Paradise Lost*. So if the criterion of success in reexpression of the content of *Paradise Lost* is reproduction of the poem's total effect on the reader, it is an unreasonable, certainly an overstringent criterion. It would, indeed, like the conventionalist sulk, rule out all paraphrase whatever, even from prose to prose. A teacher would not be able to paraphrase her textbook.

But even to call this criterion of success in paraphrase too demanding is to pay it a compliment it does not merit. It is in fact nonsensical, because it demands of paraphrase something that never was the object of the exercise in the first place. A lamb is being hanged for a sheep. No one who sets out to say in prose the content of what a poem says in poetic form intends as the goal of the task to provide an alternative way of experiencing the poem. And to fault the interpreter for failing to do what is not the point of interpretation in the first place is plain nonsense.

It is not difficult to see how Bradley has gotten into this peculiar, untenable position. For he tends to describe paraphrase of meaning as "translation," as, for example, in a passage quoted before, where he says, "A translation of such poetry is not really the old meaning in a fresh dress. . . ."[37] But if *translation* is your goal, then your goal *is* generally taken to be the production of the poem's whole effect in different words: words of another natural language, of course. And we all agree that that is an unattainable goal. *Tradutor, traditor* always to some palpable degree. No one really thinks that you can ever devise an English translation of the *Iliad* that will give the Greekless reader the same poetic experience as reading the poem in the original, although we may think that Lattimore came closer to it (for us) than Pope.

105

But once we see that literary or poetic "translation" is entirely the wrong model for content paraphrase, the claim that poetic content cannot be rendered in prose paraphrase loses any hold it might have had on us. It is plainly false. It may even be false in its most extreme form, short of truth by stipulation. I see no reason why, in principle if not in practice, it is not possible to give a *complete* paraphrase of poetic meaning, leaving nothing of the content out. But in any event, no one who claims the content of a poem can be stated in words other than those of the poem is (or need be) claiming that full content can be captured, that perfect paraphrase is possible. And surely the modest claim that we can say in plain words more or less what the content of a poem is seems an unobjectionable one. Where it seems to fail is when we either place upon paraphrase the completely inappropriate criterion of success of translation or simply make its denial true by stipulation.

Thus it appears to me that Bradley's most often repeated reason for maintaining the form–content identity thesis for poetry, namely the supposed impossibility of content paraphrase, is utterly groundless. It is not clear to me from repeated readings of "Poetry for Poetry's Sake" whether failure of paraphrase is supposed to be the way we recognize that there is form–content identity in a poem, whether it is the reason we should believe that the form–content identity thesis is true, or whether it is simply a statement of what the cash value is of the form–content identity thesis. But in any event, once it goes by the boards, there is little else in Bradley's lecture to offer in defense of the thesis. There are, however, a few further considerations to be taken stock of, and I will get to them now.

§11 Perhaps the most eye-catching claim in "Poetry for Poetry's Sake," after the nontranslatability thesis, is to the effect that both the experience we have in reading a poem and the manner in which poems are created are incompatible with the separability of form from content. Of the reading experience, Bradley writes: "In these words [in *Hamlet*], . . . the action and characters (more of them than you can conceive apart) are focussed; but your experience is not a combination of them, as

106

ideas, on the one side, with certain sounds on the other; it is an experience of something in which the two are indissolubly fused."[38] And of the creative act:

> Pure poetry is not the decoration of a preconceived and clearly defined matter: it springs from the creative impulse of a vague imaginative mass pressing for development and definition. If the poet already knew exactly what he meant to say, why should he write the poem? The poem would in fact already be written. For only its completion can reveal, even to him, exactly what he wanted.[39]

Even a casual acquaintance with Collingwood's philosophy of art will allow one to recognize, in Bradley's description of the poem's genesis, a remarkably close approximation to the concept of expression as it appears in the latter's *Principles of Art* – far too close for coincidence. And it carries with it the same defect (among others) in the later, more sophisticated formulation.

Taken as an account of how *all* poems (or works of art) come into being, it is plainly false. It may indeed be the case – I certainly believe it is so – that sometimes a poem has its beginning as vague, inchoate impression, some "I know not what" that gradually becomes clear to the poet as the work progresses, and reaches full, self-conscious clarity only in the completed utterance. It is a possible scenario and, I feel certain, an actual one on many occasions (which specific occasions it being impossible to tell).

But why should we believe that this "clarification-in-process" scenario is the exclusive one? I find it quite plausible to believe, to instance two cases in point, that Lucretius, on the contrary, had a well-formed idea of what he wanted to say in his great poem and that Shakespeare did too, at least some of the time. It seems likely that, given the length of these works, some parts were preconceived and some came into being in the the very way Bradley (later Collingwood) described. That, however, just goes to show that, as one would naturally suspect if untainted by "expression theory," the bringing into being of poems and other works of art, as well as their various parts, is a mixed bag:

different artists, different artworks, different parts, different methods and processes. Why not? The idea of a single thing called "the creative process" seems to me a damaging myth.

If, however, we accept this more moderate claim, that sometimes poems or parts of poems do, and sometimes do not, come into being the way Bradley makes out, the claim loses its power to discriminate between poems and other forms of linguistic utterance. For there seems no reason not to believe that essays, philosophical treatises, nonfiction works of all kinds, including scientific books and papers, show the same character as poems in respect of sometimes following the Bradley–Collingwood scenario of creation and sometimes not.

§12 Moving now from the creation of poems to the experience of them, I think we will see the same problem attaching to Bradley's account. Bradley says that when reading a poem, at least as one should, one does not experience form and content, words on the one side and meanings on the other, as separate entities but the two as one: "[I]t is an experience of something in which the two are indissolubly fused." But here, as in the preceding case, it is clear that if we understand the claim as a universal generalization, it is plainly false, the addition of "should" notwithstanding. And if we understand it as the more moderate claim that sometimes the form and content of a poem are experienced as "indissolubly fused," sometimes (quite properly) not, it becomes harmlessly true, harmlessly in that it completely fails to distinguish the experience of poetry from the experience of any other text or utterance.

Now Bradley is well aware that we do not, in reading poetry, always experience the fusion of form with content. We can analytically separate "them." But when we do, we cannot be said to really have "them" separate; for, by hypothesis, they cannot be separated, and therefore what we end up with is not parts of the poem: the so-called content that you get in "analytic" reading is "no part of it [the poem], but a product of it in your reflective imagination, a faint analogue of some aspect of it taken in detachment from the whole."[40]

What we have here, I suggest, in metaphysical dress, is simply the normative claim that the *proper* way of reading a poem is the way that is in conformity with Bradley's fusion claim. Dressing it up in talk about what is "in" and what is "out" of the poem is a pretty thin disguise and is strangely at odds with Bradley's "definition" of a poem, which is frankly mentalistic and another clear prefiguration of Collingwood. On Bradley's account, "an actual poem is the succession of experiences – sounds, images, thoughts, emotions – through which we pass when we are reading *as poetically as we can*."[41] A poem is, in other words, an "imaginative experience."[42]

I say that Bradley's sense of what is "in" and what "out" of the poem is at odds with his frankly mentalistic definition of "the poem" because the in–out dichotomy is always stated by Bradley as if it were between what is "in" the poem and what is "out" of the poem *because* "in your head." But since the whole existence of the poem, on Bradley's account, is "in your head," an "imaginative experience," a distinction between what is "in" the poem and what is not, based on what is "in" the poem as opposed to what is "in your head," obviously won't wash. It is *all* "in your head." So the question becomes what part of the experience "in your head" when you read the text is "the poem" and what part is not but in your head. Well, when we read "as poetically as we can," our experience "in the head" is "in the poem"; and reading "as poetically as we can" means reading in a manner in which form and content are fused, not in the analytic manner in which they are not.

But now see where we have arrived. The experience of reading a poem is supposed, on Bradley's view, to be incompatible with the thesis that form and content can be prised apart; and that is because, when we are *properly* experiencing a poem, experiencing it "as poetically as we can," we always experience form and content as fused. How do we know when we are properly experiencing a poem, experiencing it "as poetically as we can"? Why, when we are experiencing form and content as fused. And why should we think that is the only proper way of experiencing the poem, the way that is "as poetically as we can"? Because, in a word, the form–content identity thesis is true – which is to say, we have moved in a perfect logical circle.

Now I take it that we can experience poetry as a fused form and content, and we can experience it with form and content prised apart. Furthermore, I take it that both ways are valuable, proper ways of experiencing it. I also am of the opinion that every such experience is a bit of both and that our attention is divided in all sorts of other ways as well. What I have in mind here is splendidly captured in the following description by Donald Francis Tovey of how we listen to Bach's *Art of Fugue:*

> Psychologists tell us that it is impossible to attend to more than two things at once. From this it must follow that we cannot attend to all four parts of these fugues at once, and that it must be still more impossible to attend to all the details of augmentation, diminution, stretto, inversion, double, triple and quadruple counterpoint through which Bach develops his subject and countersubjects. But it ought never to be supposed that any such attention is required of the listener. Nothing prevents the listener from *hearing* all these things at once and *attending* to one thing at a time. It is even doubtful whether he need often, or ever, attend to two. If the complexity is artistic it will make a single harmonious impression all the time, and the attention will move with enjoyment from point to point according as it is wisely directed.[43]

What Tovey has given us here is plain, simple wisdom about how we experience and enjoy a complex work of art (or a game of baseball, for that matter). And if we think of the content and form of a poem, the meaning and the medium, as two-voice counterpoint, Tovey's description will suit a poem as well as a fugue. Sometimes we concentrate on the "subject," sometimes the "counterpoint," and sometimes they "fuse" in our attention. The notion that the mode of attention in which form and content, medium and message fuse is some special, favored way of attending is just not in touch with reality. It is redolent with the aroma of "aesthetic attitude" theories and has aught to do with how real people experience poetry (or any of the other fine arts).

It seems reasonable to conclude, then, that the *moderate* thesis of form–content fusion is true for the experience of reading poetry. Sometimes we experience the medium and the message as one rather than two objects of attention; sometimes we are not aware of the medium and the message but only the medium-and-message, undifferentiated. But sometimes, too, our attention flits rapidly back and forth from one to the other or concentrates for a while on one rather than the other.

The moderate thesis, however, will not do the job for Bradley of distinguishing between poetry and other forms of linguistic expression. For it is true of all kinds of written texts, as well as speech, that sometimes we are aware of a fused meaning-and-form and sometimes our attention divides them and wanders from one to the other. What is even more damaging to Bradley's viewpoint, it seems to me, is that one will be far more likely to experience form–content fusion in the nonpoetic and nonliterary cases than in poetic and prose literature. When I read textbooks or newspapers, I am concerned only with the message, not the medium. The medium is "transparent" to me. Of course, I must *experience* the medium to get the message. But just because I do not pay particular attention to it, it is perfectly fused with its meaning. It is quite different with poetry, and literary language in general, just because the medium is thick, interesting, and so, far more frequently, the object of my attention: attention-getting, in fact. So it appears that, far from the experience of form–content fusion being exclusive to poetry, it is linguistically ubiquitous and more prevalent in nonpoetic forms to boot. The form–content identity thesis for poetry again comes to nought.

§13   I have expended a good deal of effort tracing the evolution of the form–content identity thesis from Kant to Bradley and trying to refute it in Bradley's lecture "Poetry for Poetry's Sake," its most well-known and vigorously defended exposition. It is now time for us to be reminded of why I thought this was an important thing to do and to determine what conclusions we can reasonably draw from the development and ultimate failure (at least as I see it) of the doctrine that in poetry, and in the other arts, there is no viable distinction between form and content.

Two forces, I suggested early on, were behind the development in the modern era of this notion. One force was the attempt to find, for poetry, some unique knowledge claim that the special sciences, practices, and disciplines could not preempt. This is quite explicit in Bradley's lecture. The "heresy," as Bradley calls it, of paraphrasing a poem, putting its content in our words, is tantamount to "putting our own thoughts or fancies into the place of the poet's creation." But that is a mistake, for then: "What he meant by *Hamlet*, or *Abt Vogler*, we say, is this or that which we knew already; and so we lose what he had to tell us."[44] Thus, for Bradley, to paraphrase is, of necessity, to attribute to the poem knowledge we must have already got from another source, and the poem, therefore, is prevented from giving us the new and special knowledge that it alone possesses. That, at least as I read Bradley, is the implication.

Equally apparent, if not more out front in Bradley's lecture, as we saw early on, is the intention of binding poetry together with the other fine arts through the thesis of form–content identity. It is an important enough point to bear quoting from Bradley to that effect yet again. (The reiterations are numerous.) "Just as there is in music not sound on one side and a meaning on the other, but expressive sound, and if you ask what is the meaning you can only answer by pointing to the sounds, just as in painting there is not a meaning *plus* paint, but a meaning *in* paint, or significant paint, and no man can really express the meaning in any other way than in paint and in *this* paint; so in a poem the true content and the true form neither exist nor can be imagined apart."[45]

Reminded, now, of these two motivating forces behind the form–content identity thesis, and assured of their visible presence in Bradley's highly influential lecture, we should now be able to weave the identity thesis – its history, its raison d'être, its (in my view) demise – into the thematic structure of the general argument. Let us concentrate first on the identity thesis as an effort to bind together the fine arts.

In the opening two chapters I traced the high points (as I saw them) in the history of aesthetics that represented, in my view, the persistent, single-minded attempt to find some defining similarity among the fine arts. The basic strategy was to make out all of the arts to be representational, or at least "contentful," with absolute music always the problematic case: the *experimentum crucis.*

Formalism is an island in this historical stream of representation and content theories, a brief interlude in which absolute music becomes the paradigm and everything else an anomaly. And the form–content identity thesis shares that characteristic with formalism, all the while its major practitioner, Bradley, insisting that the thesis is not to be identified with formalism because the formalist "goes too far. . . ."[46] Thus it is not music as pure form that the form–content identity theorist takes as his paradigm but music as the paradigmatic art in which form and content are fused, inseparable, identical.

In Hanslick, who, as we have seen, coined the famous phrase "The content of music is tonally moving forms,"[47] the identification of form with content is, I have argued, simply a rhetorical way of *denying* that music has a "content" at all, as that word is customarily used with reference to the arts. It is therefore only a stimulus to the real form–content identity thesis, not an early version of the thing itself. To get from Hanslick to Bradley, the notion of musical "content" must be given real substance, or formalism it remains. And it is clear what that substance must be. It is the ineffable, the "I know not what"; and so it presents itself in Bradley's thesis that the content of poetry cannot be paraphrased, is unutterable except by the poem itself.

For those, like myself, who see the resort to ineffable content as a council of despair, the attempt to knit the fine arts together under its banner will hold little attraction. It is another attempt at discovering that essential sameness in the arts, with the added liability of having the worst of both worlds. Instead of, as in the case of content theories, ascribing to music something the other arts have but it does not or, as in the case of formalism, ascribing to the other arts something that music has but they do not, the form–content identity thesis ascribes to *all* of the arts something that *none* of them has: "ineffable content."

A great deal more, doubtless, needs to be said about the ineffable business in regard to music, but for now I shall leave it alone, resting in the conclusion that one motive behind the form–content identity thesis, our old friend the quest for defining sameness in the arts, failed in its purpose. It seems to me that it is vital to maintain the very distinction between music and the "contentful" arts that the identity thesis is designed to rub out. Music is the art in which form (broadly speaking) and content cannot be distinguished, the art in which the form is the "content." That is something extremely important that distinguishes music from most examples of visual and literary art, where form, or medium, and content, or subject, can be and, in experience, frequently are distinguished. It is only in recognizing this "difference" that we can come to understand the arts as we have them.

But this cannot be our last word on the form–content identity thesis. For we will recall that the quest for sameness is not the only motivating force behind it. There is still to be dealt with the other: the attempt to carve out for poetry and the other arts a class of knowledge claims all their own. Is this a sensible thing to attempt? Does the form–content identity thesis address, if unsuccessfully, a real problem in our experience of the arts? To these matters I want to turn next.

§14 If a molecular biologist were to submit her results to *Nature* in poetic form, it would be thought utterly absurd, hardly less so if John Rawls had submitted the manuscript of his *Theory of Justice* to Harvard University Press in rhymed couplets. Yet Lucretius presented his "results," at the cutting edge of atomic theory and moral philosophy, in a longish poem that has come to be thought of as one of the masterworks of Western literature. That Lucretius was able to do this and we are not implies, needless to say, a profound change in the practice of science and philosophy, as well as a profound change in the role of poetry, at least in some of its aspects, in our lives.

From this profound change, however, it seems to be a mistake to conclude that poetry must be "defended" by showing that it imparts some special knowledge, unique to itself and expressible, in each individual case, only by the poem that is supposed to contain that particular body of knowledge (whatever it might be). The practice of poetry is not a way of knowing some particular kind of thing but, in one of its offices, one of the various

114

ways we may have of expressing all kinds of things we know or believe, wish or hope, fear or value. And the reason poetry is not a viable way to express scientific results today but was in the times of Parmenides and Lucretius is not that poetry has changed but that science has.

Two things Bradley says are directly relevant here, one quite wrong, the other profoundly right. He says there is something wrong, you may recall, with the conclusion that a poem might express "this or that which we know already. . . ."[48] What is so strangely mistaken about this idea is that it overlooks one of our deepest and most persistent needs: the need, so obvious already in childhood, of being told the same things over and again. Truth saying is the office of poetry as well as of newspapers and scientific periodicals. But perhaps what separates poetry from these others (and many more organs of expression) is that it needn't necessarily be reporting the news for the first time; literary art forms need not give us the scoop, although there is no reason to believe they do not do it some of the time, and properly so. The Greeks were right, pace Plato: poets sometimes are seers. But Pope was right too: they sometimes pronounce "what oft was thought, but ne'er so well expressed."

The role of poetry and the other literary arts in our lives is not a simple one. And it cannot be my place here to tease out the strands. But thinking of literature, either poetry or prose fiction, as a source of some special kind of human knowledge, as Bradley and others have done, is, in my view, profoundly mistaken and often seems to border on a kind of "aesthetic mysticism" that is not just unhelpful to the philosophical understanding. Poetry and fiction are not special conduits to the font of wisdom. They are ways some wise folks (and some not so wise) have tried to express some of the things they have found out or others have found out (and some things that nobody has found out, because they are not the case). There is no one kind of knowledge, effable or ineffable, that is the particular province of poets. And this leads us to the point in this regard on which Bradley is profoundly right.

Bradley insisted that there is no special *subject* of art in general or of poetry in particular. (Bear in mind here his distinction between "subject" and "content.") He writes, "[I]t is surely true that we cannot determine beforehand what subjects are fit for Art, or name any subject on which a good poem may not possibly be written."[49] It was *content*, of course, not *subject*, that Bradley said was unique to the poem and its own special knowledge. But of both content and subject, *we* may want to say that there are no a priori limits on what might be poetically expressed. There may, of course, be practical limits on what might usefully be expressed, and so it may well be a foolish exercise to report results in quantum theory in blank verse. But that poetic expression of the quantum-mechanical "vision" might be both appropriate and moving is not thereby denied.

The quest for a special poetic knowledge, which motivates the form–content identity thesis, is, I have been arguing, a fruitless, misdirected one. The practice of poetry is not a method or methods of gaining some special, esoteric form of knowledge, but a method or methods of expressing knowledge (and other things too) that people have (or think they have) acquired in all of the various ways people do acquire such things, from scientific investigation to philosophical discussion, from common sense to ecstatic vision, from moral argument to religious conversion. To the extent, then, that the form–content identity thesis is a quest for special knowledge, unique to poetry (and art), it fails to connect with any valid intuition about or genuine problem in the philosophy of art. The question remaining is whether it connects with *any* valid intuition or problem at all. I think that it does, but comes to a mistaken conclusion.

§15 Throughout this chapter I have referred to two motivating forces behind the form–content identity thesis. They are the quest for the common essence of the arts, the quest for sameness that is the *bête noire* of my book, and the quest for a special poetic (or art-specific) kind of knowledge. To these I must now add a third. It appears to me that we have a deep intuition that in the arts there is an especially intimate relation between form and content not exhibited in other modes of expression. To a degree, that is a valid intuition, and the form–content identity thesis is a response to it – the wrong response, as it turns out. For it

116

construes the intimate relation of form to content as identity: an intimate relation indeed. But the real trick is to avoid that extreme conclusion, to show the special intimacy of form and content in the arts while maintaining the distinction between them. This the identity thesis fails (quite intentionally) to do.

There is currently abroad a philosophically deep way of approaching our intuition about the intimacy of the form–content relation, in Arthur Danto's second condition on something's being a work of art. On Danto's view, it will be recalled, the first condition for arthood is "aboutness." Works of art are essentially about something, or at least the question of what a true work of art is about can be sensibly raised, even if the answer is "nothing." But the aboutness criterion cannot be all there is to it, for modes of expression other than artworks are "about." So to the genus must be appended a difference. In Danto's words (quoted also in Chapter 2): "The thesis is that works of art, in categorical contrast with mere representations, use the means of representation in a way that is not exhaustively specified when one has exhaustively specified what is being represented."[50]

What Danto is saying, I take it, is that when one exhaustively specifies what the content of a work of art is, what, in other words, has been represented *by* the medium of representation, one has not exhaustively specified the relation of medium to subject, form to content, whereas, say, in a philosophical or scientific treatise one has exhaustively specified the relation between medium and content, form and representation when one has exhaustively paraphrased the content. The relation between form and content simply is, in the nonart case, that *this* form has expressed *this* content.

What is extra in the artistic form–content relation is that one must also specify the way in which the form, the medium, is employed. And that way is what makes the relation more intimate. For the *way* in which the artist employs the medium is, in effect, part of the content, because it expresses something in the artist's point of view about the content.

My point is that Danto's way of seeing the relation of medium to representation in art, as opposed to nonart, is also a way of explaining the intuition, which the form–content identity thesis was also (in part) contrived to explain, that the relation of form to content in art is particularly, uniquely intimate. Furthermore, Danto manages to do the business without obliterating the distinction between form and content, medium and object of representation. And that is crucial to the success of the enterprise.

I was somewhat cagey in my statement of the intuition that, in art, form and content are intimately connected in a special way alien to other forms of expression. I framed it in terms of degree. For I think there are other cases besides that of the fine arts where the mode of expression sometimes performs the function Danto is talking about. (Philosophical works like Spinoza's *Ethics,* the *Tractatus,* as well as the later writings of Wittgenstein come to mind, where the special or even startling modes of expression seem to "comment" implicitly on the content in ways akin to the cases of the fine arts Danto adduces. I intentionally omit mention of Plato's dialogues, as these might be construed as works of the fine arts themselves.) But I think it would be carping to place too much emphasis on these instances, which can be construed as the exception rather than the rule (unless one has a "theory" about this, which some people do). It remains the case that it is especially in the arts where we feel a particular, intimate relation between form and content. The form–content identity thesis responded to this valid intuition in, it seems to me, a disastrous way, by obliterating the distinction altogether. Danto, I suggest, gives us a way of supporting our intuition that manages also to preserve it. And whether or not one can buy into Danto's solution, any other successful competitor will have to preserve it as well.

§16   I have argued in the present chapter that the notion of a form–content fusion, in the literary arts in particular, is symptomatic of a desire to reveal in them some special kind of knowledge that only they can possess and impart: a kind of knowledge immune to the inroads of the specialized scientific, academic, and philosophical disciplines, which claim exclusive domain over the "knowledge game." My own belief is that literature has been, and continues to be, a conduit for knowledge not unique to itself, but common to the specialized disciplines as well, at least within the limits of its demesne. But this is a highly controversial belief, and stands in need of defense and amplification. That will be my project in the following chapter.

I hasten to add that any thorough defense and development of a "truth-in-literature" thesis of any kind would require not a chapter but a volume. So my goal in what follows must be more modest than that. It is to defend a moderate thesis about, principally, *fictional* literature, to the effect that, sometimes at least, one of the functions of a literary work, *qua* literary work, is to present hypotheses of a philosophical, religious, moral, or "social" kind (or what have you) for readers' consideration as to truth or falsity. This defense will be conducted against the background of a thorough and closely reasoned argument in contradiction of such theses, published recently. As usual, my theme will be differences, although in the present instance I vary it slightly. For whereas in one place I shall indeed argue at length that an implicit musical model of fictional literature, taken for granted in our thinking about the question of literary truth, is quite misplaced and wrongheaded, I shall argue in another place that a musical model for the role of the literary critic, a crucial point in the argument, is both helpful and valid. So, now, on to that task.

Chapter 5
The Laboratory of Fictional Truth

§1 The publication of Peter Lamarque and Stein Olsen's book, *Truth, Fiction and Literature*, was an event of the first magnitude in contemporary philosophy of art. I intend to defend here, in the face of some trenchant criticism by Lamarque and Olsen in that book, a version of what they call there the Propositional Theory of Literary Truth – henceforth, the Propositional Theory for short. I underscore that I will defend a *version* of this theory because I will not defend it in as strong a form as stated by Lamarque and Olsen. And I underscore that I will defend it against *some* criticism by Lamarque and Olsen because I cannot, in a single chapter in a single book, hope to defend it against all. But if at least a modest version of the Propositional Theory cannot be salvaged from Lamarque and Olsen's powerful attempt at demolition, my own literary experience will be very difficult for me to comprehend. Indeed, part of my "worldview," if I may risk being too grandiose, is going to totter. So what I am attempting here is of no small importance to me. And if, as I think, there are others who share my literary experience and the worldview in which it inheres, it will be at least of some interest to them as well.

§2 Proponents of the Propositional Theory, as Lamarque and Olsen characterize them,

> admit the reasonableness of the view that literature at the "literal level" is for the most part fictive, i.e. that characteristically its content is fictional and its mode of presentation is not that of fact-stating. But they claim that at a different level literary

works do, perhaps must, imply or suggest general propositions about human life which have to be assessed as true or
false, and that these propositions are what make literature valuable.[1]

More specifically, the Propositional Theory is founded, as
Lamarque and Olsen present it, on the distinction between two
different kinds of proposition a fictional literary work might express:

> Propositions which describe or mention particular situations
> and events, characters and places in a literary work may be
> labelled *subject descriptions*. Propositions which express gen-
> eralizations or judgements based on or referring to these de-
> scribed situations, events, characters and places may be
> labelled *thematic statements*.[2]

Furthermore, thematic statements – with which the Propositional Theory is principally concerned – "may be of two types,
explicit and *implicit*. Explicit thematic statements occur in the
literary work itself," whereas implicit statements are "extracted
from the work by the reader in interpretation."[3]

With these distinctions in hand, we are ready for a more precise statement of the Propositional Theory. In the words of Lem-
arque and Olsen, "A Propositional Theory of Literary Truth
could then be formulated as follows: *the literary work contains
or implies general thematic statements about the world which the
reader as part of an appreciation of the work has to assess as true or
false*."[4] I intend to defend a somewhat weaker form of this theory
against some criticism by Lamarque and Olsen. But before I state
their criticism, or my defense, I must make my modifications.

First, I am not saying that all works of fiction contain general
thematic statements; only some of them do. (And from now on
I will use the terms "fiction" and "fictional," "literature" and
"literary" in the general sense of "fiction that is literature," as
contrasted with literature that is not fiction and fiction that is
not literature.)

Second, I am not saying that every general thematic statement is or ought to be the subject of truth-value assessment, as part of the reader's literary appreciation. Whether it is or is not, ought or ought not to be depends on the work in which it is expressed as well as the role it may play in the work.

Third, I am not saying that the truth of a general thematic statement is ever necessary for a work's being evaluated positively or ever sufficient for a work's being evaluated positively. The truth of general thematic statements is just one literary value among many, their falsity just one literary disvalue among many. In any case, it is reader-relative plausibility rather than truth that is at issue, as we shall see.

With these amendments on the table, I can now state the version of the Propositional Theory that I want to defend: *Some fictional works contain or imply general thematic statements about the world that the reader, as part of an appreciation of the work, has to assess as true or false.*

I am basically interested, in this regard, in two closely related claims Lamarque and Olsen make, meant to cast doubt on the Propositional Theory. They are that critics do not, as part of their ordinary business, try to determine the truth or falsity of general thematic statements and that the determination of the truth or falsity of such claims is not part of literary appreciation. And the reason I say that they are closely related is that they imply one another, the way Lamarque and Olsen put matters. That is to say, if true–false determinations are not part of critical practice, then they cannot be part of literary appreciation, since critical practice deals with all aspects of literary appreciation; and going in the other direction of implication, if true–false determinations are not part of literary appreciation, then they will not be part of critical practice, since, again, critical practice deals with all aspects of literary appreciation. This reciprocal implication can be understood in the following succinct statement by Lamarque and Olsen. "Debate about the truth or falsity of the propositions implied by a literary work is absent from literary criticism since it does not enter into *the appreciation of the work as a literary work.*"[5]

I want to look, first, at the claim that literary critics do not as a rule engage in determinations of the truth or falsity of general thematic statements in or implied by literature. I will then turn to the wider, related question of literary appreciation.

§3   Briefly, the criticism argument can be stated as follows. According to the Propositional Theory, part of the appreciation of a literary work may consist in the reader's assessing the truth-value of general thematic propositions expressed therein. But if that is so, then we could rightfully expect that such assessment should also occur in the work of the literary critic, under the assumption that anything relevant to literary appreciation is also the critic's job to discuss. But critics typically engage in no discussion of the truth or falsity of general thematic statements, only the interpretive task of bringing them out. So the Propositional Theory is incompatible with the practice of literary criticism, and hence must be false. In the words of Lamarque and Olsen, "The issues of literary criticism concern aspects of literary works, and among these issues will be their handling of certain types of themes and concepts, but there is no accepted place for debate about the truth or falsity of general statements about human life or the human condition."[6] Nor is this absence a trivial matter. On the contrary, it is of the essence. "The lack of debate in literary criticism and critical discourse in general about the truth of such general propositions must therefore be understood as a feature of the literary practice itself."[7]

I confess that when I first read these observations, I was rather knocked back on my heels and felt, intuitive believer that I was in the Propositional Theory, awakened from my dogmatic slumber. For it seemed to me then, and still seems to me now, that Lamarque and Olsen are right about most literary criticism: there is, most of the time, no true–false evaluation in it of the general thematic statements. And it seemed to me then, too, that this fact – and fact it seems to be – was completely incompatible with my deeply held belief in the Propositional Theory.

Subsequent reflection, however, has convinced me that there is no incompatibility between the Propositional Theory and the uncontested fact that critics do not usually engage in verifying or disconfirming practices vis-à-vis the propositions fictional works might be thought to express. The problem is to choose the right model for the relation between critic, reader, and work.

Our problem is this. If the Propositional Theory is true, there must be some significant place in the literary experience for the confirmation and disconfirmation of general thematic statements. The most obvious place to look is critical practice. But when we look, we do not find any such proceedings. So the Propositional Theory seems to be in deep trouble.

But what about the general readership for fiction? Why not look there for the true–false evaluation we fail to find in the practices of literary critics? Perhaps it is just not the critic's job but the reader's.

Lamarque and Olsen do indeed give the reader a passing glance, but come up empty-handed: "There is no debate about truth in literary criticism, so the argument might run, because every mature reader is in possession of such reasons as would lead to broad agreement with other readers on the acceptance or rejection of the explicit and implicit thematic statements of a literary work."[8]

Notice that the possibility Lamarque and Olsen canvass is not there being no true–false evaluation among critics because it takes place among readers. Rather, it is that there is no true–false evaluation among critics because readers have already agreed on truth–value themselves. Thus in neither case does literary appreciation provide space for true–false evaluation. The latter alternative is no better than the former, as Lamarque and Olsen quickly conclude; and with that conclusion I concur.

I wish to propose an alternative designed to provide a place in literary appreciation for considerations of truth and falsity of the general thematic statements. My model is drawn from music, and it is the triadic relation of work to performer to listener.

Let us say that the job of the musical performer is to make musical works available for the listener's appreciation, which seems uncontroversial. Furthermore, let us say that, analogously, it is *one* of the jobs of the literary critic to make works of fiction *more* available for the reader's appreciation.

There is, of course, a big difference between the two cases. For very few of us can make a work of music available to ourselves for appreciation. Some of us can appreciate a piano sonata by playing it to ourselves. And a very small number of us can appreciate music merely by reading scores. But by far the vast majority of us require the performer to, so to speak, be the middle man between us and the work.

But all of us who are literate can make fictional works available to ourselves, by reading them. Nevertheless, the critic can make things that we do not notice available to us by revealing them through interpretation. And among those things are the explicit and implied general thematic statements. So we may say that as the pianist makes available to us a Beethoven sonata for our appreciation, so the literary critic makes available to us for our appreciation those great thematic statements that she perceives and we do not.

Now if one thinks, as I do, that part of the reader's literary appreciation consists in confirming and disconfirming for himself the general thematic statements he perceives in the fictional works he reads, sometimes unaided, sometimes through the writings of literary critics, one will see why it is quite compatible with the Propositional Theory that such confirmation and disconfirmation should be absent from the writings of literary critics. For confirmation and disconfirmation are part of *appreciation,* and appreciation is the job, if I may so put it, of the reader, not the critic *qua* critic. The critic's job, *qua* critic, is, among other things, to make available to the reader whatever hypotheses the fictional work may, directly or indirectly, propose. It is the reader's job to appreciate them, in part, by confirming or disconfirming them for himself. The job of the critic, like the job of the performer, is to make the work available for appreciation. And since confirmation and disconfirmation are part of appreciation, it is no business of hers to mess about with it – and she does not.

None of this, I should add, implies that readers must be – and, as Lamarque and Olsen quite rightly observe, they are not – in agreement with one another about the truth or falsity of the general thematic statements. Different readers may come to different conclusions about them. And most of these statements, at least in literary works of depth and value, will be such that the same reader may never decide one way or the other during a lifetime of thought about them. The reason for that and further elucidation of the reader's role in the verification or disconfirmation process will occupy me for the next few pages.

§4 The community of readers, in their consideration of the truth-values of the general thematic statements, constitute the "laboratory of fictional truth" to which the title of this chapter refers. What goes on in this laboratory?

To help answer this question I would like to introduce a distinction made by William James in one of his most well known and widely read essays, "The Will to Believe." James distinguished there between what he called "live" and "dead" hypotheses. "A live hypothesis," he said, "is one which appeals as a real possibility to him to whom it is proposed."[9] Contrariwise, a dead hypothesis is one that makes no such appeal, but is an impossibility to the person who considers it. Thus, as James concluded, "deadness and liveness in an hypothesis are not intrinsic properties but relations to the individual thinker."[10] What is a dead hypothesis to one person then, may be a live one to – indeed, taken for true by – another.

Fictional works present us, in the general thematic statements, explicit or implicit, hypotheses dead to some, live to others, and frequently concerning the profoundest religious, metaphysical, moral, and social questions. Works of fiction may or may not also provide reasons for believing such propositions. But what I am most interested in here are the reader's own efforts in the laboratory of fictional truth to confirm or disconfirm such hypotheses himself.

A reader may have one of three attitudes toward a general thematic statement. If it is a dead hypothesis for him, his attitude will be disbelief, and if it is a live one, his attitude *could* be belief or it could be merely inclination to believe combined with inclination not to believe, the reader being still agnostic with regard to it. It is the third kind of case that will initiate, one would think, the most active attempt on the reader's part to confirm or disconfirm. For where the question is already decided for him, he will obviously have less motivation to put his belief to the test. It is therefore those cases where the hypothesis is live and the reader agnostic with regard to it that I will talk about in what follows. But I do not think that the other cases are unimportant. To begin with, there seems to be a deep and abiding human need to hear again what is already believed, and literature seems to serve this need in a way peculiar to itself, which merits further investigation. That there is something of ritual in this I think is obvious. But that is a topic for another time.

So I am suggesting that one of the things fiction sometimes does is to propose to the reader live hypotheses, in the form of general thematic statements, which the reader, as part of the literary experience attempts to confirm or disconfirm, either in thought or in action. The action part of the process, I should add, is a can of worms, and I am not going to open it here. I shall confine myself to talking about the confirmation–disconfirmation process in mentalistic terms. Or, less pompously put, I shall discuss the obvious and, it seems to me, uncontentious claim that intelligent readers of the canon often have proposed to them live hypotheses of a religious, metaphysical, or moral content that they continue to think about and try, thereby, to evaluate during and after the reading process. Certainly Lamarque and Olsen believe this takes place. What they do not believe, and what I do believe, is that this process of critical thinking about the truth or falsity of the general thematic statements is, broadly speaking, part of *literary appreciation*.

In the next section I shall argue for the *literary* claims of the confirmation–disconfirmation process. And I think I can segue smoothly into that discussion by suggesting here that academics in general, philosophers in particular, tend to vastly underestimate the importance of the higher forms of fictional literature for the general nonacademic, nonspecialist readership of these works, as a source of what can, in a generous sense, be thought of as "philosophy." Whether or not it is an indictment of philosophy, few people outside of the Academy read Plato or Hume or Quine. What they know of the great questions of philosophy they know from novels and plays and, in our century, the movies.

Nor is this true of the modern world alone. It is even more true of antiquity, where, indeed, the epistemic claims of literature would scarcely have needed to be argued for and against which Plato launched so stout a criticism, Aristotle so stout a defense. If one is seriously interested in literature as an institution, and Lamarque and Olsen certainly are, one ignores at one's peril how deeply implicated fictional literature is and has been in the process by which an intelligent and educated public obtains what knowledge it does of the "big questions," and what motivation it is given to thinking these questions through to whatever conclusions the individual reader may draw. A world without the Greek playwrights, without Shakespeare and Cervantes, Dostoyevski and Tolstoy, Austen and Goethe would be a world in which a vast number of people remained ignorant of philosophical speculation and bereft of the means to acquire it. It is, to me, a hard saying that the philosophical and moral education fictional literature imparts to so many, and the verification processes it sets in motion, both of which they get in fictional works and nowhere else, can't be part of what they certainly would call their literary appreciation.

Now these considerations in themselves prove nothing. The general readership for literature may simply be misdescribing its epistemic experience of literary works by calling it a part of "literary appreciation," and if so, it is the task of philosophy to correct it. Nevertheless, the institution of literature, as it has existed since Parmenides and the Homeric epics, is at least prima facie evidence in favor of the idea that part of literary appreciation is, and has been since time out of mind, thinking about general thematic statements to the end of confirming or disconfirming them.

I doubt that the individual reader always or even often reaches firm conclusions with regard to the general thematic statements – because of the nature of the general thematic statements themselves, at least as they occur in serious works of fiction. For the hypotheses themselves, when they are live, usually state the most perennially contested themes, of which Kant's Antinomies might serve as examples. Thus a reader may never decide, in the process of deliberation that a profound work of fiction stimulates in him, between freedom and determinism, Voltaire or a benevolent theodicy, deism or atheism, the role of men and women in a well-ordered society, and so on. Or he may find himself on one side of the question after an encounter with *Candide,* another after an encounter with Milton. In other words, the laboratory of fictional truth, unlike the laboratory of natural science, does not necessarily aim at, or achieve, consensus. But this should not disqualify it as essentially a truth-seeking institution, for it shares this character with philosophy. And unless one has some philosophical position on philosophical truth itself, one uses philosophy as a model of truth seeking that fiction must stand favorable comparison with if it has pretensions to the truth game itself.

I have, then, been arguing that the institution of fiction, since antiquity, has contained a strong epistemic part in the form of the reader's propensity for thinking about, and attempting to confirm or disconfirm thereby, the live hypotheses that may be proposed to him in the general thematic statements, either explicit or implied. Furthermore, I have been arguing that this provides at least prima facie evidence for the truth of the Propositional Theory, in a modest version. But prima facie evidence it remains – certainly far from conclusive. I shall now say a little more on its behalf, although I hasten to add that even when I have finished, I will be far from convincing you, or indeed myself, that even my modest Propositional Theory is beyond doubt.

§5   I want now to talk about my own idea of why we should consider truth-value determination of the kind outlined just now to be part of literary appreciation, over and above the fact that it seems to play such a conspicuous role in the institution of literary fiction, on the reader's side, and has done since antiquity. I take my departure from some remarks by Lamarque and Olsen to the contrary. But I want to emphasize that the speculations directly following are not directed toward any specific argument of theirs, but rather to what I imagine to be a difficulty that many will have with my proposal and that might be at least vaguely suggested by what they say.

As I noted previously, Lamarque and Olsen do not deny that

readers are frequently stimulated by the general thematic statements of fiction to ruminate over their truth or falsity. What they
deny is that this is any part of literary appreciation:

> This question is not a question whether the general proposi-
> tions used to organize events, characters, and situations of a
> work into a significant and meaningful pattern have any ap-
> plication in contexts outside literature. Clearly they do and
> may have been so used. The question is whether assessment
> of their truth enters into the reader's appreciation of a literary
> work as a literary work.[11]

Their answer to the question, of course, is no. As they say of the
critic, with regard to what they take to be one of the central
themes of George Eliot's *Middlemarch* but which applies, pari
passu, to the ordinary reader:

> A debate about the substance of this thematic statement will
> be a debate about the possibility of free will and this is central
> in philosophy. The critic is free to join this debate, of course,
> but when he does he has moved on from literary appreciation
> of *Middlemarch*.[12]

There is something about the way this point is put that will
be very compelling, on first reflection, to many readers, because,
I think, of an implicit assumption about what appreciation of a
work of art, in general, is like. The assumption has as its basis
what I would describe, to return to musical analogies once
again, as a *musical* model of how these things go. And that
model, I suggest, is the wrong one for the literary work of art.
Here, yet again, is a *difference*.

Suppose I were to give the following scenario of a musical
"experience." I listen to the first movement of Beethoven's Fifth
Symphony with great concentration and with a pleasure intense
enough to border on rapture. So vividly has the thematic unity
of the first movement, in particular, impressed itself on my consciousness that I become convinced that Beethoven meant to
convey a hypothesis concerning it. And the hypothesis that
keeps presenting itself to me is that all humanity is unified as
the notes of Beethoven's music, in familial bonds of harmony

stronger than the dissensions and differences that separate us. To coin a phrase, Beethoven is telling us that all men are brothers, and in mulling over this proposition, in the days and weeks following my audition of the work, I come to the conclusion that this hypothesis is true. What a fine thing, I keep thinking, for a composer to be able to accomplish with his music.[13] And how much richer my appreciation of the music is because this is a part of that appreciation.

There are two reasons why a skeptical chap like myself would be highly suspicious of such a notion of musical "appreciation." The first is well known, and I will not dwell on it here. It remains, at best, highly controversial whether absolute music can possibly express such semantical content as exemplified by theses like the one about "unity" that I have just sketched. Or, to put the point more broadly, it seems impossible to me that absolute music can express what I have been calling, following Lamarque and Olsen, general thematic statements of the kind we find in works of literary fiction. There are plenty of reasons for this skepticism, but as I and others have presented them many times before, I will refrain from any further discussion of that kind here.

Rather, I am particularly interested in another objection to the picture sketched above, of the musical experience, based on what I shall call the "afterlife" of purported artistic appreciations. Musical works, unlike at least read works of fiction, novels or epic poems (say), have a self-contained appreciation time, so to speak. By that I mean that it would be common for a reader of a novel to put it down from time to time, sometimes for an extended period, and then pick it up again, with no experienced break in fictional time. I have always found this phenomenon quite remarkable. Somehow, one can leave the heroine poised on the precipice for an hour or two, or even a weekend or a week, and return with no feeling of narrative or aesthetic discontinuity. Nor need this be a less than optimal way to experience fictional works. Indeed, it is normal, as one can assure oneself by recalling that the great "three-volume novels" of the nineteenth century, those of Dickens and the rest, were published in installments in the literary periodicals of the day.

But how absurd to think one could properly appreciate a symphony, let alone a movement or section thereof, in bits and pieces. Could I listen to Beethoven's Fifth Symphony to the end of the first movement, go away for the weekend, and come back for the other three and be thought to have experienced the work properly? Yet such gaps occur in my experience of novels all the time. (Who can read *War and Peace* in a single sitting?) What this strongly suggests is that the relation of fictional time to real time is very different from the relation of musical time to real time, in that fictional time tolerates large gaps in real time and musical time does not.

Now the "gappy" experience of read fictional literature, as opposed to the continuous experience of music, suggests that real time and fictional time have a more "sloppy" relationship, if I may so put it, than the rather strict relationship between real and musical time; and this leads to the discovery of another temporal disanalogy, also describable as sloppy versus strict.

Those who savor good wine will be familiar with the notion that the appreciation includes an aftertaste; and the quality of the aftertaste matters to the quality of the wine experience. What I want to suggest is that the appreciation of fiction by the normal reader has a long, somewhat indeterminate aftertaste, which I will designate its "afterlife," whereas the appreciation of music, at least for most musically untrained listeners, ends with the end of the music: it has little if any afterlife at all, except perhaps for the accomplished musician.

The fictional experience, then, both is gappy with regard to real time and has a somewhat indeterminate outer boundary. The appreciation has a considerable afterlife. The musical experience, on the contrary, neither is gappy with regard to real time, nor has an afterlife to speak of, for most listeners. It is continuous and ends with the coda.

Now suppose there is ingrained in one, without one's really having thought about it, a preconceived notion of artistic appreciation that has *musical* appreciation as its model, in respect of the gappiness and afterlife phenomena, as, I suspect, there is in many people. If there is, then one will feel an intuitive pull toward the view that verifying the general thematic statements cannot be part of literary appreciation. For, after all, such a verification process – which is to say, mulling things over and reaching at least tentative, temporary conclusions – is just not something expected to go on, or at least not very extensively, *during* the reading experience but, mainly, in the gaps and the afterlife. And if one thinks in terms of the musical model, then one will think that the appreciation of fiction has no gaps or afterlife or, put another way, that the gaps and the afterlife of reading are not part of literary appreciation. It doesn't much matter which way you put it; I prefer the former.

I believe, however, that the musical model of artistic appreciation casts a false light on the literary experience. It assumes artistic appreciation to be, *tout court*, a neat, self-contained kind of thing, whereas the literary experience, as I have suggested, is a gappy, sloppy sort of thing.

That the literary experience is gappy, I think, will be agreed on without argument. We all know that we can put down a work of fiction and take it up again without loss of narrative continuity. But that it is sloppy as well as gappy, that it has an afterlife, and that part of that afterlife, as well as part of the gaps, consists in verifying or disconfirming the general thematic statements will certainly require more than an appeal to intuition or common experience. There is no quarrel, I presume, about whether we go on thinking about what we have read in a literary work, intentionally and, perhaps, for an extended period of time, when we have finished (say) a novel by Tolstoy or Jane Austen or other of our serious novelists, even those of lesser rank. The question before us is whether the gaps or afterlife or any part thereof can be considered literary appreciation. Am I still enjoying *Pride and Prejudice* as a literary work when I am savoring the aftertaste and mulling over serious issues it has raised?

To try to answer this question let us forget, for a moment, the crucial case of thesis verification and just consider the very general phenomenon, with contents unspecified, of thinking about, remembering, reimagining what we have experienced in the gaps or after completing a good novel. Should this be considered part of our literary appreciation of that novel or not?

I doubt that I can give, in so limited a space, a completely satisfactory answer to this question. But consider the following thought experiment. Imagine going to a concert, listening with pleasure to a Beethoven symphony, and then going about your business, the experience all but forgotten in the press of affairs. Next imagine finishing *Pride and Prejudice,* having read it with pleasure, and going about your business, the experience all but forgotten in the press of affairs, as in the case of the Beethoven symphony.

Let me suggest to you that the experience of the Beethoven, although not what I would call an optimal one, is nevertheless a full, complete one. It is the way serious music is appreciated by people who love music but do not have good musical memories, do not think about or study it. Let me suggest, further, that the experience of *Pride and Prejudice,* without the afterlife, is not merely less than an optimal literary experience but less than a literary experience altogether: less than a *full* literary experience of *that work.* What I have described is a full literary experience of a time waster: a whodunit or one of the lesser genres of sci-fi – literature intended to be read and forgotten, intended not to provoke thought, not to have an afterlife. By my lights, though, to experience *Pride and Prejudice* and its ilk without the afterlife is to have less than a full experience, not merely less than an optimal one.

This is not to say that every thought sequence, no matter how wide, long, diffuse, or irrelevant, a novel sets in train is part of the literary experience of the work. And to draw boundaries of relevance is obviously a nontrivial matter, not to be taken up here. All that must be agreed upon for present purposes is that *some* significant afterlife, suitably circumscribed, is a bona fide part of literary experience. That, I think, I have shown is neither initially implausible nor without some fairly strong intuitive appeal, if one simply imagines what the literary experience of serious works would be without it.

But I asked you to put aside, for the moment, the question of hypothesis verification and consider only the general idea of the literary afterlife. That moment is over, and we must confront the question of whether, given that at least some part of the literary afterlife can be construed as literary appreciation, hypothesis verification can be construed as part of that part, that is to say, as part of literary appreciation. For someone might well accept the more general claim but balk at the specific one. What can I say to such a person?

Perhaps another thought experiment will help. Presumably no one wishes to deny that part of literary appreciation consists in understanding the general thematic statements and their relations to the literary work that expresses them. And if I am right in my argument so far, at least some of that appreciation, perhaps a very large part of it, takes place during the afterlife of the work, as well as during the gaps. So now I ask you to imagine appreciating these general thematic statements, but without any consideration of truth-value at all. Can you do that? And if you can, would your experience still constitute full literary appreciation of the general thematic statements? I suspect not.

The logical positivists claimed, notoriously, that an unverifiable hypothesis was a meaningless one, and that meaning was spelled out *in* real or envisioned verification procedures. This is a discredited claim, and I am certainly not asserting it. But there is, I do want to claim, a grain of truth in the positivists' verification principle, and it is this. In many cases we really do not fully grasp a hypothesis, fully grasp its import, anyway, what it means to us without at least mulling over the question of whether or not it is true, which is to say, without trying to "argue" mentally for its truth or falsity, to mentally image possible means of verification. Indeed, apart from reaching a conclusion about a hypothesis, how could we determine whether, in James's terms, it was a "live" or "dead" hypothesis for us without at least some consideration of its truth or falsity? If it is a dead one, then it is dead because we are convinced of its falsity, and we ordinarily have at least some grounds for that belief; and if it is a living one, we must have at least some reason to believe that it might be true, or at least no conclusive reason to believe it is false.

Thus I suggest that fully understanding the general thematic statements and fully appreciating them as part of the literary experience require an evaluation of their possible truth or falsity.

Indeed, I think that Lamarque and Olsen all but admit something like this in the last chapter of their book, where they raise the question of the value of literary fiction. I would like to conclude with a consideration of what they have to say in this regard.

§6   Lamarque and Olsen, in their discussion of literary value, locate it largely in the presence of what they call the "perennial themes":

> One central, characteristic purpose defined by the literary practice and served by the literary work is to develop, in depth, through subject and form, a theme which is in some sense central to human concern and which can therefore be recognized as of more or less universal interest. Appreciation and consequent evaluation of the individual literary work is a matter of eliciting and supporting the identification and development of a "perennial theme."[14]

Perennial themes present, not surprisingly, just those deep questions of philosophy – religious, moral, metaphysical – that are perennially contested. And the example Lamarque and Olsen choose to illustrate their position will equally suit our purposes. It is the theme of free will and determinism, its literary setting Arnold Bennett's novel *Anna of the Five Towns*. Of the theme and its setting, Lamarque and Olsen say:

> *Anna of the Five Towns* organizes a described universe in such a way that the reader who applies concepts like "freedom of the will," "determinism," "victim of external forces beyond human control" in the appreciating of that work will come to see how, in that universe, human beings are controlled by external forces. There is no similar order in the real world that will make these concepts meaningful in this way. Daily life does not offer the sort of visible connections that artistic narrative defines. These connections emerge in the artistic presentation of the subject.[15]

Contrast this big, "perennial" theme of *Anna of the Five Towns* with what we find in trivial works of art, television soap operas, and the like, and we will have a fairly clear picture of what Lamarque and Olsen are after, which is, as I see it, thinking about themes without thinking about truth. As Lamarque and Olsen put the contrast:

> There may be a coherent vision in such [inconsequential] works, with clear choices, but very little for the mind to grapple with. . . . It makes no demands on either the intellectual, emotional, or moral nature that are not also made in daily life with its simple choices and short term goals. For literature like philosophy challenges the reader to make his own construction, to invest time and effort in reaching a deeper insight into the great themes, though this insight is "literary."[16]

The question we must now pose is whether the position Lamarque and Olsen have taken here can be made intelligible without the intrusion of truth and falsity into the equation, whether, that is to say, the notion of "perennial themes" as a (or the) source of literary value can possibly be sustained while at the same time considerations of truth and falsity, as part of the reader's literary appreciation, are denied. I think the answer must be no.

Consider, now, the perennial theme of freedom and determinism that Lamarque and Olsen perceive in Bennett's *Anna of the Five Towns*. In the novel, in the world of that work, determinism is true: "in that universe," as Lamarque and Olsen put it, "human beings are controlled by external forces." What makes the theme of *Anna of the Five Towns* a perennial one is that determinism is a live option for many of us but also that freedom of the will is as well. If only one or the other were a live hypothesis, then of course the theme of freedom and determinism would not be a perennial one; it would have been decided one way or the other. It is *perennial* because we can't decide, and so it constantly or with regularity engages and perplexes us.

But how could we appreciate the theme of *Anna of the Five Towns* as a perennial one without, at the same time, taking part in some kind of at least mental verification process? To experience a theme as perennial, it seems clear enough, we must know whether its opposing hypotheses are live hypotheses; and to know if the hypotheses are live we must have some reason or reasons for believing each; and to arrive at some reason or reasons for believing each we must go through a process of verification.

Two things that Lamarque and Olsen say, therefore, must strike one as extremely puzzling, given their, so to speak, antiepistemic stance with regard to the perennial themes. They say of the determinism in *Anna of the Five Towns* that "[t]here is no similar order in the real world that will make these concepts meaningful in this way." Well, of course, the narrative exaggerates the determinism. But if the real world did not offer us "similar order," that is, order at least suggesting that determinism might be true, then determinism would scarcely be a live hypothesis for us, and hence not a perennial theme. We all know the examples that suggest determinism, as we do the ones that suggest the opposite thesis. So I will say no more about it.

Another puzzling thing that Lamarque and Olsen say, this time about the perennial theme versus its opposite, is that the latter "provides little for the mind to grapple with and develop." But what is it that the mind is meant to "grapple with and develop"? Well, with what the hypotheses of the theme mean and, I would think, what their significance is for us if they were true (or false). Nor can this grappling with and development have any real interest for us unless the hypotheses we mean to grapple with and develop are live ones. It is hard to imagine being engaged in deep thought about the hypothesis that the universe rests on a giant tortoise or that the enslaving, buying, and selling of human beings might really be a good thing after all. These are dead issues for us. The perennial themes are perennial because they are live, live because we think they might be true.

What makes the theme of determinism in *Anna of the Five Towns* a theme to grapple with and develop? Surely not that it is an "interesting" hypothesis (whatever that would mean in the absence of any consideration of possible truth). No one, I trust, grapples any longer with the geocentric worldview, even though it might be in some sense an "interesting" view. Presumably, those themes are perennially interesting to us that present live hypotheses. These are the ones worthy of grappling with and developing. But to grapple with and develop them without raising questions of truth and falsity – without any attempt at verification – seems impossible, and if possible, an empty, profitless exercise.

§7 In this chapter and the two before, I looked at three problems in the philosophy of literature: the problems of literary representation, the form–content relation, and literary truth. In each case I argued that traditional solutions had been proposed by analogizing literature to other arts. In the first case the paradigm was the visual arts, in the second and third absolute music. In each case I argued that the proffered analogy was, if not preposterous, then at least singularly unenlightening. For the analogies are infelicitous; and a stubborn devotion to them over a long period of time has obscured crucial ways in which literature (in the first instance) differs from visual representation and (in the second) from absolute music.

In my final two chapters, I shall turn to the art that, it appears to me, has suffered more from false analogies to the other arts than any of the other arts have suffered from analogy to it: that is, the art of absolute music. If there is any place in the philosophy of art where differences have been obscured, and deserve to be acknowledged, it is here. Music, of all the arts, is the most philosophically unexplored and most philosophically misunderstood where it has been explored at all. That this is due, in large measure, to the persistent practice of basing our understanding of absolute music on literary or painterly models is not an exaggeration. It will be the purpose of the final two chapters to try to undo some of this mischief. Alas, to undo it all is as impossible as bailing dry a leaking boat.

Chapter 6

The Quest for Musical Profundity

§1   The theme of this chapter is the misapplication of a literary model to absolute music, with predictably dire results. I begin on something of a tangent. But if the reader is patient, all, I promise, will be made plain.

I concluded my book *Music Alone* (1990) with a chapter called "The Profundity of Music." In that chapter I reached a somewhat skeptical conclusion about whether absolute music could be "profound," properly so called, although I did explore a way in which I thought it might be. Much to my surprise, this chapter provoked a good deal of discussion, partly because, at least as far as I know, the subject had not been broached before.

I suppose I should not have been surprised. For I was, after all, denying that music was capable of doing (or, rather, *being*) something important, or at least was casting some serious doubt in that direction. And long experience has taught me that whenever someone denies to music any power at all, or any important property, such denial tends to be seen as treachery or barbarism or some kind of musical insensitivity only to be expected from philosophical analysis or formalism, both of which I suppose my work exemplifies. Had I denied that music can predict the future or remove warts, I am certain there would have been at least two responses in the literature to the effect that I had missed some sense in which music can predict the future or remove warts, although of course, one must not be quite so rigid or pedantic about what it means to "predict" or "remove" or what exactly the "future" or a "wart" might be.

Needless to say, that's not the whole of it. The substantive issue, for our purposes, of musical profundity, and any skepticism that might be evinced toward it, is our old familiar theme of the unity of the arts. This can immediately be inferred from the opening statement of one of the first of those who have taken issue with me on the subject of musical profundity. Here is how David A. White begins his essay called "Toward a Theory of Profundity in Music":

> Is music meaningful? Current reflection tends to be dominated by the view that it is a mistake to look for meaning in music, since music is not the sort of ordered activity to have meaning in any of the usual senses of that (itself vexed) term. But it is worth noting that philosophers, in perhaps unguarded moments, still talk about music as if it were meaningful. And one particularly enticing kind of discourse concerns those musical works described as "profound."[1]

There is an argument lurking somewhere in the vicinity here that goes (informally) something like this. In order to be profound, a work of music must be meaningful, because it must be profound *about* something. We have at least some evidence that some works of music are profound, because philosophers in their "unguarded" moments – and, I might add, plenty of musical analysts in their guarded moments as well – talk about individual works of absolute music as being profound. So "current reflection," my own reflection included, must be mistaken in denying "meaning" to music – at least to "profound" music.

Skepticism about profundity in music, then, turns out to be the result of skepticism about the meaningfulness, in some robust linguistic sense of that term, of absolute music. And if we don't have such musical meaning, then the project of construing music as a fine art through the analogy to literature must break down. And as an analogy to representation in the visual arts seems, these days, a fairly unpromising alternative, the project of bringing absolute music into the circle of the fine arts itself breaks down, if the analogy does.

Now, although it does seem to follow that if absolute music cannot have meaning, cannot have a subject matter about which it speaks, it cannot be profound, it certainly does not follow that if absolute music cannot be profound, it cannot be meaningful, cannot have a subject matter. It may be that music can have meaning, yet fail to be profound because it is unable to have profound meaning: unable to have a profound subject or be able to say anything profound about it. Furthermore, perhaps it really does not follow that because it cannot have meaning, it cannot be profound. Perhaps there is another way that something can be profound besides by having profound meaning – without, indeed, having any meaning at all.

As for the project of allying music with the literary arts, the musical project of "sameness," neither of the above possibilities is helpful, the latter quite obviously so. For since the latter alternative is profundity without meaning, proving the possibility of profundity fails to prove the possibility of meaning; and it is *meaning* that is the thing required for the sameness project in music to go through.

It is, perhaps, somewhat less obvious why the former alternative, musical meaning without musical profundity, or with the profundity completely unrelated to the meaning, is a fruitless conclusion for the sameness project. But not much reflection is required to show that it is so.

If music is to be a fine art in virtue of an analogy to literature, that analogy must be a good fit in the crucial respects. As we shall see shortly, literature is profound, in large part, in virtue of its having profound meaning – which is to say, profound subject matter about which it profoundly speaks. If music is profound in some other way, a way that has nothing to do with meaning, even if it has meaning, then, I submit, the analogy to literature would be so significantly defective as to be worthless for the purpose to which it is being put, namely, the legitimization of music as a fine art.

The question of musical profundity, then, lies at the heart of the question of musical meaning. And the question of musical meaning lies at the heart of the question of whether music can be brought into the circle of the fine arts by means of an analogy to literature.

In this chapter I shall try to answer some criticism of my views of musical profundity as laid out in *Music Alone*, and criticize some suggestions that have been made about how musical profundity might be possible. The general theme, as before, is that the quest for sameness in the arts has led us down the garden path, the garden path being the literary model of absolute music. There are many, perhaps more direct ways I could have made my point. I have chosen to do so by way of the musical profundity question mainly because it is a fresh question and therefore preferable to one of the more familiar alternatives. My first task, before I can get to the debate over my view, is to acquaint the reader with it.

§2   I shall begin the way I should have begun when I first broached the subject of musical profundity in *Music Alone,* with a very simple distinction between what I call the adjectival and the adverbial senses of the word "profound." Had I made this distinction then, I think it would have saved us a good deal of confusion now.

The *Critique of Pure Reason* is both a profound work and a profoundly influential one. What it means for a work to be profound we shall get to shortly. But what it means for the *Critique of Pure Reason* (or any other work) to be profoundly influential is easily said: it means, roughly, that it is not merely influential, or even very influential, but perhaps very very influential. Whether it may mean anything more than that we shall discuss later. For the time being, the rough gloss will do: to be *profoundly* anything is to be very very that thing.

Furthermore, we cannot infer from a work's being profoundly *anything* that it is a *profound* work. In other words, to be profoundly something is not, ipso facto, to be profound. The *Critique of Pure Reason* is a profound work and a profoundly influential one; but Norman Vincent Peale's *The Power of Positive Thinking,* although profoundly influential, at least in its own day, is, far from being a profound work, a profoundly silly one.

So much, then, for the distinction between the adjectival and the adverbial senses of "profound," except to add, emphatically, that it was solely the *adjectival* sense of "profound" that I was concerned with in *Music Alone.* And to point out that a work can be profoundly sad or profoundly unified or profoundly anything else, in answer to my guarded skepticism with regard to the possible profundity of absolute music, is just an *ignoratio;* it completely misses my point. And although I don't claim that any one of my commentators has blatantly made this blunder, I think that two of them are at least subtly committed to the (fallacious) move from profoundly to profound, or to the substitution of the first for the second, neither of which is an answer to either skepticism about musical profundity or the very tentative suggestion I made about how perhaps music might be "profound" in a full-blooded sense, appearances to the contrary notwithstanding.

With these preliminaries taken care of, I can now briefly present the view of musical profundity I put forth in *Music Alone* and then get to a more leisurely examination of the criticism and alternatives it has elicited.

§3 I began with Kant's first *Critique* as an example of a profound work, so I will stick with it. What makes this work "profound"? First, it raises, or is about, profound issues. But that, of course, is not enough. Many recent shallow books raise the profound question of the mind–body problem. Second, the first *Critique* gives searching, original, thorough, thought-provoking responses to the profound issues it addresses: it says profound things about its subject matter. We can sum this up by saying that the treatment the *Critique of Pure Reason* gives of its profound subject matter is *adequate* to that subject matter.

Moving on, now, to works of art, it seems clear that at least literary works can be, and sometimes are, profound. (I will say nothing about painting or other visual arts here.) For some literary works do indeed treat a profound subject matter in a manner adequate to its profundity. So literary works can obviously fulfill both conditions for being profound.

But what it means to *adequately* treat a profound subject matter must undergo some alteration when we move from works of philosophy, science, history, or anything else of that kind to literary works, which is to say, works of art. We must add, not surprisingly, an "aesthetic" dimension. For as I claimed in *Music Alone,* and see no reason to demur from now, a profound work of literature (or any other kind of artwork) must not only possess a profound subject matter and say things profound about it (not necessarily or frequently in a direct manner), but must also be aesthetically or artistically exemplary: of a very high quality. A work of literature may be profound in content, but if it is not a great or exemplary work of art, it is not profound *qua* literature, *qua* art. In other words, for a novel (say) to treat a profound subject matter *adequately*, it must not only say profound things about it, but say them supremely well in an aesthetic or artistic way.

I feel certain this is true – that aesthetic or artistic excellence is part of art profundity. I feel certain that one would never call a mediocre work of art "profound," even if it said profound things about a profound subject matter, except with qualifications like "Looked at as a *philosophical* work (or whatever) it is profound; but it is not a profound novel." The problem is that I do not know exactly why this is so. One might venture a Danto-like hypothesis to the effect that, since, in a work of art, *how* the work of art is "about" is part of *what* it is "about," or something of the kind, the aesthetic or artistic greatness of the work is part of what makes its subject profound. But however that may be, it does appear to me just to be so, that no one calls a work of literature profound literature, no matter how profound its subject matter or how profound the things said about it, unless the work is of supremely high artistic or aesthetic value. So I will leave it at that.

To summarize, then, for a work of art to be profound – and literature is the obvious example here – it must (1) have a profound subject matter and (2) treat this profound subject matter in a way adequate to its profundity – which is to say, (a) say profound things about this subject matter and (b) do it at a very high level of artistic or aesthetic excellence. This is my analysis of what I have called here the "adjectival" sense of "profound." It is the only sense I was or am now interested in, and the only sense according to which I was and am now denying that absolute music can, in any *obvious* way, be "profound."

This denial that music can in any obvious way be "profound" in the adjectival sense I shall refer to as the negative aspect of my position on musical profundity. It arises from my reluctance to allow that absolute music can have any subject matter or could say anything about it if it had. For if it cannot have or say anything about any subject matter whatever, then, a fortiori, it cannot have a profound subject matter or could not say anything profound about it if it could have any. Absolute music fails to fulfill both criteria of profundity in the adjectival sense and hence cannot, in that sense, be profound.

But in *Music Alone* I also made a positive suggestion about how music might in something like its adjectival sense be "profound." My idea was that although absolute music cannot be about, or be profound about, extramusical matters, it might nevertheless sometimes be about and be profound about *itself:* that, in other words, music might at times be profound about music. This positive aspect of my position I hope to develop further in another place. My purpose here, however, is to go on to discuss two responses to the negative aspect of my view, those of Aaron Ridley and Jerrold Levinson.

§4   I think that Ridley knows quite well the adverbial sense of "profound" and its inadequacy as a solution to the problem of profundity in music. Nevertheless, I do not think he succeeds in getting beyond it to what I would consider a satisfactory account of how absolute music might be profound in the adjectival sense. But to show this will require some careful work.

Ridley begins with my contention that in order to be profound a musical work must be about something profound and treat that something in a way adequate to its profundity, "[w]hich, of course," he quite rightly observes, makes music, "which isn't much good at being about things, an outsider from the start."[2] Furthermore, he claims that both the profundity condition and the adequacy condition are invalid: that, in other words, something can be profound without being about anything profound and profound without being adequate to its profound subject matter.

Ridley's counterexample to both of my conditions is *belief.* Thus "... Natasha believes profoundly in a religion," Ridley suggests by way of example and adds, as particularly worthy of emphasis, "It is clearly her belief which is being described as profound."³ Suppose her belief is in a profound religion. We need know nothing about the "adequacy" of her belief to maintain that her belief is "profound." Perhaps her belief is not "adequate" to the profound religious subject matter. It is a profound belief for all of that. So much, then, for my adequacy condition.

But, of course, Natasha's religion might be utterly silly, shallow, a singularly unprofound one:

> Would this mean that her belief could not, after all, be profound? Of course it wouldn't. . . . [B]ecause profundity is a quality of the *belief* – and not, as Kivy would have it, a quality of the subject matter which the belief somehow inherits by being adequate *to* it – the apparent triviality of what the belief is about is irrelevant to the assumption of profundity to the belief itself.⁴

A belief, then, can be profound, even though its content is not. So much, then, for my profundity of subject matter condition.

I think it ought to be pretty clear by now, from previous considerations, what has gone wrong here with the first stage of Ridley's argument. He waffles between adjectival and adverbial descriptions of belief in a way that obscures the implausibility of what he is saying. Everything Ridley says about *profoundly held* belief, about believing *profoundly*, is true; but everything he says about *profound* beliefs, if there were such, which there aren't, is false.

Let me first get rid of the notion of profound belief, in the adjectival sense of "profound." In the sense in which the *Critique of Pure Reason* is a profound work and *The Power of Positive Thinking* a shallow one, there is no such thing as a profound belief. One belief cannot be profound. A *set* of beliefs might be profound. The *Critique of Pure Reason* is a set of beliefs that Kant wrote down. And although Socrates never wrote down his beliefs, I think we can safely say that a substantial set of them must have been a profound set of beliefs.

A single belief cannot be profound, then, nor can it be adequate or inadequate to its subject matter. If Thomas Aquinas and Mrs. Grundy both believe in God, there is absolutely no sense I can make of the claim, about that one belief, that Thomas's is more adequate to the profound subject matter than Mrs. Grundy's. What *is* more adequate is the set of his beliefs in and about God.

Belief, then, turns out to be a palpable red herring. In the adjectival sense, no belief can be profound, because, although a belief may be about something profound, it makes no sense to talk about its adequacy vis-à-vis its profound subject. And as I understand the English language, "profound belief" does not mean "belief about something profound." The only sense in which *a* belief can be profound is the adverbial sense: a belief can be very very strongly held, in other words, profoundly held. But as I am not concerned with the adverbial sense of "profound," that is irrelevant to my argument.

However, if we apply what Ridley says about belief to things that can be or fail to be profound in the adjectival sense, we see that it is flat out wrong about those things. A philosophical work, for example, that is about a trivial subject matter cannot be a profound philosophical work; and a philosophical work about a profound subject matter that is not adequate to that subject matter cannot be a profound philosophical work. If I should write a book about the mind–body problem that consists of all sorts of bad arguments and silly theories, then my work is, clearly, not profound, even though it is about a profound question, because I have not treated that question adequately: my book is not adequate to its profound subject matter. And if I should write a philosophical work on the subject of bottle caps, my work cannot be profound, no matter how adequately I treat my subject, because my subject is trivial, not profound.[5]

Thus it is only by equivocating between the adverbial and the adjectival senses of "profound" that Ridley can make belief seem to be a counterexample to my claim that a philosophical work, or work of art, must be, in order to be profound, both about something profound and adequate to its profundity. It appears to me, then, that in his quest for musical profundity Ridley is off to a very shaky start.

§5 Matters do not improve in the second stage of Ridley's argument, in which he aims to show that not only needn't a thing be about something profound to be profound, the way a belief is said to be by Ridley, but that "a thing needn't be about *anything at all* in order to be profound."[6] This of course, is not very hard to show since, again, it is the adverbial sense of "profound" that is clearly intended. The example now is Natasha's gullibility. She is very very gullible, profoundly gullible in fact. But gullibility is a disposition, and dispositions aren't *about*. So Ridley has his conclusion, with which I heartily concur. That is not at issue.

What is at issue – and it becomes crucial in the latter stages of Ridley's argument – is the analysis he proposes of what it means to be profoundly gullible:

> Now imagine that Natasha is capable of being persuaded of just about anything; that most of her actions are determined by beliefs far less critically acquired than they might have been; that she is continually surprised to learn that what she has just taken for gospel is pure baloney; that her whole life is structured, at every level, by her tendency willingly to believe whatever she is told. Clearly, and (I take it) uncontroversially, Natasha is profoundly gullible. . . . This opens the door to any mental item, trait of character, habitual attitude, or propensity, which is capable of structuring significant aspects, or simply significant quantities, of a person's life. Thus one might be profoundly cheerful, profoundly mean, profoundly suspicious, profoundly courageous, and so on. And in each case it can be true of one's cheerfulness, meanness, courage, etc., that it is *profound.* This accords well with common usage, and is also quite unmysterious.[7]

Now a great deal that Ridley says here is quite uncontentious. Of course one can be profoundly gullible, profoundly mean, profoundly suspicious, and the rest; and if one is profoundly any of those things, another way of saying it is that one's gullibility is profound, one's meanness is profound, one's courage is profound. All of this does accord well with common usage.

However, there is one very crucial respect in which what Ridley seems to be saying is neither uncontentious nor in accord with common usage – indeed is, I think, completely wrong. As

149

far as I can make out, there is no requirement whatever, nor does it accord with common usage, that for someone to be profoundly gullible, "her whole life," as Ridley puts it, must be "structured, at every level," by her gullibility; nor with regard to any of the other dispositions he mentions does this appear to be the case.

It may indeed be the case that if someone structures her life around gullibility, she will be rightly judged profoundly gullible. But it is just affirming the consequent to go from being profoundly gullible to having a life structured by gullibility. It accords well with common usage to call someone profoundly gullible when she is very very gullible. And I submit that one need know nothing about the "structure" of a person's inner or outer life to pronounce the judgment "profoundly gullible" with full justification. A person may perfectly well lead a completely haphazard, unstructured life of gullibility and be justly adjudged profoundly gullible, nor would the revelation of the lack of structure around the gullibility require withdrawal of the judgment. It does not offend common usage to assert profound gullibility while denying a "structure" of gullibility. One can, of course, just stipulate that one will call someone profoundly *x* only when one is very very *x and* the structure is in place. But stipulation doesn't settle an argument.

I belabor this point beyond, perhaps, apparent cause, because Ridley makes a lot of mileage out of it later on. It is the way he tries to work his passage from the adverbial sense of "profound" to a workable theory of musical profundity. But it won't do. This step is an unwarranted one. Profoundly *x* just means very very *x*, and there's an end on't.

Furthermore, that this gratuitous addition of structure to the adverbial sense of "profound" is a mistake and unable to help us with the question of musical profundity can immediately be seen in the first use Ridley tries to make of it at the end of this second stage of his argument. Of my positive account of musical profundity, Ridley writes:

> He suggests that certain contrapuntal music might be called profound because it is in some sense about (and adequately

150

about) the possibilities inherent in music, which are themselves profound. . . . But how much simpler to say that the
music is *profoundly contrapuntal* – that every aspect of the music is informed, controlled, and given shape by the counterpoint that lies at its heart! It seems to me that this is a vastly
more natural way of speaking.[8]

I have no quarrel with the phrase "profoundly contrapuntal,"
needless to say, nor with the notion, hardly controversial, that
some music is "profoundly contrapuntal." The problem is that
profoundly contrapuntal music was not, is not, my problem. My
problem is *contrapuntally profound* music, which is quite another
thing. My problem is, as I have said so many times before, the
adjectival sense of "profound": the sense not in which the *Critique of Pure Reason* is profoundly philosophical but the sense in
which it is philosophically profound. For a work can be profoundly philosophical, to appropriate Ridley's words, in being
"informed, controlled, and given shape by" philosophy without
being a profound philosophical work at all.

And as for music, *all* of the art music of the Renaissance was
profoundly contrapuntal: that was, after all, the golden age of
polyphony. But only *some* of the works of the masters were contrapuntally profound: profound musical works in a contrapuntal
way. The *Kleinmeisters* wrote yards and yards of profoundly contrapuntal music. Only the likes of a Josquin, however, could
achieve contrapuntal profundity.

Nor, by the way, do I think that profoundly contrapuntal music need be "informed, controlled, and given shape by the counterpoint," any more than a profoundly silly person's life need
be "informed, controlled, and given shape by" his silliness. All
that is required is heaps and heaps of counterpoint, however
haphazard it may be. And the reason I suspect that someone
might think it odd to call such stuff *profoundly* contrapuntal is
that he or she is mixing up the profoundly contrapuntal with
the contrapuntally profound, which, of course, cannot be haphazard, cannot lack the inner structural logic that *profound* counterpoint requires.

However, the last point is beside the point. Even if we give

Ridley his analysis of what it means to be profoundly contrapuntal, he cannot reach an interesting conclusion about the question of musical profundity. For that question, with regard to counterpoint, is how music can be contrapuntally profound, not how it can be profoundly contrapuntal. The latter is no more difficult to understand than how music can be profoundly boring.

§6 In the third stage of his argument Ridley finally faces the music in earnest and endeavors to apply to it what has gone before. His interest is confined to "music which is profound in virtue of its *expressive* properties."[9] It is here that his principal chicken comes home to roost.

The strategy, given what has gone before, will be to say that a musical composition is profound when it is profoundly some expressive property: cheerfulness, to take Ridley's example. But, as we have seen, Ridley will not say that a musical work is profoundly cheerful, or whatever, just because it is very very cheerful. For "there is a difference between being profoundly cheerful and being merely regularly or relentlessly cheerful."[10] And given Ridley's previously expressed views on being profoundly gullible, namely, that one's life must be structured around the disposition if it is to be profoundly instantiated, the nature of the "difference" will not be surprising. So, of the "defiance" that Ridley supposes Beethoven's Fifth Symphony to be *profoundly* expressive of, "The quality of defiance . . . appears to structure the expressive content of the symphony as a whole. . . ."[11]

I have already registered my objection to this move. There is no reason in the world to believe that being structured around a property is a necessary condition for its being profoundly instantiated. The way I understand the English language, to be profoundly *x* is just to be very very *x*; and to be very very *x*, as far as I can tell, hardly requires being "structured" around *x*. Indeed, things without any "structure" at all can be profoundly *x*. When you are very thirsty, a drink of water is *profoundly* satisfying.

But suppose we give Ridley his premise about structure. What have we got? Well, if Ridley is saying that it is a degree – that is to say, the degree to which something is x is high enough for it to be profoundly x only if that thing is structured around x – then being profoundly x still means being x to some certain very high degree. And we are still stuck with the adverbial sense of "profound," which is irrelevant to the question of musical profundity that I originally raised.

I think at this point in his argument Ridley must be beginning to realize this himself. For the next step is in the direction, not surprising from my point of view, of *content*, of "aboutness," which is the only way to get to the adjectival sense of "profound."

Back to Natasha. "Now suppose it is *Natasha* who is profoundly defiant, in a way analogous to that in which Beethoven's Fifth is defiant. . . . [A]lthough her defiance is not *about* anything in particular, it certainly does suppose an attitude *towards* things in general."[12] In contemporary philosophical lingo, Natasha's defiance, by being a conscious mental state, takes an "intentional object." But how can that be true of absolute music? Ridley replies:

> I am not suggesting, of course, that music literally *has* an outlook of some kind. . . . But I am suggesting that, in experiencing certain pieces of music intently, and responsively, and so coming to grasp their profoundly expressive qualities, we at the same time gain an intimation of the outlook on the world implicit *in* those qualities: so that, for example, in grasping the profoundly defiant character of Beethoven's Fifth Symphony we gain an intimation of what it would be to have a defiant outlook on the world, of what it would be to view the world as threatening but outfaceable.[13]

Well, we do not quite have "content" here, but we are getting close. Music can be expressive of qualities that imply attitudes or, indeed, that, like defiance, are attitudes. Ridley is saying that when these qualities are profoundly instantiated in absolute music, they can somehow get us to know what it would be like to have the attitudes they imply or are toward the world. That is how I understand him, although I am not quite sure whether he means that the music enables us to feel what it would be like or know what it would be like. Let us call this "quasi-content." And in regard to it, let us consider two questions. Can absolute music possess quasi-content? And, if it could, would that give us any reasonable grounds for calling at least some works of absolute music "profound"?

That Ridley is in immediate trouble with regard to the first question should be readily apparent from the quotation he adduces to illustrate what he has in mind. It is from Michael Tanner, a philosopher whose opinion certainly carries weight, deservedly so in such matters. Of this quotation Ridley says, "The responses described in this passage reflect rather fully, I believe, the kind of engagement with music which I have suggested is central to understanding the expressive qualities of certain musical works as *profound*."[14] There is no need to discuss the content of the passage from Tanner. It suffices to say that it talks about Tanner's experiences of Bach's *St. Matthew Passion* and Wagner's *Tristan und Isolde!* They are works with texts, and with regard to texted works all bets are off. There is no need to ascribe quasi-content to Bach's passion music or Wagner's music dramas. They have real content, in the full-blooded sense of the concept, and profound content into the bargain. Who would demur from that? Certainly not I. But how can the "responses" of Tanner to these kinds of texted works "reflect rather fully" a response to a work of absolute music like Beethoven's Fifth Symphony, which does not have a text? Quoting Tanner on Bach's *Passion* or Wagner's great music drama is just an empty rhetorical gesture. Ridley might just as well have quoted A. C. Bradley on Shakespearean tragedy. Of course, these works can be profound. They have profound subject matter to which they are adequate (although the role of *music* in the affair is no easy task to explicate).

Ridley's problem is to convince such skeptics as me that *absolute music* can possess even such quasi-content as he ascribes to Beethoven's Fifth Symphony. He has an uphill fight.

That one of the things Beethoven's Fifth Symphony could be expressive of is defiance let us grant; and let us grant too that the Fifth is *profoundly* defiant. I think I know how this might be established – by pointing to various musical figures, melodies, harmonies, and structural features that contribute to the expressive quality I am claiming to perceive in the work.

What I do not see is the next step – how it might be established that the defiance Beethoven's Fifth is expressive of conveys to us "an intimation of what it would be to have a defiant outlook on the world, what it would be to view the world as threatening but outfaceable." I do know how I would establish that *King Lear* tells us what it would be to be defiant, to outface a threatening world. I would quote his defiant speeches and describe his defiant behavior: that, I would say, is what it is like to be defiant and to outface a threatening world; it is in those speeches and actions.

What should I point to in Beethoven's Fifth Symphony to convince you that it tells what it is like to outface a defiant world? There are no speeches. There are no actions. What *is* it like to be defiant and outface a threatening world *according to Beethoven's Fifth Symphony?* It is just avoiding the issue to say that it gives only "intimations." Even "intimations" must have a content, must be discussable. Lear evinces a certain *kind* of defiance. We might compare it to the defiance of Faust or, in "real life," Patrick Henry or Giordano Bruno. Which of these is the defiance of the Fifth more like? Does the question even make sense?

We are up against the same old problem that has been with us since Hanslick dug in his heels against just the sort of argument Ridley is trying to run. It is always easy to make a claim about what some piece of absolute music is "saying." The difficult part is making it good. What we can point to in Beethoven's Fifth Symphony is what makes it expressive of defiance. What we cannot point to is anything more about that defiance, even in the limited sense of what I called "quasi-content."

But let us grant Ridley his quasi-content: let us grant that Beethoven's Fifth Symphony gives us "intimations" of what it might be like to be defiant. How can *this* work our passage from the Fifth's being "profoundly defiant" to its being "profound" in any sense other than "profoundly defiant"? Certainly it cannot make the Fifth "profound" in the adjectival sense. *Love Story* and *Anna Karenina* are both profoundly sad; and certainly if Beethoven's Fifth can give us an "intimation" of what it would be like to be defiant, *Love Story*, soap opera though it is, certainly has the power, a fortiori, to give us an "intimation" of what it would be like to have whatever attitudes profound sadness entails. But *Anna Karenina* is profoundly sad, and profound in part because of its profound sadness, just because it can give us more than an "intimation" of what the attitudes involved in this sadness are like. It speaks *profoundly* about these attitudes, as *Lear* and *Faust* speak profoundly about defiance. And that Beethoven's Fifth Symphony cannot do. It cannot speak at all.

Once more, then, I conclude that Ridley cannot get beyond the adverbial sense of profundity to any sense relevant to my concerns. And at this point in the argument Ridley himself has obviously come to the same conclusion. For in the final stage of his argument he explicitly describes his position as so far dealing merely with the adverbial sense of "profound" and attempts to ameliorate the situation, not, in my view, successfully.

§7   What Ridley sees his view lacking, as so far developed, and rightly so, is a *normative* element. For, after all, in the adverbial sense of "profound," a work can profoundly instantiate the worst as well as the best properties: a work can be profoundly ugly as well as profoundly beautiful, profoundly silly as well as profoundly sensible. As Ridley states the objection:

> Surely, it will be objected, the account given here simply *ignores* what is most interesting about profundity, musical or otherwise. It simply ignores the kind of metaphysical or moral content characteristic of the profound – the kind of content which Peter Kivy attempts to capture. . . . Indeed, the present essay gives only an adverbial account of profundity. . . . Thus the essential link with *evaluation* is severed. When we call something profound, after all, we are surely – among other things – meaning to commend it.[15]

The problem, obviously, is that Ridley wants to go from "X is profoundly ϕ" to "X is profound"; but if "ϕ" is "silly" or "shallow" or some other negative quality, it seems hardly plausible to go from "His novel is profoundly silly" or "profoundly shallow" or whatever to "His novel is profound." There are a number of steps in this last stage of Ridley's argument, and we will have to go through them carefully. There is, I think, something wrong with each. Let us begin with a return to Natasha.

How can one connect a trivial property profoundly instantiated with *value?* In my original account of musical profundity, I suggested that what it would be for some subject matter or content to be profound was "something of abiding interest and importance to human beings" that was at the same time "not just of great concern but *worthy* of great concern, in some suitably strong sense of 'worthy'...."[16] That was half of my value component in glossing the adjectival sense of "profound" (the other half being the aesthetic and adequacy conditions). Ridley is apparently trying to use that kind of value component to put a normative component into the adverbial sense. For he writes of Natasha's gullibility, not, one would think, a very profound subject, although profoundly exemplified in her: "It still seems to me appropriate to call Natasha's gullibility profound . . . ," and adds: "If you're *interested* in Natasha, then her profoundly gullible quality will strike you, without doubt, as worthy of regard (of reflection, of contemplation), because it will strike you as *valuable* in your efforts to *understand* her."[17]

Now this strategy cannot possibly bestow a value component, at least of the kind I was explicating in *Music Alone*, on such profoundly exemplified properties as Natasha's gullibility. No doubt, Natasha's psychiatrist might find her gullibility of deep and abiding interest, and it is indeed worthy of his interest, since she is in his care. But my conditions spoke of abiding interest and importance to human beings, obviously not every human being in the world, but at least a broad spectrum of human beings in my cultural neck of the woods. Thus it cuts no ice with me that for *any* profoundly instantiated property there is at least one person who finds it, for some personal reason or other, of deep and abiding interest, and rightly so, given who that particular person is. However, this is beside the point. What we are interested in is the profundity of *music*. So let us see what this strategy can do for musical works that profoundly instantiate "negative" properties.

157

Ridley quotes the philosopher Ernst Bloch to the effect that Richard Strauss's *Elektra* is profoundly "hollow": the " 'brilliant hollowness' that disturbs Bloch would almost certainly count as a profound quality of *Elektra*."[18] Now one can't think of a quality any more incompatible with a novel's or play's or philosophical treatise's being profound than its being hollow, empty of significant content. Being "hollow," I should say, is just about the opposite (along with "shallow") of having profound subject matter. *Elektra*, being an opera, hence having a text, mise-en-scène, and the rest, is not a very felicitous example. But, in any case, if the *music* of *Elektra* is not only hollow but profoundly hollow, it seems equally damning of *its* profundity, except in the adverbial sense, where its being profound simply means that it is profoundly hollow. How can we get from the profound hollowness of *Elektra* to the normative component of profundity in the adjectival sense?

The case of *Elektra*'s profound hollowness is analogous, Ridley wants to argue, to the case of Natasha's profound gullibility:

> And similarly with the Strauss example: If I'm genuinely interested in *Elektra,* and really want to understand it, or what's off-putting about it, I may well be glad to recognize (with Bloch's help) just how profoundly hollow it is. . . . But my recognition of *Elektra*'s hollowness as profound is conditional upon my desire to understand *Elektra,* and the value which that recognition has for me lies in the understanding of *Elektra* which it yields.[19]

But, as in the case of Natasha's gullibility, this example hardly gives the normative element of profundity that I was seeking in *Music Alone.* Understanding *Elektra* may have *value* for someone; and understanding the profound hollowness of the music might be instrumental in achieving that understanding – and hence have *instrumental value.* But that seems completely beside the point. What we want is value that accrues specially to profundity. And Ridley has given us nothing of the kind. All sorts of features of music, profoundly instantiated or not, have instrumental value in helping us to understand the music that possesses them. Furthermore, and more important, Ridley gives us no way of determining what is worth taking an interest in and what is not, which, it seems to me, must be part of any understanding of profundity in the adjectival sense. Anyone might take an interest in any profoundly instantiated property, no matter how worthless the property or how worthless the work that possessed it, and perceiving that property would then have value to that person, in the instrumental way of helping her understand that worthless work through that worthless but profoundly instantiated property. Is there anything here resembling what we think of as valuable about the profound? I think not.

Of course, Strauss's *Elektra* is not a worthless work, but a very important work in the development of modernism in our musical world, whether you think it is hollow or hallowed. And if it is hollow (which I do not believe), that hollowness is surely worthy of our interest, study, and understanding. If that is so, however, then the value conditions are satisfied not for the profundity of *Elektra*; rather for the profundity of a person's *understanding* of *Elektra*: the set of beliefs, written down or not, with the hollowness of *Elektra* as its profound subject matter. Perhaps Bloch's essay, from which Ridley quotes, is such a profound set of beliefs. But that scarcely makes *Elektra* a profound work – only a profound subject matter for a profound work. We are no closer, I conclude, to a suitable value component for the adverbial sense of "profound."

At this point Ridley makes a distinction between what he calls "work profundity" and "world profundity." The defiance of Beethoven's Fifth Symphony is an example of work profundity: "defiance plays a structuring role within the work, and is interesting and valuable for that, at least for anyone with a desire to understand Beethoven's Fifth Symphony." And the attitude implied in this defiance is an example of world profundity: "an attitude for which the world falls under the description 'threatening but outfaceable'. . . ."[20]

With this distinction in hand Ridley now tells us what the "world profundity" is that Beethoven's mighty Fifth Symphony imparts, through the attitude of defiance that it is expressive of: "The attitude contains one possible answer to the metaphysical question, What is the world really like? (Answer: threatening.)

And one possible answer to the moral question, How ought one to regard such a world? (Answer: as something to be out-faced.)"[21]

Now if my Uncle Harry put his arm around my shoulder and, with great earnestness, imparted the intelligence that the world is threatening and one should try to outface it, I would think him a Polonius for enunciating such a platitude. Yet Ridley would have us believe that this banality is the profound content of one of the most profound of musical utterances (if profound musical utterances there be), what E. M. Forster called "the most sublime noise that has ever penetrated the ear of man." I cannot credit it. If *this* is what the mighty Fifth tells us, then, indeed, *parturient montes, nascetur ridiculus mus.*

Indeed, Ridley, throughout his discussion, does not talk about any of the things that I would adduce to support the belief that Beethoven's Fifth Symphony is musically profound. He has not talked about the incredible thematic economy and concentration with which the master has constructed the sonata movement, the wonderful fugatto passages of the scherzo's trio, the miraculous harmonic bridge between the scherzo and the finale. In a word, he hasn't talked about the *music*. If there is profundity in Beethoven's Fifth Symphony, *there* is where to look for it. If not there, then the game is lost.

§8 Let me conclude this discussion of Ridley's quest for musical profundity by suggesting the difference, in this regard, between what my program was and is and what I perceive his to be (whether on not he so perceives it).

I began my account of musical profundity in *Music Alone* with the intuition that, like some exemplary works of literature or philosophy, some exemplary works of absolute music are not merely great works of art, but profound ones. I had a vague idea of what it might mean for a novel or play or a treatise in philosophy to be profound, and also a vague suspicion that there might be some problem applying this sense of profundity to absolute music, as I understand it. So I tried to state as clearly as I could what I thought people were saying about works of philosophy, literature, and the like when they called these works "profound"; and I then tried to see whether the works of absolute music that I and my friends in the musical world tended to call profound really could be in the sense I had made clear, at least to myself. Though I was skeptical that absolute music could be profound in what I have been calling the adjectival sense, in the end I made a positive suggestion about how, after all, it might be so. My program was, then, to take what I perceived to be an accepted, bona fide, presystematic sense of the word "profound," the adjectival, and see if works of absolute music we generally call "profound" really satisfied the conditions of this sense.

I perceive Ridley to be doing something quite different. He does, indeed, start with an accepted, presystematic, altogether *echt* sense of the word "profound," as I have done, namely, the adverbial sense: the sense in which something can be profoundly this or profoundly that. But he knows that just being (say) profoundly sad or profoundly defiant, in the sense of being very very sad or very very defiant, which is the sense I understand in these adverbial expressions, cannot make a musical work the kind that would generally be described as "profound." So he piles on to this adverbial sense various other conditions, the structuring condition being the most prominent, until he arrives at what he calls "work profundity," and "world profundity," hoping thereby that these beefed-up senses of "profound" will gather up those works that musical people, by and large, are inclined to call "profound."

My problem with this strategy is that these two senses of "profound," what Ridley calls "work profundity" and "world profundity," are made-up senses. I do not believe anyone uses "profound" in Ridley's sense of the word. It is a constructed sense of "profound": the word has become a term of art.

We could, of course, stipulate that from now on only works of absolute music that are "profound" in Ridley's constructed sense of "profound" are to be called "profound." I don't know why we should do that, but we could. But in any case, Ridley's project, as I see it, is irrelevant to mine. I have tried to apply what I take to be a presystematic sense of "profound," which I have called the adjectival sense, and asked some hard questions about whether absolute music can ever be profound *in that sense*. Ridley has done something else. Perhaps it is as worthwhile as what I have tried to do. But it does not answer my question, nor does it invalidate my answer. Ridley and I are doing profoundly different things: which is to say, very very different things.

§9 The second of my critics, Jerrold Levinson, sees quite clearly what my project is and pursues that very project himself, as far as I can see. He is, in other words, looking for adjectival profundity in music, as I was, and where we differ is in where we see that profundity to lie. Levinson, I guess, thinks that I am more skeptical than I should be about some very straightforward things that absolute music can be profound about, and is skeptical about the rather less than straightforward way that I think music might just possibly be profound. And I, in my turn, am very skeptical about those straightforward ways Levinson thinks absolute music can be profound.

My skepticism was fueled by very strong reservations concerning whether absolute music can be "about" anything: whether it can have a subject matter or say anything about a subject matter it might, per impossible, have. For if absolute music cannot be about anything, cannot have a subject matter, then, a fortiori, it cannot have a profound subject matter or say anything profound about it.

Levinson's optimism concerning the possibility of profound absolute music is born of his skepticism about my skepticism about the possibility of absolute music's having a subject matter or the capacity to "say things" about absolute music.

The first step in the direction of a notion as to how music might be profound is to show how music can have a subject matter. For, obviously, unless music can have a subject matter, be "about" something, it cannot say anything about it; and saying something profound about a subject matter is, at least on my view, a necessary condition for profundity in the adjectival sense. I assume that Levinson thinks likewise, because the first step in his article "Musical Profundity Misplaced" is to make out a case for musical "aboutness."

He begins: "The profundity of music, it is often said, has something to do with its emotional or, perhaps more broadly, human content."[22] Naturally enough, given the long tradition of connecting music with expressive properties, Levinson straightaway gloms on to "emotional content" and tries to make an argument for the view that music can be about the emotions it displays:

> If musical works have expressive properties, if composers generally intend them to have such, if listeners generally expect them to have such, and if it is widely acknowledged that a considerable (though not the greatest) part of the interest in music resides there, I don't see why we should be barred from saying that one of the things music as a whole is *about*, i.e. is concerned with, is emotional expression. . . . In addition, if we consider that when music is expressive of emotional states, listeners who grasp that are often led to reflect, if obscurely, on such states – possibly through inhabiting them temporarily in imagination – and that this result must often be envisaged by the creators and and transmitters of music, then it is hard to see what can be wrong in allowing that some music is about emotional states and their expression – when it is often an express point of the music to bring such to the consciousness of listeners.[23]

The argument in this densely packed passage proceeds in two stages. Here is how I see the argument of the first stage, in the form of four propositions:

(1) Musical works have expressive properties.
(2) Composers generally intend that their works have the expressive properties they do.
(3) A considerable part of the interest of a musical work resides in its expressive properties.
(4) One of the things music as a whole is about is [therefore?] expression.

I am assuming that proposition (4) is meant to be the conclusion of an argument, of which propositions (1)–(3) are the premises, although it is not altogether clear what the argument exactly is. I take the phrase "I don't see why we should be barred from saying . . ." to mean to suggest not that propositions (1)–(3) imply (4), but that they are meant to imply the possibility of (4). That is to say, I take Levinson to be saying that (1)–(3) are stating necessary but not sufficient conditions for (4); if they are false, (4) could not possibly be true, but if they are true, (4) could still be false.

I think it is clear that (4) does not follow from (1)–(3). I take it, then, that Levinson is making the weaker claim: (1)–(3) state necessary conditions for (4), and they do in fact obtain. Hence (4) could be true. I shall argue that (2) and (3) are false, or at least not obviously true, and hence in need of independent support.

Is it true that composers *generally* intend that their works have the expressive properties they do? The answer is negative. But a statement that might be mistaken for it is true. The expressive properties of musical works are generally the direct result of the intentional acts of composers. An example will help.

Bach intended the first fugue in Book 1 of the *Well-Tempered Clavier* to be in C, to be a stretto fugue, and to have many other musical qualities. The piece is also noble and joyful in expressive character. But I do not think Bach intended it to be noble and joyful at all. These came with the territory, so to speak. They are the unintended result of Bach's other, intentional choices. I say this because, as I hear this fugue, the expressive properties play no significant role in the musical happenings. And for this reason alone it seems absurd to say the fugue is "about" joy or nobility. To be sure, the expressive properties are neither accidental nor unintentional in the sense of not anticipated by Bach; they may or may not have been anticipated – that all depends merely on whether or not Bach was ever aware of what expressive properties his other choices were imparting to his work. But they were not intentionally put there to perform a musical function in that piece. Thus it is false to say, as proposition (2) does, that expressive properties were *generally* intended, generally put in works with malice aforethought. In many cases they were not and are of little or no musical significance.

It is just as obviously false, then, to assert, as proposition (3) does, that a considerable part of the interest of absolute music resides in its expressive properties. A very large amount of the stuff has expressive properties of little if any real interest whatever. And even where expressive properties do play an important role in the musical proceedings, it is doubtful that the music is usefully seen as being organized around them or written principally for the purpose of displaying them. Indeed, it is, I believe, the rare case rather than the general case of which one can truthfully assert, "A considerable (though not the greatest) part of the interest in such music resides there [in the expressive properties]." The claim is contentious at best, and false, in my opinion.

One thing that certainly is true in this regard is that during a certain period in the history of music, roughly, the Romantic period, certain musical compositions of the absolute kind do display expressive properties so prominently as to make them at least one aspect of such works demanding top billing and our careful attention. Nor do I wish to deny that some of these works, perhaps many of them, have expressive properties as part of their structural "plan." After all, it is no accident that Brahms's First Symphony progresses as part of its musical plan not only from C minor to C major, but from the "tragic" to the "triumphal," from the dark emotions to the light.

But it begs an important question to go from the fact, which I do not deny, indeed assert, that many works of music have expressive properties as part of their structure to the conclusion that these properties, therefore, make up some emotive, semantical content. My own view is that, like other "phenomenological" properties of musical works, "turbulence" or "tranquillity" or the like, they are part of absolute music's "syntactic" fabric and require no further musical explanation than that.

As for composers' claims that they have "meant" this or that or the other in their music, claims that no doubt increased in number and conviction in the nineteenth century, they must be evaluated not merely by the sincerity or vehemence of their expression but by a reasonable estimate of the enterprise itself. If a composer claims that he did something in his music that mature philosophical reflection (or plain common sense) concludes *cannot* be done, we quite rightly follow reason in the matter and dismiss the expressed intention as irrelevant to musical appreciation.

In the present instance, it may perhaps be true that a composer intended to "say" profound things about emotions in his music. That he could not, hence did not, settles the matter.

But does such a failed intention not suggest, if it is an important one in the compositional process, a failed composition? And if it *were* true, of which I by no means am convinced, that most of the great works of absolute music of the Romantic era were written with the end in view of saying profound things, or even just plain ordinary things, about the emotions, would it not imply the intolerable result that most of that repertoire, which comprises some of the most valued absolute music we possess, is an artistic failure? Or, to put the thing more modestly, if some purportedly great works of absolute music were composed with one of the dominant ends in view being the making of statements about the emotions, which I am inclined to believe is true, wouldn't it follow, on the view I am arguing for, that at least these works are artistic failures, because one of the dominant intentions behind their creation must be, on my view, a failed intention? And isn't that also an intolerable conclusion?

I see no reason to think that the failed intention to say things about the emotions should render what we take to be the great instrumental works of the nineteenth century artistic failures. Many artists have failed in their intentions because they have had crazy ideas about the world, or about what art can accomplish. Of course, if enough of an artist's intentions fail, then his works will be failures. But if enough of the crucial intentions succeed, then the fact that some intentions fail, no matter how deeply felt they may be or how important to the artist, does not spell artistic disaster for the works.

In the case in question, no matter how widespread the failed intentions of work-meaning may have been among the great Romantic composers, one intention of supreme importance, which one must presume almost all of them had, was to compose musical works that were *musically* coherent, well constructed, and as full as possible of inherently interesting musical invention: harmonic, melodic, contrapuntal, formal, orchestral, and so forth. In other words, it is likely that almost every great composer of the nineteenth century intended, when he wrote symphonies or string quartets or sonatas or any other forms of "pure" instrumental music, to produce perfectly wrought musical compositions, capable of being appreciated as such, no matter what other intentions he may have had. And where they failed, because of programmatic or other "semantic" intentions, as some think Liszt, Berlioz, Richard Strauss, and others sometimes did, to write compositions completely satisfying musically, those compositional failures, whatever their other artistic virtues, have put such compositions lower in our estimation.

What I am saying is that the pure musical parameters, when masterfully handled by the "great ones" – by Schumann, Mendelssohn, Brahms, Tchaikovsky, Mahler – are enough to overcome any failed intention to "say" things in their instrumental compositions. That intention – the intention, quite simply, to make perfectly wrought musical structures – when it succeeds, is enough to ensure musical success, whatever crackbrained or plausible intentions, impossible or possible, may fail. In instrumental music, the pure musical parameters are always trump. And that is why, I surmise, a person such as myself, who does not perceive meaning, pictures, or narratives in the great works of absolute music the nineteenth century produced, can still derive such a rich and deep aesthetic satisfaction from them.

The second stage of Levinson's argument goes on in this way:

(5) Where music is expressive of emotional states, listeners are frequently led, when they recognize these emotional states, to reflect, if obscurely, on them.
(6) Perhaps listeners perform this reflection on these emotional states by temporarily "inhabiting" them in imagination.
(7) This effect on listeners must frequently be envisaged by the creators and transmitters of music.
(8) Therefore, there seems to be nothing wrong [does that mean it is *right?*] in saying that such music as described by (5) and (6) is "about" the emotions it is expressive of.

This second stage seems much more to me like a straightforward argument than the first, and I will so treat it. Proposition (5), I think, is flat out false, but I cannot prove that, nor can Levinson prove its truth. For it is an empirical claim that could be confirmed or disconfirmed only by the boring and laborious process of polling listeners. For myself, I cannot but think it beyond belief that very many listeners to absolute music are led in any systematic way – indeed, in any way whatever – to think about emotions. Almost *anything,* I suppose, can provoke someone to think about almost anything. It seems a slender thread on which to hang a theory of musical "content."

Proposition (6) immediately raises a question about its central concept, "inhabiting" an emotion. What does it mean for someone to "inhabit" an emotion in imagination? I suppose the most likely candidate is imagining that one is feeling the emotion. But that in itself raises questions. Nor do I see what I might find out about an emotion by imagining I am feeling it, beyond what I already know. To make proposition (6) intelligible, let alone believable, a great deal more of explaining would have to be done. And it would be pointless, in any event, to undertake that task until we had determined that proposition (5) was true, since it is obviously pointless to try to figure out how something occurs if it doesn't occur.

Propositions (5) and (7) are related in much the same way as (1) and (2). For even if (5) were true, which I doubt, (7) does not follow from it for the same reason (2) does not follow from (1). I think it would be an extremely rare case indeed in which a composer, in the compositional process, planned his music in such a way as to make his listeners think about emotions, to make them reach conclusions about them, and so forth. That just is not what composers do when they compose instrumental music or what their teachers have taught them to do. If someone thinks it is, it is incumbent on that person to provide us with the evidence. Until I have seen such evidence, I remain highly skeptical. And I would require evidence, by the way, beyond the occasional, vague remark of a Haydn or a Beethoven that he meant to educate humanity or reveal truths. Such talk is cheap, and usually ends where it begins, whereas the musical listener

– which is to say the listener who is musical – goes elsewhere for an emotional or moral education.

Proposition (8) I take to be the conclusion of an argument of which propositions (5) and (7) are the premises. But it is, it seems to me, a completely unwarranted one. Even if it were true that listeners are frequently led to think about the emotions they hear in music, and even if it were true that composers frequently envisaged this, it would emphatically not make music "about" these emotions, any more than coffee mugs are "about" coffee, even though the perception of them causes people to think about coffee, which makers of coffee mugs well know.

"Aboutness," I take it, is more than the result merely of a contingent connection between what we perceive and what that perception causes us to think, however regular the connection might be. "Aboutness" is a semantic concept; and the causal connection between perceiving music's expressive properties and, frequently afterward, "obscurely" thinking about them is hardly enough to make absolute music a "language," even in the most distant, scare-quote way.

It seems to me, then, that Levinson has failed to make out a plausible case for musical "aboutness." And without "aboutness" the case for musical profundity must also fail. But perhaps some might think this a logical quibble or my concept of "aboutness" overly stringent and restrictive. So let us grant, for the sake of the argument, that Levinson has established the possibility of musical aboutness and ask ourselves whether, even then, a case can be made for musical profundity based on this kind of "aboutness." For profundity does not just require being able to say *something* about *something*; it requires being able to say something *profound*. I do not believe, even given the concept of musical aboutness as a gift, that Levinson can make his case for musical profundity.

§10 As we have just seen, Levinson's case for musical aboutness is based on the expressive aspect of music. Not surprisingly, therefore, one of the ways Levinson thinks music can be profound is by being profound about our emotions or about our emotive life. In addition, it can be profound, Levinson says, about what he calls "modes of growth and development" and can be what might be called "metaphysically" profound as well:

> So, finally, what might it plausibly mean to say that a piece of instrumental music was profound . . . ? The following, it seems, are still worth considering: 1) it explores the emotional or psychic realm in a more insightful or eye-opening way than most music; 2) it epitomizes or alludes to more interesting or complex extra-musical modes of growth and development than most music, and gives us a vicarious experience of such modes; 3) it strikes us as touching, in some fashion or other, on the most fundamental and pressing aspects of human existence – e.g. death, fate, the inexorability of time, the space between aspiration and attainment.[24]

The problem is, as Levinson well knows, that these are empty claims and can be made convincing only by providing real, full-blooded examples of music expressing profound thoughts about profound subject matter. In the absence of such examples, why should we believe the claims? As Levinson himself observes of them, "Of course these are just suggestions, brief promissory notes which only a more extensive analysis could redeem."[25]

But these promissory notes have been out a long time. Why have they not yet been paid? May I suggest it is because the account is bankrupt?

Let us run through Levinson's three possibilities for musical profundity briefly. Levinson offers no example in the essay on musical profundity of what music might "say" about the emotions, but he does in another of his essays, called "Truth in Music." Levinson makes the following suggestion there: "A work that expresses emotions ϕ and θ in successive passages suggests that in the experience of a single individual θ could *naturally* succeed ϕ."[26] Thus, on Levinson's view, the mournful first subject of Mozart's G-minor Symphony (K. 550) with the happy second subject is stating that in the experience of a single individual happiness could *naturally* follow unhappiness. It scarcely needs pointing out that whatever this assertion is, it is scarcely profound. And if the whole G-minor Symphony is a series of such assertions, their sum can scarcely make a profound utterance or a profound work.

Now I do not suggest that Levinson offers this kind of thing as an example of how absolute music can be profound about the emotions. But it *is* the kind of thing he offers as an example of how music can be truthful about the emotions, can, indeed, be "about" the emotions in the first place. And this seems to be all he has to offer to date on that regard. In the absence of any other more promising example of how music can say things about the emotions, this is what we have to work with, and it will never, in its paucity of propositional potential, add up to profundity. Levinson's first promissory note seems to have bounced.

What are we to make of the second claim, that profound music "epitomizes or alludes to more interesting or complex extramusical modes of growth and development than most music . . ."? Of course, we would like to know just what work "epitomizes" and "alludes" are doing in this sentence. And although Levinson does not tell us directly what he means, he does refer us, in a note, to an essay by the late Monroe Beardsley for further elucidation. I think we can get a good idea of what Levinson might have in mind by looking there.

In an essay called "Understanding Music," Beardsley discusses the perennial question of whether music can have extramusical "content" in any sense related to that in which linguistic utterances have "extralinguistic" content. In other words, can music *mean* in anything like the linguistic sense?

After rejecting, quite rightly, some of the more flamboyant claims made on behalf of musical "meaning," Beardsley turns to Nelson Goodman's theory of "exemplification" for a more plausible, if less ambitious account of musical reference. On Goodman's account, artworks refer to the properties they "exemplify." His now-familiar example of this relation is the tailor's swatch of cloth, which exemplifies – is a sample of – its color (say) or its texture (but not its shape or weight) and, insofar as it exemplifies one of these properties, at the same time refers to it.

Not every property of an artwork is one that it exemplifies

171

and (hence) refers to. How can one distinguish the exemplified properties of (say) a piano sonata from the others? According to Beardsley, "[T]he properties of the sonata that are exemplified by the sonata are just those properties which are *worthy of note* in the context of concert-giving and concert going (and recording, too): that is, they are those properties whose presence or absence, or degree of presence, have a direct bearing on the sonata's capacity to interest us aesthetically."[27]

Now "development," "growth," and "change" are terms that we consistently find ourselves applying to absolute music. And the quality that all of these terms seem to be picking out would be an exemplified quality, if any were. So, Beardsley concludes, "the idea that music exemplifies – indeed, exploits and glories in – aspects of change that are among the most fundamental and pervasive characteristics of living seems to me to be true."[28]

Given, then, that Levinson himself has directed us to Beardsley's essay for further elucidation, given too that Levinson's "epitomize" and "allude" are pretty good synonyms for Goodman's and Beardsley's "exemplify," one can fairly conclude, I would think, that Levinson is running here a Goodman–Beardsley analysis of what it might mean for a piece of music to epitomize or allude to extramusical modes of growth and development. Such a piece of music would exemplify extramusical growth and development, and (hence) refer to them. Profound music, on this analysis is, then, music that exemplifies and (hence) refers to more interesting extramusical modes of growth and development than does less profound or trivial music.

My first problem with this analysis concerns the step from exemplifying growth or development to either exemplifying or referring to *extramusical* growth or development. There is no doubt, to take an obvious example, that the first movement of Beethoven's Fifth Symphony, and particularly its development, exemplifies, if any piece of music does, *musical* growth, *musical* development. But what licenses us to say that it refers to (or exemplifies) any other kind of growth or development besides the musical? There is no doubt that texts can fix such external reference. The wonderful resolution to D major in the last measures of *The Marriage of Figaro* seems unmistakably to exemplify musical "resolution," but the "resolution" of the plot, and the alienation of the various characters as well, nor is it too much to say that *our* alienations and (one hopes) resolutions are also alluded to. The text and dramatic situation make that clear. With Beethoven's Fifth Symphony, however, or any other work of absolute music, there is no such linguistic connection with an extramusical reality; and the assumption that an extramusical connection exists at all is just that: a completely unfounded *assumption*.

To be sure, the first movement of Beethoven's Fifth has perhaps caused some people to think about extramusical growth: perhaps the growth of embryos or of human beings or of the cosmos since the Big Bang, or who knows what. And it may indeed regularly cause people to think of examples of "growth" and "development" (although I know of no evidence that it does, except among philosophers). But it will seldom lead anyone to have profound thoughts about these things, because few of us, obviously, are capable of having profound thoughts about "growth" or "development" or anything else. If, however, the first movement of Beethoven's Fifth Symphony should stimulate profound thoughts about growth and development in some "genius" listener, it would be the thoughts, not the notes, that were profound. I don't see how Beethoven or his symphony could claim the credit. (All sorts of unprofound things have occasioned profound thoughts in those capable of them.)

Suppose, though, that we grant extramusical exemplification and reference as a gift. Where are we then? Hardly closer, I think, to musical profundity.

Even if Levinson can show that Beethoven's Fifth Symphony exemplifies and refers to profound subject matter, whether it be growth, or development or anything else, he has not shown that the *work* is profound. For as I pointed out earlier, it takes more than a profound subject matter to make a profound work. Even I can make reference to the human condition. (I just did.) What I cannot do is say anything profound about it, nor (for a different reason) can Beethoven's Fifth Symphony, for all of its musical magnificence. Even if it could achieve reference to the profound, as long as it is bereft of profound things to say about it, it is bereft of profundity.

I move on, now, to Levinson's final "promissory note." Music, he says, "strikes us as touching, in some fashion or other, on the most fundamental and primary aspects of human existence – e.g. death, fate, the inexorability of time, the space between aspiration and attainment."

Those are a veritable gaggle of metaphysical profundities that Levinson tells us music is "touching, in some fashion or other." But the promissory notes get harder and harder for us to imagine ever being made good. What, to begin with, is the "fashion" in which music is supposed to "touch" these profound questions? If it is the Goodmanian combination of exemplification cum reference, then what we have just said about these two will suffice. If there is some other analysis of how absolute music can be understood as "touching" these profundities, then we are owed it; and I have no doubt that in due course Levinson will try to pay this debt. But until then, the account seems in the red.

Furthermore, Levinson's rather too easy assumption that absolute music strikes "us" as touching all of these metaphysical profundities seems to me far from plausible. Perhaps it strikes a few of "us" that way, a few philosophers with theoretical axes to grind. I doubt if it so strikes the general public of music lovers or the general population of musicians and musically trained amateurs.

§11 Experience has taught me that proposals for how music might be about one thing or another are limited only by the ingenuity of philosophers in thinking them up. And since the ingenuity of philosophers is limitless, so are the proposals. It would be a life's work to keep up.

Indeed, the Goodman–Beardsley theory of exemplification gives us a machinery for generating "aboutness" in regard to *any* quality a piece of music can be said to exemplify, which amounts to *any* quality a piece of music can possess *qua* music. Is it a minuet? Then it exemplifie "minuetness," and hence is about minuets (or about dances?). Does it resolve to the tonic?

Then it exemplifies resolution and hence is "about" it. Is it turbulent music? Then. . . . And so on in infinitum. But however philosophical ingenuity may produce candidates for aboutness in music, it is a hollow logical victory, simply a parlor trick, unless it can be shown that that aboutness is something we should care about, something that makes the music interesting or valuable to us. It sometimes does matter, musically, that a piece of music is turbulent in such and such a place or resolves to the tonic at another. But what is *added*, what makes it matter more, if we then say, "So it must be *about* turbulence, so it must be *about* resolution"?

The obvious answer is: in order for aboutness to matter in music, the music must say something interesting or useful or in some other way valuable *about* what it *is* about. Naked aboutness is nothing at all.

In the case of produndity, of course, in order for aboutness to achieve it, what the music is about must be profound *and* something profound must be asserted about this musical content. It is very hard to see how this second condition can be fulfilled.

Indeed, it is very difficult to see how much of anything either interesting or valuable – forget about profound – can be said by music about what it is about, even if the minimal, Goodman–Beardsley aboutness is achieved. Of course I cannot prove it is impossible. But let me try to underscore the difficulty with an example.

In "Truth in Music," Jerrold Levinson tries to show, with considerable philosophical ingenuity, that Beethoven's Sonata for Violin and Piano in C minor, Op. 30, No. 2 asserts, in one of its very crucial musical places, a false proposition. This work, one would be forced to conclude, is significantly false.

Now if we find a philosophical or scientific work seriously false, it is a heavy judgment against it. Yet with regard to the "falsity" Levinson thinks he has revealed in this much-admired work of Beethoven's, he is forced to conclude that "none of this prevents the C minor Violin Sonata from being overall probably the finest of Beethoven's efforts in that medium."[29] One wonders, then, what the cash value of this kind of truth and falsity is if it should leave the works it inhabits of just about the same musical value, whatever the truth-value? "Who cares?" one is tempted to ask. And Levinson, who has far more invested in musical truth and falsity than I, seems almost to feel the same way. For of the kinds of falsity he has identified in musical works Levinson remarks: "I want . . . to caution readers who sense a threat to some favored piece of music that I do not mean to imply that if a piece of music admits of . . . falsity it is *necessarily*, or even *probably*, a bad piece of music."[30] Isn't Levinson himself essentially saying "Who cares?"

Of course, Levinson is not out to establish, in the essay under discussion now, either that the truths music can express can be profound or even, as we have just seen, that they can be of any great importance at all to the music at any level below profundity. And this, I suggest, is because one cannot get much beyond bare reference, if one can even get there, for absolute music. One can perhaps get the music to be "about." But to make it say anything interesting, let alone profound about anything, seems beyond the ingenuity of philosophy, at present, to achieve. Of course, one can never prove the negative, so I will be forced to leave it at that.

But let me reemphasize that an account of how music "touches" profound questions must be rich enough not merely to attain bare reference but to attain some recognizable profundity of comment on what is referred to. Without that, there is only the relation to profundity that even the mediocre of us can attain in our work. A cat can look at a king, and reference to the profound is what most of us can attain. It is going beyond that to speaking profoundly about the profound that achieves work profundity. And it is that further step that absolute music can never take, even if, as I doubt, it can take the preliminary step of exemplification of and reference to extramusical profundity. This does not make absolute music less worthy than philosophy or poetry or science or tragedy. It does make it *different*. And difference is my theme.

§12   It is time now to extract what moral we can from the quest for musical profundity, and the failures of the quest that I have just chronicled. The quest for profundity in music comes out of a genuine and general feeling – intuition, if you want to beg the question – that certain works of absolute music are limitless in their "musical substance," whatever that might be. They are the works one feels one can explore forever, the works that always bear rehearing, the works one takes on summer vacation, when baggage space is limited and the nights empty. I suppose that those who think this way will have some "odd" cases of their own. But I cannot imagine anyone's list not having Bach's *Well-Tempered Clavier, Musical Offering, The Art of Fugue,* and the major organ works; the thirty-two piano sonatas of Beethoven, along with the late quartets and the major symphonies; and select instrumental works of Haydn, Mozart, Schubert, and Brahms. Those, at least, are the core, the canon; and there is not much to be gained, for present purposes, by arguing over the details.

But if there is bona fide musical profundity, what is its foundation? And if there is not, if it is just a "feeling" and nothing more that we have about the "profundity" (so called) of the works above-mentioned, where does that leave absolute music in the pantheon of the arts, in the hierarchy of human values?

The question of musical profundity, then, is really a special case of the question, Why does instrumental music matter? Why should it be mentioned in the same breath as great (or even good) literature and painting?

Some eighteenth-century thinkers, including Kant, as we have seen, had a ready answer: "It doesn't. It shouldn't." It is wallpaper for the ears and should be accorded equal treatment with the stuff on your walls. For such thinkers, Muzak would have been the expected destiny of absolute music, not its ultimate degradation.

For Western literature, "profundity," I guess, is the ultimate value. If absolute music is also to have that ultimate value, it must, so I suspect its defenders think, be capable of profundity too – and profundity about the same kinds of things. The question of musical profundity is the question of music's ultimate worth.

But profundity is the top of a scale. And the question of musical profundity is, as I see it, not so much whether its best examples can ever really reach the top of the scale as whether it is on the scale at all: whether, that is, absolute music has to any degree whatever that substance that the scale quantifies and measures. But if it does not possess that substance at all – namely, *extramusical subject matter* – what can its value possibly be to us? Why should we, as we seem to do, take it so seriously? It is the quest for "sameness" in yet another guise.

In the following chapter I will not, then, as might have been expected, try to argue for musical profundity in a way more successful than those ways I have found wanting. I will leave that alone for now.

What I do want to tackle is the question that lies at the heart of the flap over musical profundity: the more general question, which I am frequently asked, usually in an aggressive manner given my so-called formalist proclivities, What really matters to us, in absolute music, if formalism is true? (Nothing: therefore formalism is false.) Again, the quest for sameness – the compulsion to see music as another example of literary or painterly values – drives the argument.

Can we have musical value *and* musical "difference"? To this crucial question I now turn my attention. But let me caution the (perhaps) overly expectent reader that I will not – cannot – in what follows give a complete account of musical value (whatever such an account would look like). What I will do, in keeping with the theme of my book, is to show how *one* value of music accrues to *one* musical *difference*. I should add, however, that it is a very crucial difference, and hence a very crucial value.

Chapter 7
The Liberation of Music

Zip. I was reading Schopenhauer last night.
Zip. And I think that Schopenhauer was right.
Lorenz Hart

§1 Whatever the value of the literary arts in human life, and
however this value is connected with the pleasure we take in
them, few would deny that both the value and the pleasure are
deeply beholden to what we are used to calling its "content."
Literature is language, and it speaks to us as language does, of
many and various things. Aristotle thought at least some of it
more philosophical than history. And except for an occasional
flirtation with "formalism," philosophers of art and literary theorists have, from Plato and Aristotle onward, seen literature as
a way some people – people we admire very much – have of
telling us how things are with us, them, and our world. They –
the philosophers and theorists, that is – do indeed differ greatly
on the "what" and the "how" of literary "speech," and some
in our own day have even doubted that literature does or can
have direct reference to us and our world, but only to the world
of the text itself. Yet however the thing is done, however reference is achieved, few would deny that the value of and our
pleasure in literature have a great deal, though not of course
wholly, to do with what it "says," one way or another, about
one thing and another.

Of the arts of visual representation, something like the same
sort of thing can be said – but neither so strongly nor so unequivocally, nor, I think, with quite the same philosophical clout.
Whether the visual arts of representation "say," in any full-
blooded sense of that word, can be seriously doubted. None
except formalists, however, would deny that what the visual arts
of representation mean in our lives, the value we place on them,

179

as well as the pleasure we take in them, has intimately to do not only with their formal and sensual elements, but with their representational subject matter: *what* it is they represent. Indeed, as concerned as we are with the physical, painterly, or sculptural medium of the visual arts of representation, it makes little sense to suggest that it can be valued or enjoyed in vacuo. It is a medium of representation, and we can neither value nor enjoy it, *qua* medium, apart from what it represents, *qua* medium. We cannot have the *how* without the *what*, which is to say, we cannot enjoy how the painterly or sculptural medium represents what it does without cognizing what it represents. This seems obvious and hardly in need of argument.

The difficult case is absolute music. If so much of what we enjoy and value in the arts of literature and visual representation is involved with content, with subject matter, where does that leave the apparently contentless, subjectless art of instrumental composition? Schopenhauer was so impressed with considerations of this kind that he was willing to argue from them to the conclusion that, appearances to the contrary notwithstanding, absolute music (*in*correctly so called) must be a representational and, indeed, linguistic art after all.

I shall play with three themes from Schopenhauer in what follows, and the second of them has now been alluded to, namely, the theme of music as an art of hidden, hermeneutical representation. This theme, as will become apparent, I repudiate. But this discordant theme is introduced by a simple first theme that, unadorned, I fully endorse. Of the art of absolute music, Schopenhauer states, with boldness, "It stands quite apart from all the others."[1]

Had Schopenhauer developed this theme as boldly as he stated it, he would, I believe, have gotten far closer to the truth than he did. But after recognizing a radical difference between music and the other fine arts, he then cashed out that difference not in any radical way, rather in the event, merely as a difference in the *what* and *how* of music's reaffirmed representationality. For Schopenhauer, the nonmusical arts are representational not of our familiar world of space, time, cause, and human intention, but of the Platonic ideas that lie behind. Music is distinguished

180

in being representational *not* of these Platonic ideas but of what Schopenhauer conceives of as the underlying metaphysical reality of the whole shebang: the striving noumenal will. The argument is straightforward. Accept the representationality of the other fine arts and the similarity of our experience of music to our experience of them; accept how deeply our experience of the nonmusical arts is imbued with their content – accept all of this and you are compelled to accept the representationality of music in some form or other. "That in some sense music must be related to the world as the depiction to the thing depicted, as the copy to the original, we can infer from the analogy with the remaining arts, to all of which this character is peculiar; from their effect on us, it can be inferred that that of music is on the whole of the same nature, only stronger, more rapid, more necessary and infallible."[2]

I shall return to Schopenhauer's murky and cumbersome metaphysics later on, when we encounter the third, and main, Schopenhauerian theme. For now, let me just say that, shorn of its metaphysics, Schopenhauer's view characterizes absolute music as having a hidden content, not apparent on its artistic surface, but in need of hermeneutical revelation. Stated this way, metaphysics aside, Schopenhauer's view is now widely held among musical scholars and analyists. This requires some brief explanation.

§2   Archibald, as I shall call him, is looking at a picture of a man sitting at a table, writing. At the man's feet lies what Archibald takes to be a pet animal of the four-legged variety; and the man seems to Archibald to have a peculiar ring around his head, which Archibald presumes is a funny kind of hat. Let me add that Archibald, except for his name, is your average ten-year-old.

Archibald, I want to say, is taking in what might be called the manifest representational content of the picture. Anyone who could not see at least this much in the representation – who could not see the man, the table, the ring around the man's head, the four-legged creature, the act of writing – we could fairly call illiterate with regard to visual representation.

But you and I would see something beyond what Archibald sees. We would see Saint Jerome with his halo and his lion. We would see the seated figure as a saint because we have imbibed enough elementary iconography and background information to know that the ring is a halo, that Saint Jerome's "familiar" is a lion, and so forth. We have some superficial acquaintance with the inner, nonmanifest content of the picture. Archibald does not.

Let me caution that I am launching no profound philosophical argument here meant to explicate, with logical rigor, the boundary between manifest and hermeneutical content in the visual arts of representation or in literature. All I mean to do is illustrate, with this intentionally crude example, that we commonly recognize such a distinction and are in some kind of vague agreement, if not about where hermeneutical content begins, then at least where total illiteracy begins. If Archibald cannot even see the saint as a human being or the lion as an animal with four legs, we are likely to say that he is not seeing the picture as a *picture*, whatever his visual experience may be.

I press this point because when we are told, either by Schopenhauer or by his late-twentieth-century reincarnations, that absolute music has a hidden, nonmanifest content that the commentator in question will now reveal, the claim is made against the familiar background of a practice in which the commentator upon a literary work, or a work of the visual arts, digs beneath the manifest content of the work to reveal the hermeneutical content underlying it. But we must not be lulled by this familiar background into missing a rather startling incongruity between the cases. For in the case of absolute music there is no manifest content. And that is a nontrivial fact. In the familiar case, the manifest content is medium for the hidden content, whereas in the case of absolute music, there is no manifest content to serve the purpose.

There is a familiar plausibility to the notion that one can appreciate a representational work at a certain "level," as Archibald does, without perceiving the levels beneath. Archibald can enjoy how well the representation of a man and his pet is brought off without yet perceiving it as a representation of Saint Jerome and his lion. Think, though, of the position I am in, or that Hanslick or Schenker is in, before the musical hermeneutist reveals to us what something we thought was absolute music represents, something we have been enjoying all of our lives under the impression that it represents nothing. Archibald is a connoisseur, a mavin compared with us. We are perceiving no representational content at all in a work that is supposed to derive a major portion – perhaps the whole – of its aesthetic payoff from its representationality. A ten-year-old is closer to appreciating rightly the picture of Saint Jerome than Hanslick, Schenker, and I are of appreciating Beethoven's Fifth Symphony rightly (or at all?). Perhaps you are prepared to dismiss my musical experiences as of no account. But what about Hanslick's and Schenker's?

I say that this is a nontrivial stumbling block for any account of absolute music on representational grounds. It is so, let me remind you, because the argument from Schopenhauer is founded on the premise that our appreciation of the obviously contentful arts – literature, painting, sculpture – is largely appreciation of content represented or presented. From this premise, and the further one that our "experience" of music seems like our "experience" of those other, contentful arts, it is supposed to follow that absolute music must, despite appearances, be contentful as well. So if it now seems as if absolute music, unlike the contentful arts, can be richly appreciated without experiencing its content at all, the argument begins to look very doubtful indeed. For absolute music is strikingly dissimilar to the other, contentful arts in this respect. To be able to richly appreciate a contentful work of art in complete ignorance of its content seems bizarre in the extreme.

This deep chasm separating absolute music from the arts of content and representation has for a long time seemed to me conclusive against any account of absolute music as some kind of occult representation or narrative. But I want, for the sake of argument, to put such considerations aside and take a look at two actual cases of musical analysis in the hermeneutical vein.

In the preceding chapter we encountered suggestions from philosophers as to where one might look for representational, even
propositional, content in absolute music. But philosophers tend,
in Levinson's words, to only issue "promissory notes." Musical
analysts and scholars, on the other hand, are in the business of
cash transactions. So I want to see if they can really deliver the
goods, in terms of believable musical analysis of a representational or contentful kind. Can the musical hermeneuticists really
convince us that absolute music has the content they say it has?
And can we convince ourselves that that content, even if music
has it, constitutes a plausible account of what we value and
enjoy in absolute music? My answers to both questions will be
negative. And I hope to go on from there to give, if only in bare
outline, an account of my own.

§3   I dare say that no more central or obvious cases of absolute
music could be adduced than Bach's *Art of Fugue* or Haydn's
late symphonies. If these are not absolute music, one hardly
knows what else might answer to that description. And yet I
am about to examine the claims of two professional practitioners
of the discipline of musical analysis, each claiming, for one of
the above-mentioned, remarkable content of, I suppose one
might say, a, "philosophical" kind. I begin, chronologically,
with Bach's *Art of Fugue.*
    The eternal symbol of the musical art at its most abstract, its
most absolute, is surely Bach's musical homage to the fugue and
its near relations. If it has been praised, it has been praised for
that, if criticized, criticized for that: praised for its perfection of
sonic form, criticized for its lack of "human values" (under the
odd assumption that musical structure in its highest form is not
one of them).
    But the temper of the times made it inevitable, I guess, that
even such a bastion of music at its most absolute should finally
be assaulted by the musical content crowd. It would seem to be
far easier to show that *The Art of Fugue* is a dark saying and
encoded pronouncement in defense of its human value than to
take on the difficult and so far neglected task of showing the

human value in a musical structure altogether without content, hidden or otherwise. And so we have from Hans Eggebrecht, most sober and scholarly of German musicologists, an analysis of Bach's unfinished contrapuntal last testament, purporting to show "that Bach relied upon a specific extramusical idea to control the invention and development of the musical materials in *The Art of Fugue.*" although Eggebrecht raises our suspicions concerning this rather extraordinary claim with two fairly damaging disclaimers, to wit, that his views "cannot be proved" and that what he is presenting is "a personal subjective theory."[3] What these odd expressions of self-doubt amount to – particularly the strange specter of a theory that is "personal" and "subjective" – is not clear. But the kind of "extramusical" analysis Eggebrecht offers is suspicious enough without his disclaimers, because it seeks "an aesthetic meaning concealed within the work's musical substance,"[4] a view of how music might mean or represent that, in our preliminary discussion of Schopenhauer, we have already found dubious indeed.

Every commentator on *The Art of Fugue*, hermeneutist or not, will agree that the musical climax of the work begins at the place in the great unfinished fugue were Bach introduces as the third theme his own name spelled out in notes: B-flat, A, C, H (which is to say, B-natural, in German notation). The whole subject also includes the notes C-sharp and D (an important musical fact that I shall return to presently).

Example 1

We can identify this as the beginning of the musical climax, independently of knowing that the third theme spells "Bach," because we can show that the three subjects so far introduced can be combined with the main theme of the work. Thus it appears that Bach intended the final fugue, which breaks off shortly after the introduction of the Bach theme, to be a quadruple fugue in which the third theme was his own name and the fourth the ground theme of the work, as yet not heard in the unfinished fugue. Needless to say, it can hardly be a coincidence that the ground theme can be combined with the others simultaneously. So it seems to follow both that the final fugue of the work was to be a quadruple fugue – triple fugues being the most ambitious theretofore – and that the final climactic stroke would be the combining of the three themes, already introduced, with the main theme, not yet heard in the piece. On this all students of *The Art of Fugue* now agree.

For most folks, I would think, that the third subject of the fugue spells out Bach's name in German musical notation is an amusing conceit that, once known, plays no future part in the appreciation of Bach's massive musical architectonic. That the master died, apparently, shortly after introducing this theme lends that musical event a poignancy no lover of Bach can escape. But for most of us the thing ends there. Not so, however, for Professor Eggebrecht.

"Until now," Eggebrecht observes, "it has been generally accepted that the B–A–C–H motto was simply the composer's way of autographing *The Art of Fugue*."[5] But Eggebrecht's understanding of this seemingly innocent play is quite different, and heavy with significance. To begin with: "It is quite possible that Bach did not so much engrave his name in the closing fugue to denote authorship, but rather to say: 'I desire to reach, and am in the process of reaching, toward the *Tonic* – I am identified with it.'"[6] As evidence for this puzzling interpretation Eggebrecht offers the following: "An examination of the musical materials indeed confirms that the tonic note (d) is the central reference pitch of every movement. In fact, d is both the starting pitch and goal pitch of the overall musical structure in the work as a whole. Therefore, the addition of a *double discant clausula* to the pitches B–A–C–H in the third subject of the closing fugue is very significant."[7]

For those not initiated into this musicological jargon, a double discant clausula is, simply, two cadences (*clausulae*), one right after the other for emphasis, in the highest voice, that is, the *discant*.

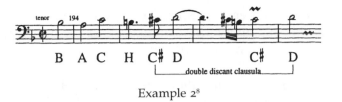

B A C H C# D   C# D
⌞____double discant clausula____⌟

Example 2[8]

Thus Eggebrecht's argument seems to be that the *double* cadence on the tonic is meant to call our attention emphatically to the tonic, and to the resolution to it, while the fact that the theme in which the double cadence is embodied spells out the composer's name tells us that the composer is saying, "I desire to reach, and am in the process of reaching the *Tonic* – I am identified with it."

There is something rather breathtaking in the combination of audacity and insouciance with which Professor Eggebrecht travels, in the course of four sentences, from two simple musical events to this astonishing assertion. Suppose Bach had really intended to say what Engelbrecht thinks he said in his music. *Could* he have said it?

Of course not. In order to say this one must employ a linguistic artifact in an appropriate rule- and convention-governed way. Music simply is not such an artifact. So if Bach did intend this, it is a necessarily failed intention. And it is tempting to let the discussion end with this, it seems to me conclusive refutation.

But it might be well, instead, to go on. For even though it is impossible to say such things in music as Eggebrecht claims Bach says in *The Art of Fugue* – and these claims get more ambitious as his book proceeds – it would be a nontrivial fact that Bach even intended to say them, failed though that intention must perforce be from the start. As will become apparent, I am not convinced that the evidence adduced proves anything of the kind.

§4   It makes little sense, it should be apparent, for Bach, or anyone else, to have the intention of delivering the message that he desires to reach the tonic, that he identifies with it. If that escapes being nonsense, it is hard to imagine how. And before long Eggebrecht amplifies this message into one heavy with religious and metaphysical significance:

> Because Bach connected the pitches B–A–C–H to this emphatic cadential process, I cannot believe that he only intended to say: "I composed this." Rather, appending the double discant clausula to the B–A–C–H motto seems to say, "I am identified with the *Tonic* and it is my desire to reach it." Interpreted more broadly, this statement could read: "Like you I am human, I am in need of salvation; I am certain in the hope of salvation, and have been saved by grace."[9]

It bears repeating that, whatever Bach's intention, his music cannot say what Eggebrecht construes. If it cannot say, "I seek the tonic," it cannot, a fortiori, say, "I seek salvation." But what evidence is there that he even intended it?

I think we can cut to the core of the problem with the simple observation that the double discant clausula could be used, not to say anything, but to *represent* any number of things. In particular, it could be used to represent the seeking and achieving of any goal you like: salvation, to be sure, but, as well, victory over your enemies, getting home after a long journey, solving a problem, living happily ever after, and so on.

I say it *could* be used to represent any of those things. But how do we claim to know which of them it does represent? And, prior to that, how do we claim to know that it represents anything at all?

I think we know that the wonderful resolution and cadence to D major in the last scene of *The Marriage of Figaro* represents the resolving of the conflicts and the unraveling of the plot entanglements because the text and mise-en-scène make it apparent. And we know Bach interlarded his vocal works with many such examples of "tone painting," which are easily recognized through the texts they accompany. But *The Art of Fugue* has no text. So how do we claim to know what, if anything, of the many things the double discant clausula could represent it does represent? Why, in particular, assume it represents *religious* things?

The most, indeed the only, obvious connection between *The Art of Fugue* and religion is the fact that when the unfinished work was first published, by Bach's son Carl Phillip Emanuel, he appended to it as a coda what is reputed to be his father's last completed work, the chorale prelude, *Vor deinen Thron tret ich hiermit,* supposedly dictated by the blind composer to his son-in-law Altnikol. And Eggebrecht remarks somewhat disingenuously, after introducing his religious interpretation of *The Art of Fugue,* "Indeed, there is an unmistakable similarity between the conviction established in this interpretation and the hymn text of Bach's last chorale setting. . . ."[10]

I say that the drawing of this connection is somewhat disingenuous because Eggebrecht well knows – indeed devotes an entire chapter to – the history of how the chorale prelude became attached to *The Art of Fugue;* and he well knows, in particular, that it was no part of J. S. Bach's intention that it should conclude his monument to the fugue. Thus he writes, "Although I will use the traditional association of this chorale with *The Art of Fugue* in order to help clarify my interpretation, it should be remembered that the chorale does not really belong to the work at all."[11]

It is hard to think of a better reason to consider Bach's last chorale prelude irrelevant to the interpretation of *The Art of Fugue* than Eggebrecht's own admission that "it does not really belong to the work at all." But it is instructive to consider the case further.

Suppose Bach had really concluded *The Art of Fugue* with the chorale prelude? If he had, if the chorale prelude really were a part of the work, then we would have license, by virtue of its associated text, to give *The Art of Fugue* a religious interpretation, perhaps even the one Eggebrecht puts on it. This consideration is instructive because it gives us a clue to Eggebrecht's whole strategy – a not uncommon one in music analysis these days. If the chorale had been part of the work, the work would have had a religious text; and if it had a religious text, there would be no difficulty in putting a religious interpretation on various of the musical parameters, seeing them, in effect, as "tone painting." Thus, I suggest, Eggebrecht's strategy throughout his analysis is to try to discover "hidden texts" in *The Art of Fugue*. Let us pursue this thought further.

§5 Eggebrecht's problem is this. Toward the end of what appears to be the intended climax of the concluding, and hence climactic, moment of *The Art of Fugue*, Bach introduces as the third subject of a quadruple fugue his own name spelled out in notes. Were that to be the only place where the Bach theme occurs, we would be hard put to see the whole *Art of Fugue* as somehow "about" Bach, let alone about his religious salvation. So if one is convinced that there is deep religious significance in this appearance of the Bach theme and that, in consequence, this significance is the ruling extramusical principle of the work, one had better find that Bach theme all over the place. For if it is merely a lone occurrence, it would have only the kind of casual interest that accrues to such musical tricks. And, indeed, Eggebrecht sees as many Bach themes in *The Art of Fugue* as Senator McCarthy saw communists in the State Department. And his methods of detection are pretty much as disreputable.

Eggebrecht has two methods for detecting – or, I would have to say, manufacturing – Bach themes. One I call "tune-tinkering," the other Eggebrecht calls "alpha-numeric symbolism." They are, in my view, equally fallacious. Let us take a look at tune-tinkering first.

The tones B–A–C–H, in that order, spelling out the composer's name, appear in only one place in *The Art of Fugue*, where the third theme of the projected quadruple fugue is introduced, although had Bach completed the fugue, they would have continued to appear until the close. However, the tones B–A–C–H, along with the associated tones, C-sharp and D, occur with great frequency throughout the entire work, although not in the order that spells out "Bach." "In this study," Eggebrecht tells us, "we shall call this group of six variously ordered pitches the B–A–C–H sphere."[12] And because these pitches as a group – the B–A–C–H sphere – are a ubiquitous presence in the work, "the presence of these elements," says Eggebrecht, "also support [*sic*] our view that the B–A–C–H–C#–D theme is a symbol which unlocks the hidden meaning of this work."[13]

Those familiar with Rudolph Reti's book, *The Thematic Process in Music*,[14] will be well acquainted with the method by which Eggebrecht "locates" the appearance of the B–A–C–H theme in *The Art of Fugue*. Roughly, it works this way. Remove any notes you wish, without independent justification of why you are removing just those notes, until you have left only the notes that constitute the theme you are looking for. Eggebrecht has, indeed, refined this method even beyond Reti's by disregarding not only the notes that don't belong to the theme but the order in which those notes appear that do, which is tantamount to arguing that the use of the word "dogged" in a poem has deep religious significance, since, by leaving off the last three letters and reversing the order of the first three, you get the word "god."

The method of Reti and his ilk has been so thoroughly discredited by myself[15] and others that its reappearance yet again, in the work of an established musical scholar, gives one pause to wonder whether rational persuasion in matters musical is ever possible. But, yet again, the method, if that is not paying it too high a compliment, of finding a theme by tinkering with the notes until you get it is a self-fulfilling one. It cannot fail to find what it is seeking because the only rule for tinkering is, "Tinker until you get what you have already decided *must* be there."

What is especially egregious about Eggebrecht's hunt for the B–A–C–H theme is that, as any first-year theory student can tell you, the notes of what Eggebrecht calls the "B–A–C–H sphere," B–A–C–H–C#–D, constitute the ascending and descending upper tetrachord of the natural D-minor scale. *Of course* this group of notes appears with great frequency in a work every movement of which is in D minor: it is part of the very grammar of D minor. And to discover its ubiquitousness is about as surprising as discovering that every sentence in *Paradise Lost* has a verb. Thus the presence of the B–A–C–H sphere does not require, for its explanation, any symbolic interpretation at all, but is accounted for completely by the musical syntax. It cannot, therefore, be adduced as evidence for a symbolic interpretation.

§6 If possible, Eggebrecht's other method for finding B–A–C–H themes in *The Art of Fugue* is even more outrageous than the one just canvassed. It is, in a word, "numerology." We are now in the world of Nostradamus and Revelation. I will adduce one example.

First, affix a number to each letter of the alphabet, "A" being 1, "B" being 2, and so on, with the pair "I" and "J" being assigned the number 9, and the pair "U" and "V" the number 20. "By this method," Eggebrecht now points out,

> the surname "Bach" is represented by the number fourteen. That is, "Bach" can be numerically represented by the sum of the numbers which represent the letters B, A, C, and H (2 + 1 + 3 + 8 = 14). Correspondingly, the name "J. S. Bach" can be represented by the number forty-one (9 + 18 + 14 = 41), and the full name, "Johann Sebastian Bach," by the number one hundred fifty-eight.[16]

Having conveyed this intelligence, Eggebrecht then observes, "At this point, it is imperative that we distance ourselves from the grotesque speculation about alpha-numeric symbolism which runs rampant in many treatises on Bach."[17] It sounds like very good advice. But as far as I can see Eggebrecht goes right on to ignore it. Here follows a typical application of alpha-numeric analysis, as Eggebrecht employs it.

The second subject of the unfinished quadruple fugue has, Eggebrecht has determined, exactly forty-one pitches, thus, by alpha-numeric symbolism, spelling out the name "J. S. Bach." It is, I suppose, a nice question in numerology whether one counts pitches or counts note characters. For if you count note characters, the second subject, because of two ties over the bar, has forty-three of those. Perhaps it seems more reasonable to you to count pitches instead of note characters. But you can be assured that if it were necessary to count note characters rather than pitches to get forty-one, that is what Eggebrecht would have counted. And it is just this kind of freedom to choose that makes numerology, like tune-tinkering, a method that cannot fail to produce the results desired.

But now suppose that the composer really has "signed" his

name, albeit cryptically, in the second theme as well as unequivocally in the third. What can we really make of that? Here
is what Eggebrecht makes of it:

> Though this relationship is pure conjecture, I wish to stress
> again that my interpretation does not regard any symbolic
> reference to "Bach" in *The Art of Fugue* simply to mean: "I
> have composed this." Instead, the forty-one pitches contained
> in the restless second subject might well express the thought:
> "I, J. S. Bach, am the one who is running toward the goal,
> though I am yet living an imperfect human existence. . . ." Be-
> cause of a possible connection between the alpha numeric
> symbol (forty-one) and the restless motion of the second sub-
> ject, I shall consider the second subject of the closing fugue to
> be a musical representation of Bach's goal-directed but human
> existence.[18]

It is instructive to follow the course of the argument, in this
passage, for it is a pattern familiar to anyone who has ever
delved into the pages of what might be called crypto-history, of
which books meant to prove darkly concealed conspiracies are
a prime example. The inferences always go from *possible* to *actual*, the reverse of the order of Aristotle's well-known and in-
contestable precept. Were it the other way round, pigs would
indeed have wings. But in the books I am describing what is
shown to be possible in Chapter 1 somehow, on the strength of
that, has become true in Chapter 2, and what is possible in 2
true in 3, and so on. Likewise, in the passage just quoted, we
begin with a "conjecture," which becomes, erelong, a "possible
connection" and ends up a baldly asserted truth: "I shall consider the second subject of the closing fugue to be a musical
representation of Bach's goal-directed but human existence."

But possible does not make true. Eggebrecht has not here or
anywhere else provided a shred of evidence to show that Bach
intended the second subject of the final fugue to represent what
Eggebrecht considers it to represent, namely, Bach's goal-
directed human existence. That is simply woven from whole
cloth out of mere possibility; and to accept possibility for truth
is simply to indulge in fantasy, however it might masquerade

as rational argument. Of course Bach could have used such a running figure to represent running toward a goal. He probably did so more than once in the cantatas. But the fallacy of going from the tone painting in the cantatas to representation in Bach's instrumental music has been well known since Pirro and Schweitzer and, as a general fallacy of going from texted music to absolute music, since Deryck Cooke's *The Language of Music*. I see no reason to refute the inference yet again.

It is my conclusion, then, that Eggebrecht has failed to reveal any extramusical content in Bach's *Art of Fugue* or any intention on Bach's part to express such content, aside from "spelling" his name in notes in the finale. It nevertheless remains an interesting question as to what significance it would have if the content Eggebrecht ascribes to Bach's work, or content like it, really were contained therein. For, after all, one might object that even though Eggebrecht has provided bad arguments – indeed, no arguments at all – for believing such content is there, it may be there for all of that; the conclusion of a bad argument may nevertheless be true.

I shall return to this point later. But first I would like to have before us one more example of the musical hermeneuticist's trade, just to assure the reader that Eggebrecht's venture is not, in our times, by any means an isolated one. For this purpose I shall leave behind the murky atmosphere of German religious mysticism for the healthy daylight of New World analysis. Unfortunately, as I will try to show, the hermeneutical venture fairs no better in this more salubrious intellectual climate.

§7   As I said earlier on, Haydn's last twelve symphonies, the London Symphonies, have an honored place among what many people would take to be the paradigmatic instances of absolute music. And they are far more familiar to the listening public than Bach's fugal essay, so problematic from the performance point of view. Whether it is more or less surprising that they too should gain the attention of the neo-Schopenhauerians I can't say. But gain it they have, in a book by David P. Schroeder called *Haydn and the Enlightenment: The Late Symphonies and Their Audience*.

It is Professor Schroeder's hypothesis that Haydn tried – and I guess Professor Schroeder thinks succeeded – in expressing, particularly in the late symphonies, certain moral precepts characteristic of the Enlightenment, but in particular of the work of Anthony Ashley Cooper, third earl of Shaftesbury. Thus a substantial part of the book is an attempt to convince, with the usual historical arguments, that Haydn was acquainted with the philosophy of Shaftesbury and to present that part of the philosophy he thinks Haydn was expressing in his music.

I am not concerned here with whether Schroeder has succeeded in demonstrating that Haydn was familiar with the philosophy of Shaftesbury, either directly, through his reading of the author's major work, the *Characteristics,* or indirectly, through what Leonard Meyer has happily called "intellectual scuttlebutt." The point, in my opinion, is contentious. What is far more interesting from the philosophical perspective is whether, even given the premise that Haydn was familiar with Shaftesbury's philosophy, we can establish either the intention to express it in his music or the successful carrying out of that intention. My own view is that we cannot.

§8 Let us take a fairly representative example of what Professor Schroeder is up to. Here is what he says about the conclusion of Haydn's Symphony No. 92:

> With the final appearance of the closing theme at bar 225, the two polar forces of the movement are heard, as in No. 83, simply standing side by side. The conclusion does not provide a resolution but instead presents a coexistence; like No. 83, there is a message here concerning tolerance.[19]

Tolerance, needless to say, is high on the list of Enlightenment virtues, and certainly part of Shaftesbury's philosophical agenda. So this is one example of how Haydn expresses Shaftesbury's thought in his music. He has sent us, by musical means, a "message concerning tolerance."

But here is a puzzlement. Schroeder fails to tell us what Haydn's message concerning tolerance *is.* Is Haydn recommending tolerance of Catholics but not atheists? That was a very common form of "tolerance" among philosophers in the Enlightment. Or, genius that he was, was he perhaps advanced in his thinking in tolerating atheists as well? What about Jews? I would like to think that Haydn's "message" was against anti-Semitism as well, but I rather doubt that he managed to escape that common and pernicious form of intolerance so prevelant then, as now, in Austria.

Did Haydn believe in the kind of toleration that embraces freedom of expression? If he did, would that include freedom to blaspheme or freedom to speak against the sovereign?

Clearly the way to answer these questions is to look more closely at Haydn's "expression" of tolerance, namely, the music. With the hypothesis in hand that Haydn was delivering us a message concerning tolerance in the first movement of Symphony No. 92, what we should do to determine that message more precisely is to comb the work for further indications as to whether Haydn was recommending tolerance for atheists and Jews as well as Catholics and Protestants; whether he was advocating freedom of expression and, if so, whether he meant for us to tolerate the public utterance of blasphemy and treason. What was Haydn's message concerning tolerance? I know how to determine Locke's: by looking closely at the texts. I have Haydn's "text" before me. I shall look.

Now everyone knows I am speaking nonsense. No matter how closely I study the score of Haydn's Symphony No. 92, I can never find such a message about tolerance. And anyone who claims to do so we know is making it up. I think Schroeder must know this, which is why he never tells us what that message is. Indeed, when he gets even the least bit more detailed, as he does in his description of the message concerning tolerance in Symphony No. 83, which that of 92 is supposed to duplicate, we begin to squirm uncomfortably. This is what he says:

> In the conclusion of the first movement of No. 83, Haydn can be seen to be demonstrating a very fundamental yet difficult truth: opposition is inevitable, and the highest form of unity is not the one which eliminates conflict. On the contrary, it is one in which opposing forces can coexist. The best minds of

Haydn's age aspired to tolerance, not dogmatism. It is precisely this message that can be heard in many of Haydn's late symphonies.[20]

Here is a little more for us to get our teeth into. Haydn, in Symphony No. 83, is demonstrating a fundamental truth, namely, that opposition is inevitable and the highest form of unity is not one that eliminates conflict, but rather one in which opposing forces can coexist.

What will perhaps stand out most prominently here for members of the philosophical profession is the startling, I am tempted to say mind-boggling, claim that Haydn, in his music, is presenting a *demonstration*, a *proof* of this moral truth. Indeed, our author seems to be saying not only that Haydn has presented an argument for this truth, but a successful one. What kind of demonstration? What are its premises? Does Haydn think that conflict is inevitable because of some constant, unalterable human nature? Does he try to prove that tolerance, in the face of conflict, is better than repression on (say) consequentialist grounds? Or is Haydn a deontologist in ethics? How can one "argue" in music, even if one is a Haydn, which is to say, a transcendent genius?

No wonder Schroeder is reluctant to tell us what Haydn's message concerning tolerance is. The result of the attempt just has to be nonsense.

§9 "Let's get real," as my students used to say in a now-outmoded argot. In order for one to say anything about anything, one must first succeed in referring to it: reference is the minimal necessary condition. And philosophers who bother about music are in some disagreement about whether music can even do that, that is, refer, let alone express propositions about what is referred to as we have seen in the last chapter. Furthermore, even those who think that music can refer will not think that it can refer to tolerance.

Musical reference is thought to occur, by those who countenance it, where music is called expressive of the emotions. These folks think that where a piece of music is expressive (say) of sadness, it, ipso facto, refers to sadness. Others who agree that music can be expressive of emotions do not think that that implies reference to the emotions.

There is also disagreement about the variety of emotions music can be expressive of, some thinking that "sad" and "happy" pretty much exhaust the repertoire, others expanding it to more of the common emotions, such as anger, fear, and the like. But there is hardly a philosopher I know of who thinks music's power to be expressive goes beyond that, to the more "conceptual" emotions and attitudes such as "pride" and "envy," because music does not have the capacity to provide the conceptual materials such "conceptual" emotions require. And for it to be expressive of a concept such as "tolerance," or any other moral or philosophical notion, seems beyond credibility. Thus music does not fulfill even the minimal necessary condition for delivering a "message concerning tolerance," namely, the possession of power to *refer* to it.

But even if we grant that in the various places in Haydn's late symphonies singled out by Schroeder, reference to tolerance has successfully been made, this still leaves us light years away from the music's being able to convey any message about it, even one telling us whether Haydn was in favor of it. If I carry a sign around that has "TOLERANCE!" painted on it, how are you to know whether I am recommending or denouncing it? Such a sign might be carried by the Grand Inquisitor as well as by Thomas Jefferson, each with a different intent. So even if, per impossible, Haydn succeeded in referring to tolerance in his late symphonies, he could not *say* anything about it, even whether or not he endorsed it. So much, then, for Haydn the moralist.

§10 But look here, I can imagine Schroeder replying: we know Haydn's message concerning tolerance as follows. In the first part of my book I give an account of what Shaftesbury said about tolerance, and historical evidence that Haydn knew what Shaftesbury said. In the final part of my book I show where and how Haydn referred to tolerance in his music. A reasonable conclusion to reach, therefore, is that Haydn's message concerning tolerance in the late symphonies is identical to Shaftesbury's message concerning tolerance in the *Characteristics*, including, of course, the endorsement. If you want to know what Haydn said in his late symphonies about tolerance, read what Shaftesbury said in the *Characteristics*.

A few observations on this line of argument. To begin with, it would obviously be a very bad inference to go from the fact that Haydn referred to Shaftesbury's views concerning tolerance to the conclusion that he endorsed them. Such a line of argument would lead us from the fact that Kant referred to Hume's position on causality in the *Critique of Pure Reason* to the conclusion that Kant endorsed it, which is, of course, the opposite of the truth.

Second, it would be bizarre indeed to say that Shaftesbury's doctrine concerning tolerance is expressed in Haydn's late symphonies if all Haydn succeeded in doing was to refer to Shaftesbury's doctrine, albeit with approbation. Haydn would then essentially be saying, "For my views on tolerance, see Shaftesbury." The doctrine is expressed in Shaftesbury, not Haydn. All Haydn provides is a footnote, poor compliment to one of the greatest composers in the Pantheon.

To put this point another way, if a book on Shaftesbury successfully expresses Shaftesbury's views on tolerance, I could apprise myself of them either by reading Shaftesbury or by reading the book on him. Who would ever claim that one could listen to Haydn's late symphonies in lieu of reading Shaftesbury, as one could read a secondary source in lieu of reading him? The only way one could possibly hear Shaftesbury in Haydn would be by first reading Shaftesbury (or a gloss of him). And once one did that, it is hard to see what the point would be of listening to Haydn. I certainly might want a second or third opinion on Shaftesbury's doctrine and go to the secondary literature to get it. That I should get it from Haydn's music seems to me a suggestion too silly to consider further.

§11 Let me make an end to my discussion of these two musical hermeneuticists, Eggebrecht and Schroeder, by offering a general remark on their individual projects and on my own project, to which I have been trying to apply them.

Eggebrecht and Schroeder, each in his own way, has tried to find extramusical content in what one would have thought to be a paradigm of absolute music, which is to say, *contentless* music. In Eggebrecht's case, the content is religious and "metaphysical," in Schroeder's moral and "philosophical." Both, I have argued, have failed completely to demonstrate either that the content really is there or that the composers had any intention of putting it there.

But others unknown to me may have been, or perhaps will be, more successful than Eggebrecht and Schroeder in showing that music like *The Art of Fugue* or Haydn's London Symphonies has the kind of content Eggebrecht and Schroeder are talking about. So it is reasonable for me to ask whether, if *The Art of Fugue* or Haydn's London Symphonies had the content Eggebrecht and Schroeder, respectively, ascribe to this music, this would solve my problem, which is, it will be recalled, what in or about absolute music we enjoy and value.

To answer this question, let us remind ourselves what content Eggebrecht and Schroeder are ascribing to the works in question. According to Eggebrecht, Bach is saying in *The Art of Fugue*, "Like you, I am human; I am in need of salvation, and I have been saved by grace." And according to Schroeder, Haydn is saying in various places in his late symphonies, "Opposition is inevitable, and the highest form of unity is not the one which eliminates conflict. On the contrary, it is one in which opposing forces can coexist." Could the expression of these sentiments, or sentiments like them, be what we enjoy and value in absolute music?

How could they possibly be? They are, naked and unadorned by argument or elucidation, utter banalities. If this were the heart of their matter, and if their matter were what mattered, what we enjoyed and valued, then *The Art of Fugue* and Haydn's London Symphonies would provide the value of a sampler or welcome mat or a message from the Hallmark Co.

But surely "naked and unadorned by argument or elucidation" gives the game away. Of course, it might be objected, what any great work of art says can be trivialized by a thumbnail sketch of its content. The "intellectual" sister in Leonard Bernstein's *Wonderful Town* offers the following gloss of *Moby Dick:* "It's about this *whale*." Well, it *is* about this whale; that about sums it up. So if *Moby Dick* is valued and enjoyed, in some very large measure, for its content, then it joins the rank of the trivial, as must Shaftesbury's *Characteristics*, which is epitomized by Schroeder's representation of Haydn's message in the late symphonies, and the works of many great theologians, whose content is correctly described by Eggebrecht's spare account of Bach's message in *The Art of Fugue*. But fully elucidated and argued for, the content of all of these works, the musical ones included, lifts them to the level of masterpieces.

The emptiness of this reply, however, is not difficult to see. It is just the very possibility of elaboration of content that makes works of literature or philosophy so different from works of absolute music. Even if we could attribute the minimal content to *The Art of Fugue* and Haydn's late symphonies that Eggebrecht and Schroeder have, which I do not think we would do, that is all we could do without entering Disneyland, whereas the interpreter of *Moby Dick* or the *Characteristics* can dig into the text to fill out what such trivial descriptions as "It's about this *whale*" only hint at or abstract. There is no need for me to dilate upon the procedures by which the interpreter, closely examining the literary or philosophical text, puts flesh on the dry bones of such formulas as "It's about this *whale*" or "It's a treatise on toleration." Back and forth the interpreter goes, from interpretation to text, text to interpretation, until the full story emerges. It is just that commerce between interpretation and text that immediately breaks down, at least if you are sane, once the barest philosophical or literary or religious construction is put on a work of absolute music. And it is for just that reason that one reads through as elaborate an analysis as Eggebrecht's of *The Art of Fugue* or Schroeder's of Haydn's late symphonies, only to come away with empty banalities that cannot advance us one whit in our understanding of what we value or enjoy in these wonderful works. With regard to absolute music, content analysis is the light that fails.

§12 If musical representationalism is supposed to be an answer, then, to the question of why we should care about absolute music, it turns out, so I have been arguing, to be an utter failure: a failure because of its initial implausibility and a failure again, initial implausibility aside, for possessing a kind of musical content scarcely interesting enough to care about – scarcely interesting enough to make us say, "Why, *that* is why I love *The Art of Fugue* or Haydn's London Symphonies."

But this brings us again, face to face, with our original dilemma. If absolute music has no content, why on earth are so many people so interested in it? Why, in a word, do they love it so much?

When I am asked this question, my answer is always quite simply: I do not value, enjoy, or love music *in spite of* the fact that, unlike the literary arts and arts of visual representation, it has no content. On the contrary, I value, enjoy, and love absolute music just *because* it has no content. And that brings me to the third, and major, of my themes from Schopenhauer, indeed, the theme that has given this chapter its title.

Schopenhauer believed that our ordinary workaday lives, as well as the lives of scientists and practical men, are dominated by what he called the "fourfold root of the principle of sufficient reason," which is to say, we are in a way driven to see, reason about, deal with our world – the world of "appearance" – in terms of cause and effect, motive and action, premise and conclusion, space and time. We are in thrall to a kind of Hobbesian tyrant of a will forever impelling us to reason, seek, and possess, only to find that our conclusions and possessions give us no rest, but make another starting place for yet further reasoning, seeking, and possessing, in a never-ending and restless quest for peace and finality. That, for Schopenhauer, is the human condition, were it not for art.

It is through art, either in the external form of an object of contemplation or in the inward form of an impulse to create such an object, that we are lifted, if only temporarily, from our servitude. As Schopenhauer puts his point in one of his most eloquent passages:

When, however, an external cause or inward disposition raises us out of the endless stream of willing, and snatches knowledge from the thraldom of the will, the attention is now no longer directed to the motives of willing, but comprehends things free from their relation to the will. Thus it considers things without interest, without subjectivity, purely objectively; it is entirely given up to them in so far as they are merely representations, and not motives. Then all at once the peace, always sought but always escaping us on that first path of willing, comes to us of its own accord, and all is well with us. It is the painless state, prized by Epicurus as the highest good and as the state of the gods; for that moment we are delivered from the miserable pressure of the will. We celebrate the Sabbath of the penal survitude of willing; the wheel of Ixion stands still.[21]

The insight I would like to rescue from Schopenhauer's metaphysics is the notion of *liberation:* of music's liberating power. But liberation from what? And why music rather than, as Schopenhauer believes, the fine arts *tout court?* Let us tackle the second question first.

I do not ask you to accept Schopenhauer's metaphysical structure of the world. I certainly cannot accept it myself. In particular, I certainly cannot accept Schopenhauer's notion that the representational and contentful arts liberate us from our world of cause and effect, premise and conclusion, motive and action, space and time. On the contrary, far from retreating to a world of Platonic ideas, as Schopenhauer would have it, I am far more inclined to believe that the visual arts of representation and the contentful literary arts are, pace Aristotle, eminently particular, presenting our world in ways transformed, to be sure, but reveling in its haecceity. General or particular, however – and I am inclined to think that varies with artist and with style – the representational and contentful arts scarcely liberate us from the labor of thought about the world in just those terms Schopenhauer designates as the fourfold root of the principle of sufficient reason. And when it is the world of Shakespeare's *Lear* or Verdi's *Otello,* the labor of thought and the act of confrontation are so frought with difficulty that we will avoid such works, for all of their rich rewards, except on those occasions when we feel up to the task. We are not relieved of the problems of life by much of the arts of visual representation and literature. We are plunged into them more often than not. This is my first demur to Schopenhauer's theme of liberation.

§13 My second demur naturally has to do with Schopenhauer's characterization of music. In what I called his first theme, Schopenhauer recognized the striking disanalogy between music and the other fine arts. This, I think, was an insight – but a failed insight, in the event, because Schopenhauer cashed out this perceived disanalogy merely in terms of his idiosyncratic metaphysics of representation, simply giving absolute music a metaphysically "deeper" object of representation than he gave the contentful arts of literature, painting, and sculpture.

In what I call Schopenhauer's third and major theme, Schopenhauer, again insightfully, recognizes an element of liberation in the general vicinity of the fine arts. But, again, his insight falls short of the goal because he fails to realize what I take to be its peculiar relevance to absolute music alone. If one, then, puts the first and third themes together in their proper contrapuntal relation, one gets the result that, first, absolute music is strikingly dissimilar to the contentful arts, not, however, because it has a dissimilar content but because it has no content at all, in the sense of "content" at issue here. (Obviously it has *musical* content: themes, harmonies, counterpoint, etc.)

Second, one gets the result, so I shall argue presently, that the disanalogy lies in the liberating quality that absolute music alone of the fine arts possesses and the contentful arts, just because of their content, palpably lack. Or, to put it more precisely, it is neither a "lack" in music that it possesses no content, nor a "lack" in the contentful arts that they possess no power to liberate. On the contrary, it is a defining virtue of the contentful arts that they do *not* liberate us from our workaday world but engage us, albeit in ways characteristic of the fine arts. And it is a defining virtue of absolute music, so I shall argue, that it does not engage us in our workaday world but liberates us from it. That is my contention. Now I must try to convince you of its truth.

§14 To begin with the familiar, there is nothing very new or surprising about the idea that absolute music is a pure sonic structure or design. It was an idea familiar in the Enlightenment, and thought by those who entertained it then as quite damning of the whole enterprise of music without text. From Hanslick onward it was an idea explored to just the opposite end: to redeem absolute music from the representational and contentful arts as a thing worthy unto itself, and not an appendage to them of doubtful value. Our century has designated this view of absolute music, unhappily, musical "formalism." And I say "unhappily" because the designation suggests, quite mistakenly, that if one construes absolute music as pure, contentless sonic structure, one must think that only its musical *form* matters.

But that is not the nature of my musical formalism, which my friend and fellow tiller of the soil, Philip Alperson, has described as "enhanced formalism" – a view that accords value and pleasure not merely to musical "form," properly so called, but to all of the sensual and phenomenological properties that absolute music possesses, including, most importantly, its *expressive properties*. Nor does my musical formalism fail to recognize that the cognizing and enjoyment of musical structure is not some bloodless intellectual exercise but a deeply moving and exciting experience. It is, no doubt, far too late in the day to give up the "formalism" tag in favor of some more suitable label. For like many other labels of the kind, it has taken on a philosophical life beyond its original, literal meaning. And only confusion would result from giving it up now. Most philosophical practitioners know that "formalism" is not a doctrine, in any of the arts, that either promotes or allows interest only in "form" in its most restrictive sense. So I will continue to refer to my position now and in the future as musical formalism and require that you remember it is "enhanced formalism" that I mean by it.

Now if musical formalism is true, even in its "enhanced" version, which countenances expressive properties as part of musical structure, one can well ask why such a structure should be of interest and value to human beings. Why should we be interested in, not to put too fine a point on it, organized but meaningless noise?

I have suggested elsewhere that this question does not admit of any simple, single answer.[22] There is not one property of absolute music that makes it interesting or valuable to us: there are many. And only detailed study *of* music – the musical nuts and bolts – can reveal to us all of its many intriguing aspects.

But once these intriguing aspects are isolated and explained, there remains that gnawing question with which these remarks began, of why, in comparison with the contentful arts, absolute music should hold the fascination that it does for us; but not only that, why it should be held in such deep reverence that the figure of a Bach or a Beethoven can hold the same pride of place for many of us as that of a Shakespeare or a Michelangelo. How can that be? Our provisional answer is: we value and enjoy absolute music not in spite of its lack of content but *because* of it; its lack of content is a value to us, not a disvalue. That answer must now be fleshed out.

§15   Consider another familiar claim. Works of absolute music, like works of the contentful arts, create, so to speak, "worlds" for us to cognize and contemplate. These worlds are as varied and individual as the artists who have created them. They range from the complex world of the *Iliad* to the miniature, simple world of Goethe's poem about a trampled violet; from the violent, almost unbearably painful world of *King Lear* to the light-hearted, inconsequential world of a play by Kaufmann and Hart; from the vast world of the Sistine ceiling to the constricted world of Van Gogh's shoes; from the incredibly intricate and musically demanding world of the six-voice Ricercare in the *Musical Offering* to the transparent simplicity of *Eine kleine Nachtmusik.*

But what is crucial for our purposes is that worlds of absolute music, unlike the worlds of the contentful arts, are, as it were, "worlds apart," which is to say, they are worlds of musical sound that make no contact with – no reference to – the world in which we live and move and have our being. From that world they are apart.

This is not to say that it is altogether clear just what relation the world of a contentful work bears to *the* world or how that relation is logically constituted. The problem is particularly nasty when, like Tolstoy's *War and Peace,* the work intermingles the factual with the fictional, real names with made-up ones. In spite, however, of such genuine difficulties, and even attempts to jar the contentful arts loose from the "real" world altogether, the fact remains that those readers and gazers not in thrall to various of the postmodern theses that construe texts as solely about texts – which, I dare say, are most of us – the world of our lives is deeply implicated in the worlds of our novels and plays, statues and paintings. And only academics, whose professional world is constituted only by texts, are likely to think that texts are the only objects of artistic concern.

But just because the world of our lives is so deeply implicated in the world of our contentful artworks, we cannot have genuine, aesthetically rich encounters with such works without these works, intentionally and purposefully, setting in motion our intellectual and emotional engagement not only with the worlds of the works themselves but with our own world as well, which imbues even the most remote fantasy or the most escapist romp. And such intellectual and emotional engagement accrues to the worst as well as the best: the soap opera as well as the profoundest Shakespearean tragedy, the Norman Rockwell as well as the canvases of Cézanne.

But thinking about our world and its problems, and inevitably our problems in our world, is hard and painful work. And that is partly why some of the most profound literary works, and such paintings as Goya's *The Disasters of War* and Picasso's *Guernica,* elicit in us what psychologists used to call an "approach–avoidance conflict."

From Aristotle's *Poetics* to the most recent issue of the *Journal of Aesthetics and Art Criticism,* the paradox of this conflict, the paradox of aesthetic pain, its value, its nature, why we should seek it, has been the subject of the closest philosophical scrutiny. Yet whatever the result of such inquiry has been, or will be, the brute fact remains that our encounters, particularly with our profoundest, most valued, most serious examples of the contentful arts, are fraught with the deepest satisfactions but also with the deepest agony of thought about our deepest, most recalcitrant moral and metaphysical questions.

Of course, this is not to suggest that the pain of serious thought is some kind of irrelevant and undesirable side effect of serious contentful art. If that were so, there would be no paradox of aesthetic pain. The fact of the matter is that the agony of thought that *King Lear* or *Faust* elicits is not some unfortunate appendage to an otherwise satisfying experience, but an integral part of the experience itself: part of the very reason we value such works and derive the deep satisfaction we do from them. To contemplate the beautiful, the awesome, the finely wrought aesthetic world of *Lear* or *Faust* or *Bleak House* is to have a deeply satisfying experience. But you cannot have that experience without the other: the experience of gnawing, persistent, ultimately irresolvable thought about our world, with its moral agonies and metaphysical mysteries. It's part of the territory.

But it is freedom from just this agony of thought that absolute music provides. Absolute music gives us the world of the work without the world of the world.

This is by no means to suggest that music is a world without thought. As I have argued elsewhere, absolute music is not a thing of the nerve endings but a thing of the mind: a thing of *musical* thought.[23] What I am suggesting is that in the contentful arts our thought processes work both in the world of the work and in the world of the world, whereas in absolute music our thought processes, at least ideally, are at play in the world of the work alone. That, it appears to me, is music's blessing and *difference*.

How the mind works in our appreciation and enjoyment of music is a topic of great complexity that I cannot enter into here. I will say only that whether you are listening at the level of a lay music lover or at the level of a Mozart, or at any level between, what you are doing is perceiving that and how musical events are taking place, under whatever description you understand them, and in so doing you are enjoying those musical happenings. It is in this sense that I am insisting that absolute music is an object – an intentional object – of the mind, and the pleasure we take in it a pleasure of the mind, at whatever level of musical expertise we find ourselves.

Furthermore, as I have been arguing, what is so distinctive about this pleasure is its complete freedom from connection with our workaday world and its problems. It is both the blessing and the curse of the contentful arts that their worlds are, to borrow some familiar philosophical jargon, possible-world versions of our own and so must, as part of their nature, engage us in thought processes that bear with them a heavy burden. A passage in a long-forgotten novel of James Hilton's captures my thought: "Then she went to the piano and he took out his violin and they began to play Mozart. The music streamed into the room, enclosing a world in which they were free as air, shutting out hatreds and jealousies and despondencies, giving their eyes a look of union with something rare and distant."[24]

It is the blessing of absolute music that it frees our thought to wander in worlds that are completely self-sufficient: worlds where all is resolved, so to speak, with no loose ends, worlds that when they are grasped satisfactorily, give us that to think about which, for the duration of the experience, completely frees us from, so to speak, the failure of thought and gives us thought processes that, if the composer is up to it, can only succeed, can only resolve to a satisfactory conclusion.

It is of course true that the visual arts have produced examples of nonrepresentational objects, paintings, sculptures, "constructions" in our own century, and there is no reason to doubt that in such cases the same kind of liberating quality I have attributed to the experience of absolute music may well accrue to the experience of these artistic objects as well. But the fact remains – and it is a fact in need of explanation – that no artistic practice in the Western world has approached absolute music in significance as an art of this "liberating" kind. So although absolute music is not altogether unique in this regard, it is singular enough to require the special attention I, following Schopenhauer, have bestowed on it.

Furthermore, the power of liberation of which I speak may

not be limited to the fine arts at all. The experience of pure mathematics immediately comes to mind; and it may, for all I know, provide the same feeling of liberation in its experience as I have attributed to the experience of absolute music. This fact, if fact it is, does not trouble me in the least, as I see no reason why the experience of liberation should be exclusive to the fine arts. But let me just add that if the experience of pure mathematics does share this liberating quality with absolute music, that neither makes mathematics fine art nor makes music mathematics.

§16 I have spoken at length of the liberating *value* of music, as opposed to the contentful arts, and I underscore "value" to introduce some remarks concerning that philosophically troublesome concept. The quality of liberation is not *the* value of absolute music. There is no such thing as that. Absolute music has diverse values, which is to say, we enjoy many things about it. All of these things that have to do with its aesthetic structure and surface, when suitably described, we also enjoy in the other arts that possess them. A poem or a painting, as well as a sonata, may have unity and thematic structure, expressive and dynamic qualities, tension and release, and the rest. When we perceive these qualities we enjoy them, and when we enjoy them we value the works in which they inhere.

Of course, to the extent that a musical work has the aesthetic qualities we value and enjoy, to that extent it will fascinate and enthrall; and to the extent that it fascinates and enthralls, to that extent it will liberate. In other words, if you are busy perceiving and enjoying musical design and structure, you will not be worrying about the problem of evil or the comparative merits of sense over sensibility.

Thus the value of liberation is keyed to the other values of a musical work. But it must be observed that the liberation value of a work may well exceed its other values, in a way that might merit censure. If, for example, I were utterly enthralled at a certain stage of my musical life with the music of Leroy Anderson, you might well chide me for my lack of musical taste and sophistication, for not preferring Bach or Haydn, even though

Leroy Anderson is more liberating for me at this point than Bach or Haydn would be, since their musical virtues would go unperceived and unappreciated for the most part, and my mind, therefore, would not be as musically occupied when listening to their music.

To this, first of all, there might be the reply that if I were to cultivate the music of Bach and Haydn, there would be so much more to enthrall me than ever there could be in the music of Leroy Anderson that the "liberation sum" could be represented as correspondingly higher. Furthermore, unless I were a musical vegetable, the likelihood is that I would, in the course of time, find the music of Leroy Anderson to pall and seek musical satisfaction in more worthy examples. But even if it were the case that liberation is invariant with other musical values – that is, even if it were the case that Leroy Anderson, now and forever, provides as much of it for the person who enjoys Leroy Anderson, but not Bach and Haydn, as Bach and Haydn provide for their devotees – it does not obviate the fact that one value absolute music has, across the board, is liberation. Nor does it render us incapable, on other grounds, of placing more overall musical value on Bach and Haydn than on Leroy Anderson.

Thus it appears that the liberating quality of absolute music, as a value of absolute music *tout court*, is compatible with all of the usual grounds we have for valuing one piece of absolute music over another, unless we bring in values of "content" and "meaning" (in which case, of course, it will not be a value at all, being incompatible with those other "contentful" things). But it is those values that I am denying apply at all, so about them nothing more need be said.

I might add by the way that in making use of Schopenhauer's notion of artistic liberation in my account of absolute music, I am by no means buying into the well-known Schopenauerian pessimism, although anyone looking back over the twentieth century from our present vantage point might well think Schopenhauer a wide-eyed optimist in the light of what two world wars and the Holocaust have revealed to us about the human condition. The point is that I intend my appeal to the blessings of musical liberation to be consistent with a rather wide range of views with regard to the moral and physical state of human beings. Anyone, pessimist or optimist, who does not *sometimes* find the world a burden and the kind of release I am talking about something devoutly to be wished, is hard for me to imagine as a human being "completely formed." In any case, I don't think there could be too many such Pollyannas. I hope not, anyway; and this account of absolute music is not written for them. For them liberation is no value at all.

§17 So far I have been speaking in rather vague terms about the experience of liberation from this veil of tears that only absolute music, among the fine arts, can provide. And before I close I think it incumbent on me to say something more about what exactly this experience is like. To inaugurate the discussion let me return briefly to Schopenhauer.

In the quotation from *The World as Will and Idea* that I introduced earlier, there is an attempt to characterize the experience of freedom that, on Schopenhaur's view, all of the fine arts are supposed to convey and that, on my view, only absolute music among them can. Let me extract that characterization for examination, somewhat contrary to Schopenhauer's intentions, as a possible description of that experience of liberation that, as I am insisting, only absolute music, among the fine arts, is capable of providing.

Here, you will recall, is what Schopenhauer says: "Then all at once the peace, always sought but always escaping us on that first path of willing, comes to us of its own accord, and all is well with us. It is the painless state prized by Epicurus as the highest good and as the state of the gods; for that moment we are delivered from the miserable pressure of the will."

Few of us, I think, will be at all attracted by Epicurus's vision of the good life as being constituted wholly by the absence of pain, all else being sacrificed to that pallid, bloodless state. Most of us, I am sure, want the passion as well as the prose and are willing to pay the price of an acceptable level of pain.

Furthermore, as a characterization of the experience of musical liberation, Schopenhauer's Epicurean metaphor will strike any lover of the art of music as hopelessly inadequate in capturing either the quality or the intensity of it. Schopenhauer is ascribing to the experience a negative quality, an absence of something, whereas what we are experiencing, most of us would say, is a positive quality, the presence of something. But, you are bound to ask, how can liberation *from* something impart a *positive* quality to our experience? Is not the experience of liberation from, by very definition, the experience of an absence, a lack, a negativity?

Let me try to answer this question, and in the negative, by turning for assistance from Schopenhauer to another great philosopher, the Socrates of Plato's *Phaedo*. Socrates is discovered to us in that dialogue on the last day of his life, just having been released from his leg irons, upon awakening. I will let Plato set the scene:

> ... Socrates sat up on his couch and bent his leg and rubbed it with his hand, and while he was rubbing it he said, "What a strange thing, my friends, that seems to be which men call pleasure! How wonderfully it is related to that which seems to be its opposite, pain, in that they will not both come to a man at the same time, and yet if he pursues the one and captures it, he is generally obliged to take the other also, as if the two were joined together in one head. ... Just so it seems that in my case, after the pain was in my leg on account of the fetter, pleasure appears to have come following after."[25]

One of the things Socrates is urging here, and the thing I want to call attention to, is that, in being released from pain, he is experiencing pleasure; or to put it more precisely, experiencing the cessation of pain is, ipso facto, to experience a positive pleasure: the cessation of pain just *is* a pleasure. My own experience, for what it is worth, has been the same, at least where severe pain is concerned. When I have been in severe pain and been released from it, the experience has seemed to me a pleasurable one: not merely the negative absence of pain, but the positive presence, therein, of pleasure – and, I should say, one of the most intense pleasures of which I am capable. Socrates' observation on this regard, I think, is dead right.

But now we can compare what Schopenhauer is talking about

213

with what Socrates is talking about to some useful purpose. Briefly put, Schopenhauer is describing, in his Epicurean figure, the *absence* of pain, a negative quality of *indifference,* and Socrates is describing the *cessation* of pain, a positive quality of *pleasure.* "Liberation" from pain is a description applicable to both conditions, signifying in the former case the *state* of being free of pain, in the latter the *process* of being freed from pain. I want to suggest that it is the latter, the process of being freed from pain, wherein the liberating power of absolute music lies, thus conforming to our experience of this liberation as involving a positive quality of pleasure rather than a negative quality merely of the absence of pain. But I must amplify this somewhat.

§18   There is, it appears to me, a very important difference between the absence of pain and the cessation of pain experientially. I can best bring this out with examples. Suppose someone has gone for a considerable period of time without having been in any real pain. She awakens one morning during this protracted period, as she has many times before, totally free of pain. As likely as not, she will not be aware that she is free of pain. Why should she be? It is just what the course of her life has been, fortunately for her, during this period. Her freedom from pain is the background against which her life has been played. What she *would* notice would be a change. If she were to awaken one morning with severe back pain, she would notice that.

Compare this case with that of someone suffering from a severe toothache. He is in agony. But his dentist anticipated this eventuality and prescribed a powerful narcotic just in case. Our toothache sufferer pops one of these pills, and in a few minutes his agony rapidly begins to subside. That experience, of the cessation of pain, is as deliciously pleasurable as the pain was excrutiatingly the opposite.

What seems to emerge from these two examples is that the positive pleasure of the cessation of pain, as opposed to the quiescent, negative state of the absence of pain, requires that the subject be conscious of and attending to the process of cessation or at least attending to the absence of pain with the memory of its former presence still vividly held before the mind. For when the memory fades and the attention falls away, the subject then lapses into the quiescent state of the mere absence of pain. That at any rate is how these matters appear to me.

But if this is right, then my position with regard to how pleasure accrues to music's power to liberate cannot be right unless, in listening to music, we *are* aware of this liberation, as the sufferer from a toothache is aware of the cessation of pain in experiencing the positive pleasure it brings. Is it plausible to think that this is so: that part of the experience of absolute music, at least some of the time, is the conscious, closely attended to realization that one is both involved in thought on the world of musical sound while, at the same time, liberated from the burden of thought on the world in which one lives, strives, and all too often suffers? Let me suggest to you, in concluding, that this is not an implausible conjecture.

No experience of absolute music can be, needless to say, a perfect one. But what is a perfect one? What is the ideal case? I used to think that it would be the case of total absorption, exemplified perhaps, if the story is true, by the eight-year-old Donald Francis Tovey becoming engrossed in the reading of a musical score – a string quartet, I think it was – and being discovered applauding when he had finished. His explanation of this odd behavior – the applauding, that is – was that his concentration had been such as to make him completely oblivious to anything but the music in his head, which came to seem to him an actually present performance and which, in this abstracted state, he instinctively reacted to by clapping (an intriguing instance of self-congratulation, as the "performance" was his own).

But whatever the value of such a trancelike state of musical concentration might have for the professional musician, it is not, I now tend to think, partly because of the points I am making now, the ideal case of musical concentration when the object of such concentration is the appreciation of absolute music as it should be for a musical audience. For when the awareness of the world from which the world of musical sound liberates you is completely lost, then the positive pleasure that that liberation can bring is lost to you too. And although that sense and pleasure of musical liberation is not the whole of what we value in absolute music, it is certainly not the least of what we value either, and it has a kind of overarching effect on all else that we do value in the experience.

The view I have been presenting is, as I characterized it earlier, "enhanced formalism." It can also be described, and frequently is, in a derogatory way, these days, as the doctrine of "musical autonomy." Its defenders are becoming few, and embattled, particularly in musicological circles. And in urging it on you, I cannot do better than to quote one of its few remaining defenders in the historians' camp, someone on whose side, in musical matters, I am always happy to find myself. Thus Leo Treitler writes in a recent article:

> Belief in the absolute autonomy of music and in the permanently closed-off character of the experience of music has given us some bad history, indeed, but that is not sufficient cause to abandon the belief that a provisional personal engagement with a musical utterance for the moment unrelated to anything else is not only a possible but a necessary condition of eventual understanding of it in its most dense connections.[26]

Surely no one can accuse Leo Treitler of being oblivious to the social and historical context in which Western art music has been made since its very beginnings. That he should also, even with misgivings, be a defender of musical autonomy is all the more to be taken seriously.

But as I described my musical formalism as "enhanced formalism," perhaps it might be appropriate for me to describe my version of the autonomy of absolute music as "enhanced autonomy." And this for the following reason. If musical autonomy, *sans phrase*, is the doctrine that takes Tovey's experience of the string quartet as its ideal case, that is not my musical autonomy. For me the experience of absolute music is not, to appropriate Treitler's phrase, "permanently closed-off" from the world of the world. At the risk of sounding paradoxical, I am suggesting that absolute music is always connected to the world by its very *disconnection* from it. And in that sense, enhanced by the con-

216

nection of its disconnection, my musical autonomy is "enhanced autonomy." For it is the autonomy that says that the genius of absolute music is to make you think of aught but itself and, in so doing, of its (and your) liberation from the world. This is not its tragedy. It is its difference, and its triumph.

Epilogue

This book has no thesis. It does have a theme. It may seem that this book has a thesis. One could easily read me as aligning myself with those, notably Wittgensteinians, who have argued that there is no common, definitional thread tying what we now call the "fine arts" together into a system. For in my first two, historical chapters, I tried to trace, to the present moment, the failed attempts to produce such a thread (or threads) in the form of a "definition" of "art." And I followed that historical exercise with five "case studies" purporting to show ways in which choosing the "wrong model" has led to binding pairs of arts together in ways alien to one of them.

But it would be a mistake, as I pointed out early on and want to reemphasize now, to read this book as arguing that the quest for a definition of art is unfruitful or impossible. What I am arguing for is that at least some of us in what is called "the philosophy of art" pursue another project: looking for differences among the arts rather than accidently finding them in flawed definitions. Indeed, the case can be made that in looking for differences, the search for sameness is forwarded rather than thwarted, under the assumption that a theory put under stress is, if it survives, a stronger theory than one that is never tested at all.

So I say that my book has a theme rather than a thesis. Its theme is the pursuit of differences among the arts. It is not a rival project to that of defining art but part of the same enterprise: the philosophical understanding of the fine arts in all of their particularity, as well as their commonality.

Where do we go from here? Where I would like to go, and in

the company of others rather than alone, is on to further studies of artistic differences. Where *all* others should go I cannot say. But I think that the pursuit of differences, if it should become the monolith that the pursuit of sameness has been since the Enlightenment, would have as evil an effect on the philosophy of art.

I think the Enlightenment, surprisingly, was more sensitive to differences than was either German Romanticism or twentieth-century analytic philosophy. And I would like here, as elsewhere, to renew the Enlightenment spirit. If, in this book, I have seemed to be extreme in my quest for differences and rejection of sameness, I have aimed at the extreme only to regain the mean. In that spirit, the spirit of the Enlightenment, my epigraph will serve not only as my beginning but as my end: "Now from hence may be seen, how these Arts *agree*, and how they *differ*."

Notes

1. How We Got Here, and Why

1. Paul Oskar Kristeller, "The Modern System of the Arts," reprinted in *Essays on the History of Aesthetics,* ed. Peter Kivy (Rochester, N.Y.: University of Rochester Press, 1992).
2. See Jerome Stolnitz, "On the Origins of Aesthetic Disinterestedness," *Journal of Aesthetics and Art Criticism* 20 (1961): 131–44.
3. Plato, *Ion,* trans. W. R. M. Lamb (Cambridge, Mass.: Harvard University Press; London: William Heinemann, The Loeb Classical Library, 1962), pp. 417 (532E) and 421 (583E).
4. See Ann E. Moyer, *Musica Sacra: Musical Scholarship in the Italian Renaissance* (Ithaca, N.Y.: Cornell University Press, 1992).
5. See Umberto Eco, *Art and Beauty in the Middle Ages,* trans. Hugh Bredin (New Haven, Conn.: Yale University Press, 1986), chap. 1 and passim.
6. See David Summers, *The Judgment of Taste: Renaissance Naturalism and the Rise of Aesthetics* (Cambridge University Press, 1987).
7. Kristeller, "The Modern System of the Arts," p. 38.
8. Ibid., p. 4.
9. On the latter see Rudolf Wittkower, *Architectural Principles in the Age of Humanism* (London: Alec Tiranti, 1962). On the former, at least as in regard to classical Greek architecture, see the strange but stimulating book by Indra Kagis McEwin, *Socrates' Ancestor: An Essay on Architectural Beginnings* (Cambridge, Mass.: MIT Press, 1993).
10. It is much to be regretted that philosophers of art, in general, know little about the "philosophy of architecture" in the eighteenth century. I am certainly no exception, and so offer my estimate of the role of architecture in the early fine arts discussion with caution and only very tentative conviction.

11. Noel Carroll, "Historical Narrations and the Philosophy of Art," *Journal of Aesthetics and Art Criticism* 51 (1993): 314.

12. See Peter Kivy, "Is Music an Art?" in *The Fine Art of Repetition: Essays in the Philosophy of Music* (Cambridge University Press, 1993), pp. 360–73.

13. Ibid.

14. Pietro de' Bardi, Letter to G. B. Doni, in *Source Readings in Music History*, ed. Oliver Strunk (New York: Norton, 1950), p. 364.

15. Giulio Caccini, Foreword to *Le nuove musiche*, in *Source Readings in Music History*, ed. Strunk, p. 378.

16. Thomas Reid, *Essays on the Intellectual Powers of Man*, in *The Works of Thomas Reid*, ed. Sir William Hamilton (8th ed.; Edinburgh: James Thin, 1895), vol. 1, p. 504.

17. Ibid.

18. Francis Hutcheson, *Inquiry Concerning Beauty, Order, Harmony, Design*, ed. Peter Kivy (The Hague: Martinus Nijhoff, 1973), p. 81 (sec. 6).

19. Ibid., p. 46 (sec. 2).

20. Reid, *Essays on the Intellectual Powers*, p. 504.

21. Ibid.

22. Ibid.

23. This is not to say that Reid lacked influence in the nineteenth century. He seems to have influenced the French aestheticians, as James Manns has revealed in "The Scottish Influence on French Aesthetic Thought," reprinted in *Essays on the History of Aesthetics*, ed. Kivy, pp. 285–303. And his was, as is well known, the "textbook" philosophy of nineteenth-century American undergraduates. But he was not in the mainstream after his own time.

24. Immanuel Kant, *Anthropology from a Pragmatic Point of View*, trans. Mary J. Gregory (The Hague: Martinus Nijhoff, 1974), p. 114.

25. Immanuel Kant, *Critique of Judgement*, trans. J. H. Bernard (New York: Hafner, 1961), p. 60.

26. Immanuel Kant, *Critique of Aesthetic Judgement*, trans. James Creed Meredith (Oxford: Clarendon Press, 1911), p. 66.

27. Immanuel Kant, *Critique of Judgment*, trans. Werner S. Pluhar (Indianapolis: Hackett, 1987), p. 70.

28. See Pluhar's footnote to this passage, ibid., p. 70n, and Theodore E. Uehling, Jr., *The Notion of Form in Kant's "Critique of Aesthetic Judgment"* (The Hague: Mouton, 1971), pp. 22–6.

29. Uehling, *The Notion of Form*, pp. 24–5.

30. Kant, *Critique of Aesthetic Judgement*, trans. Meredith, p. 190.

31. Uehling, *The Notion of Form*, p. 25.
32. For a more thorough exposition of this point, see Peter Kivy, "Kant and the *Affektenlehre:* What He Said and What I Wish He Had Said," in *The Fine Art of Repetition*, pp. 250–64.
33. Kant, *Critique of Aesthetic Judgement*, trans. Meredith, p. 194.
34. Ibid., p. 199.
35. Ibid. Kant's thought here is expressed as follows: "In jest (which just as much as the former [i.e. music] deserves to be ranked rather as an agreeable than a fine art) the play sets out from thoughts which collectively, so far as seeking sensuous expression, engage the activity of the body."
36. Arthur Schopenhauer, *The World as Will and Representation*, trans. E. F. J. Payne (Indian Hills, Colo.: Falcon's Wing Press, 1958), vol. 1, p. 233 (book 3, §49).
37. Ibid., p. 257 (book 3, §52).
38. Ibid., pp. 261–2 (book 3, §52).
39. The first volume of Schopenhauer's *World as Will and Representation*, from which I have been quoting, was published in 1818. Hegel's *Lectures on the Fine Arts* was first published by G. H. Hotho in 1835. This book represents a compilation of Hegel's lecture notes and manuscripts of 1823, 1826, and 1828–9.
40. G. W. F. Hegel, *Aesthetics: Lectures on the Fine Arts*, trans. T. M. Knox (Oxford: Clarendon Press, 1975), vol. 2, pp. 901–2.
41. Ibid., p. 899.
42. Ibid., p. 899n.
43. For the German text, see G. W. F. Hegel, *Werke in zwanzig Bänden*, vol. 15, *Vorlesung über die Aesthetik, Dritter Teil* (Frankfurt am Main: Suhnkamp, 1970), p. 145.
44. Hegel, *Lectures on the Fine Arts*, vol. 2, p. 923.
45. Ibid., p. 960.
46. Hegel, *Werke*, vol. 15, pp. 223–4.
47. Hegel, *Lectures on the Fine Arts*, vol. 2, p. 892n.
48. Roger Fry, "An Essay in Aesthetics," in *Vision and Design* (New York: Meridian Books, 1960), p. 17.
49. Clive Bell, *Art* (New York: Capricorn Books, 1958), part 1, chap. 1, "The Aesthetic Hypothesis."
50. Ibid., p. 30.
51. On this see Peter Kivy, *Music Alone: Philosophical Reflections on the Purely Musical Experience* (Ithaca, N.Y.: Cornell University Press, 1990), chap. 1.
52. Bell, *Art*, p. 27.

53. Ibid., p. 30.
54. Fry called his view an expression theory and acknowledged Tolstoy as an influence. Bell too spoke, with as close to purple prose as he could get, of the "aesthetic emotion." But the emotion was, of course, defined in terms of the form that evoked it, leading, in Bell, to a notorious vicious circle in which the aesthetic emotion is distinguished from other emotions by the fact that it is caused by significant form, and significant form is distinguished from other forms by the fact that it is the form that arouses the aesthetic emotion. This is all quite well known. In any event, formalism it was, "aesthetic emotion" to the contrary notwithstanding.
55. Roger Fry, "Some Questions in Aesthetics," in *Transformations* (Garden City, N.Y.: Doubleday Anchor Books, 1956), p. 10.
56. Ibid., p. 11.
57. Bell, *Art*, p. 28.
58. Clive Bell, *Old Friends* (London: Cassell, 1988), p. 76.
59. Eduard Hanslick, *On the Musically Beautiful: A Contribution towards the Revision of the Aesthetics of Music*, trans. Geoffrey Payzant (Indianapolis: Hackett, 1986), pp. 28–9.
60. Edmund Gurney, *The Power of Sound* (London: Smith, Elder, 1980), pp. 164–5.

2. Where We Are

1. The phrase is Paul Ziff's, coined in "The Task of Defining a Work of Art," *Philosophical Review* 62 (1953): 58–78.
2. Bell, *Art*, p. 17.
3. De Witt H. Parker, "The Nature of Art," reprinted in Eliseo Vivas and Murray Krieger, *The Problems of Aesthetics: A Book of Readings* (New York: Holt, Rinehart & Winston, 1960), p. 90.
4. Ibid., p. 91. I have not quoted the passage stating the second of Parker's grounds for rejecting the search for a common property because it is not relevant here.
5. Actually, there is a far more impressive and prophetic anticipation of Wittgensteinian aesthetics in the essay "Of Beauty" (1810) by the Scottish philosopher Dugald Stewart. Stewart proposes there, not for "art" but for "beauty," a cluster analysis that has all the logical structure of Wittgenstein's "family resemblance" concept. I am not the first to notice this. See Dugald Stewart, *Works*, vol. 4, *Philosophical Essays* (Cambridge: Hilliard & Brown, 1829), part 2, essay first. See also Peter Kivy, *The Seventh Sense: A Study of Francis*

Hutcheson's Aesthetics and Its Place in Eighteenth-Century Britain (New York: Burt Franklin, 1976), pp. 203–6 and 258n.

6. Morris Weitz, "The Role of Theory in Aesthetics," reprinted in *Philosophy Looks at the Arts,* ed. Joseph Margolis (3d ed.; Philadelphia: Temple University Press, 1987), p. 146.

7. Ibid., p. 148.

8. Ibid.

9. Ibid., p. 149.

10. Ibid.

11. Ibid., p. 150.

12. Ibid., p. 149.

13. Morris Weitz, selections from *The Opening Mind,* in *Aesthetics: A Critical Anthology,* ed. George Dickie, Richard Sclafani, and Ronald Roblin (2d ed.; New York: St. Martin's Press, 1989), p. 158.

14. Arthur Danto, "The Artworld," in *Philosophy Looks at the Arts,* ed. Margolis, p. 162.

15. Arthur Danto, *The Transfiguration of the Commonplace: A Philosophy of Art* (Cambridge, Mass.: Harvard University Press, 1981), p. 82.

16. Ibid., pp. 147–8.

17. Ibid., p. 148.

18. Ibid., p. 152.

19. There is at least a hint in Danto's *Transfiguration of the Commonplace* (p. 152) that he might endorse some version of "emotive aboutness" for music, at least as I read him.

20. Jerrold Levinson, "Truth in Music," in *Music, Art and Metaphysics: Essays in Philosophical Aesthetics* (Ithaca, N.Y.: Cornell University Press, 1990), p. 280.

21. Ibid., p. 288.

22. I am not suggesting that it was Levinson's intention here to defend Danto, who as a matter of fact is not mentioned in Levinson's essay.

23. Kendall Walton, "Listening with Imagination: Is Music Representational?" *Journal of Aesthetics and Art Criticism* 52 (1994): 47–61. Some of the points I make here about Walton were made independently by Stephen Davies, "General Theories of Art versus Music," *British Journal of Aesthetics* 34 (1994): 315–25.

24. Walton's general theory is to be found in his *Mimesis as Make Believe: On the Foundations of the Representational Arts* (Cambridge, Mass.: Harvard University Press, 1990).

25. Walton, "Listening with Imagination," p. 51.

26. Ibid.

27. Ibid., p. 52.

28. Ibid.
29. Francis Bacon, *The Advancement of Learning* (1605), in *Critical Essays of the Seventeenth Century*, ed. J. E. Spingarn (Oxford: Oxford University Press, 1957), vol. 1, p. 5.
30. This point is made quite effectively in an article by Thomas Miller with direct reference to Kant. See his "On Listening to Music," *Journal of Aesthetics and Art Criticism* 52 (1994): 215–23. But the general idea is not new and was given a gestalt-psychological account in, for example, Victor Zuckerkandl, *Sound and Symbol: Music and the External World*, trans. Willard R. Trask (New York: Pantheon Books, 1956), and in other of his works.
31. Roger Scruton, "Representation in Music," reprinted in Scruton, *The Aesthetic Understanding* (London: Methuen, 1983), pp. 62–76.
32. Richard Kuhns, "Music as a Representational Art," *British Journal of Aesthetics* 18 (1978): 122.
33. The great complexity of this problem is pursued relentlessly by Paul Grice in his work on meaning. See his *Studies in the Way of Words* (Cambridge, Mass.: Harvard University Press, 1989).

3. Reading and Representation

1. Edmund Burke, *A Philosophical Enquiry into the Origin of Our Ideas of the Sublime and Beautiful*, ed. Adam Phillips (Oxford: Oxford University Press, 1990), p. 157.
2. Plato, *The Republic*, trans. John Llewelyn Davies and David James Vaughan (London: Macmillan Press, 1950), p. 340 (598–9).
3. Ibid., p. 90 (397).
4. Ibid., p. 87 (394).
5. Aristotle, *Poetics*, trans. Richard Janko (Indianapolis: Hackett, 1987), p. 10 (1450b).
6. Paul Thom, *For an Audience: A Philosophy of Performance* (Philadelphia: Temple University Press, 1993), p. 27.
7. Aristotle, *Poetics*, trans. Janko, p. 7 (1449b).
8. Plato, *Republic*, p. 340. "And now, I continued, we must proceed to consider the case of tragedy and its leader, Homer" (598).
9. Aristotle, *Poetics*, trans. Janko, p. 41 (1462b).
10. Aristotle, *The Poetics*, trans. W. Hamilton Fyfe (Cambridge, Mass.: Harvard University Press; London: William Heinemann, The Loeb Classical Library, 1953), p. 115 (1462b); emphasis mine.
11. My colleague Tim Maudlin tells me that he seems to recall the first

reference to silent reading to be in St. Augustine. How widespread it was then, among those who could read at all, I do not know.

12. William Faulkner, *The Hamlet: A Novel of the Snopes Family* (New York: Vintage Books, 1956), p. 95. Having just listed Faulkner as a major exception to the narrative scheme I am dealing with here, I suppose it is necessary to explain why my first example is from Faulkner. The reason is, simply, that many of Faulkner's novels exhibit that scheme. *The Hamlet* does, even though the narrative is peculiarly in Faulkner's style, and more jagged and broken than the typical cases of other authors.

13. R. M. J. Damman, "Emotion in Fiction," *British Journal of Aesthetics* 32 (1992): 19.

14. To keep the record straight, Eula is not a Snopes, but later becomes one by marriage.

15. Joseph Conrad, *The Secret Agent* (Garden City, N.Y.: Doubleday Anchor Books, 1953), pp. 18 and 19.

16. To say that secco recitative has no musical interest in itself is not to say that it has no musical *function*. On this see, Peter Kivy, *Osmin's Rage: Philosophical Reflections on Opera, Drama and Text* (Princeton, N.J.: Princeton University Press, 1988), pp. 153–61.

17. Edward J. Dent, *Opera* (Harmondsworth: Penguin Books, 1949), p. 40.

18. George Eliot, *The Sad Fortunes of the Rev. Amos Barton: Scenes of Clerical Life* (Harmondsworth: Penguin Books, 1973), pp. 53–4.

19. Ibid., p. 54.

20. Charles Dickens, *Bleak House,* ed. Geoffrey Tillotson (New York: Signet Classic, 1980), p. 883.

4. On the Unity of Form and Content

1. A. C. Bradley, "Poetry for Poetry's Sake," in *The Problems of Aesthetics*, ed. Vivas and Krieger, p. 575.

2. Ibid., p. 569. Unfortunately, Bradley is not entirely consistent. In the very last sentence of the note that he appended to the lecture some years after it had been written, he says: "Poetry, whatever its kind, would be pure as far as it preserved the unity of form and content; mixed, so far as it failed to do so – in other words, failed to be poetry and was partly *prosaic*" (ibid., p. 577; my emphasis). This is a disasterous statement and I cannot but think that it was a hasty afterthought rather than a well-considered pronouncement. For if it is combined with Bradley's statements in regard to poetry,

painting, and music, it suggests that he thought poetry, painting, and music are arts, by virtue of exhibiting form–content identity, and no kind of prose whatever could be art, since the implication of the above quotation is that where poetry loses form–content unity, it becomes prose. In other words, prose does not possess, in any form, the necessary condition for being art, namely, form–content identity, since poetry, when it loses that, becomes "prosaic." This is an intolerable conclusion, and I can't believe Bradley could have subscribed to it. (Did he not think the great novels of the nineteenth century were art?)

3. Ibid., p. 573.
4. Lucretius, *De rerum natura,* trans. W. H. D. Rouse and M. F. Smith (Cambridge, Mass.: Harvard University Press; London: William Heinemann, The Loeb Classical Library, 1975), revised by Martin Ferguson Smith, pp. 78–9 (book 1, lines 936–50). Lucretius repeats these lines, almost verbatim, in book 4, lines 1–25.
5. See the *Essay on Criticism.*
6. Kant, *Critique of Judgment,* trans. Pluhar, p. 182.
7. Ibid.
8. Ibid., pp. 181–2.
9. Ibid., pp. 185–8.
10. Ibid., p. 181.
11. Ibid., p. 182.
12. Ibid., p. 184.
13. Ibid., p. 62.
14. Ibid., p. 185.
15. Ibid., p. 196.
16. Unintended, that is to say, under the assumption that Kant was no formalist with regard to art – an assumption I make and that others share.
17. Hanslick, *On the Musically Beautiful,* p. 29.
18. Bradley, "Poetry for Poetry's Sake," p. 572.
19. Walter Pater, "The School of Giorgione," in *The Renaissance: Studies in Art and Poetry,* ed. Donald L. Hill (Berkeley: University of California Press, 1980), p. 106.
20. Ibid., pp. 109, 111, 117, 118. Pater also talks of the various arts as, in individual cases, aspiring toward one another, and Hegel sometimes talks this way too. On the possible Hegelian sources, see the editor's note to "The School of Giorgione" (p. 389). But as the editor remarks, "This famous phrase is not a translation of Hegel, and Hegel never quite makes Pater's point."

21. Ibid., p. 102.
22. Ibid., p. 106.
23. Ibid., p. 109.
24. Bradley, "Poetry for Poetry's Sake," p. 564.
25. Ibid.
26. Ibid., p. 568.
27. Ibid.
28. Ibid., p. 569.
29. Ibid., p. 572.
30. Ibid., p. 565.
31. Ibid., p. 567.
32. Ibid., p. 572.
33. Ibid., p. 576.
34. Ibid., p. 575.
35. Ibid., p. 572.
36. Ibid., p. 574.
37. Ibid., p. 572.
38. Ibid., p. 571.
39. Ibid., p. 575.
40. Ibid., p. 571.
41. Ibid., p. 562; my emphasis.
42. Ibid.
43. Donald Francis Tovey, "A Listener's Guide to *Die Kunst der Fuge*," in *Essays in Musical Analysis: Chamber Music*, ed. Hubert J. Foss (Oxford: Oxford University Press, 1944), p. 76.
44. Bradley, "Poetry for Poetry's Sake," p. 575.
45. Ibid., p. 569.
46. Ibid., p. 667.
47. See note 17.
48. See note 44.
49. Bradley, "Poetry for Poetry's Sake," p. 566.
50. Danto, *The Transfiguration of the Commonplace*, pp. 147–8.

5. The Laboratory of Fictional Truth

1. Peter Lamarque and Stein Haugom Olsen, *Truth, Fiction, and Literature: A Philosophical Perspective* (Oxford: Clarendon Press, 1994), p. 321.
2. Ibid., p. 324.
3. Ibid.
4. Ibid., p. 325.

5. Ibid., p. 334.
6. Ibid., p. 332.
7. Ibid., p. 333.
8. Ibid., p. 332.
9. William James, "The Will to Believe," in *Essays in Pragmatism,* ed. Alburey Castell (New York: Hafner, 1951), p. 89.
10. Ibid.
11. Lamarque and Olsen, *Truth, Fiction, and Literature,* p. 331.
12. Ibid., p. 336.
13. Anyone who thinks I am setting up a straw man here need only consult any number of recent "interpretations" of the canon of absolute music to discover that my made-up interpretation of Beethoven's Fifth is subdued in comparison.
14. Lamarque and Olsen, *Truth, Fiction, and Literature,* p. 450.
15. Ibid., p. 454.
16. Ibid., p. 455.

6. The Quest for Musical Profundity

1. David A. White, "Toward a Theory of Profundity in Music," *Journal of Aesthetics and Art Criticism* 50 (1992): 23. I will have nothing further to say about Professor White's article because, alas, repeated readings of it have failed to reveal to me an intelligible position with which to grapple. Perhaps that is his fault, perhaps it is mine.
2. Aaron Ridley, "Profundity in Music," in *Arguing about Art: Contemporary Philosophical Debates,* ed. Alex Neil and Aaron Ridley (New York: McGraw-Hill, 1995), pp. 260–1.
3. Ibid, p. 261.
4. Ibid.
5. Of course, my book might be ostensibly about bottle caps but really about something profound. And if my book were adequate to that hidden subject matter, then it could be profound.
6. Ridley, "Profundity in Music," p. 263.
7. Ibid.
8. Ibid., p. 264.
9. Ibid.
10. Ibid.
11. Ibid., p. 265.
12. Ibid.
13. Ibid., p. 266.

14. Ibid., pp. 266–7.
15. Ibid., p. 267.
16. Kivy, *Music Alone,* pp. 203 and 214.
17. Ridley, "Profundity of Music," p. 268.
18. Ibid.
19. Ibid.
20. Ibid., p. 269.
21. Ibid.
22. Jerrold Levinson, "Musical Profundity Misplaced," *Journal of Aesthetics and Art Criticism* 50 (1992): 58.
23. Ibid.
24. Ibid., p. 59.
25. Ibid.
26. Jerrold Levinson, "Truth in Music," in *Music, Art and Metaphysics,* ed. Levinson, p. 298.
27. Monroe C. Beardsley, "Understanding Music," in *On Criticizing Music: Five Philosophical Perspectives,* ed. Kingsley Price (Baltimore: Johns Hopkins University Press, 1981), p. 67.
28. Ibid., p. 70.
29. Levinson, "Truth in Music," p. 303.
30. Ibid., p. 301.

7. The Liberation of Music

1. Schopenhauer, *The World as Will and Representation,* vol. 1, p. 256.
2. Ibid.
3. Hans Heinrich Eggebrecht, *J. S. Bach's "The Art of Fugue": The Work and Its Interpretation,* trans. Jeffrey L. Prater (Ames: Iowa State University Press, 1993), pp. xvii–xviii.
4. Ibid.
5. Ibid., p. 6.
7. Ibid.
8. Example from ibid., p. 7.
9. Ibid., p. 8.
10. Ibid.
11. Ibid., p. 30.
12. Ibid., p. 43.
13. Ibid.
14. Rudolph Reti, *The Thematic Process in Music* (London: Faber & Faber, 1961).
15. For my critique of Reti, see *Music Alone,* chap. 7.

16. Eggebrecht, *"Art of Fugue,"* p. 22.
17. Ibid.
18. Ibid., p. 23.
19. David P. Schroeder, *Haydn and the Enlightenment: The Late Symphonies and Their Audience* (Oxford: Clarendon Press, 1990), p. 163. "Toleration" would have been the more usual word in the eighteenth century, but "tolerance" had been used for the same concept as early as the sixteenth century.
20. Ibid., p. 88.
21. Schopenhauer, *The World as Will, and Representation*, vol. 1, p. 196.
22. See, in particular, Peter Kivy, "The Fine Art of Repetition," in *The Fine Art of Repetition*, pp. 327–59.
23. On this see my *Music Alone*, passim, but especially chap. 6.
24. James Hilton, *We Are Not Alone* (Boston: Little, Brown, 1937), p. 158.
25. Plato, *Euthyphro, Apology, Crito, Phaedo, Phaedrus*, trans. H. N. Fowler (Cambridge, Mass., Harvard University Press; London: William Heinemann, The Loeb Classical Library, 1966), pp. 209–11.
26. Leo Treitler, "Postmodern Signs in Musical Studies," *Journal of Musicology*, 13 (1995): 12.

Bibliography

Aristotle. *The Poetics.* Translated by W. Hamilton Fyfe. Cambridge, Mass.: Harvard University Press; London: William Heinemann, The Loeb Classical Library, 1953.

Poetics. Translated by Richard Janko. Indianapolis: Hackett, 1987.

Bell, Clive. *Art.* New York: Capricorn Books, 1958.

Old Friends. London: Cassell, 1988.

Burke, Edmund. *A Philosophical Enquiry into the Origin of Our Ideas of the Sublime and Beautiful.* Edited by Adam Phillips. Oxford: Oxford University Press, 1990.

Carroll, Noel. "Historical Narrations and the Philosophy of Art." *Journal of Aesthetics and Art Criticism* 51 (1993): 313–26.

Conrad, Joseph. *The Secret Agent.* Garden City, N.Y.: Doubleday Anchor Books, 1953.

Damman, R. M. J. "Emotion in Fiction." *British Journal of Aesthetics* 32 (1992): 13–20.

Danto, Arthur. *The Transfiguration of the Commonplace: A Philosophy of Art.* Cambridge, Mass.: Harvard University Press, 1981.

Davies, Stephen. "General Theories of Art versus Music." *British Journal of Aesthetics* 34 (1994): 315–25.

Dent, Edward. *Opera.* Harmondsworth: Penguin Books, 1949.

Dickens, Charles. *Bleak House.* Edited by Geoffrey Tillotson. New York: Signet Classic, 1980.

Dickie, George, Richard Sclafani, and Ronald Roblin, eds. *Aesthetics: A Critical Anthology.* 2d ed. New York: St. Martin's Press, 1989.

Eco, Umberto. *Art and Beauty in the Middle Ages.* Translated by Hugh Bredin. New Haven, Conn.: Yale University Press, 1986.

Eggebrecht, Hans Heinrich. *J. S. Bach's "The Art of Fugue": The Work and Its Interpretation.* Translated by Jeffrey L. Prater. Ames: Iowa State University Press, 1993.

Bibliography

Eliot, George. *The Sad Fortunes of the Rev. Amos Barton: Scenes from Clerical Life.* Harmondsworth: Penguin Books, 1973.

Faulkner, William. *The Hamlet: A Novel of the Snopes Family.* New York: Vintage Books, 1956.

Fry, Roger. *Transformations.* Garden City, N.Y.: Doubleday Anchor Books, 1956.

Vision and Design. New York: Meridian Books, 1960.

Grice, Paul. *Studies in the Way of Words.* Cambridge, Mass.: Harvard University Press, 1989.

Gurney, Edmund. *The Power of Sound.* London: Smith, Elder, 1980.

Hanslick, Eduard. *On the Musically Beautiful: A Contribution towards the Revision of the Aesthetics of Music.* Translated by Geoffrey Payzant. Indianapolis: Hackett, 1980.

Hegel, G. W. F. *Aesthetics: Lectures on the Fine Arts.* Translated by T. M. Knox. 2 vols. Oxford: Clarendon Press, 1975.

Werke in Zwanzig Bänden. 20 vols. Frankfurt am Main: Suhnkamp, 1970.

Hilton, James. *We Are Not Alone.* Boston: Little, Brown, 1937.

Hutcheson, Francis. *Inquiry Concerning Beauty, Order, Harmony, Design.* Edited by Peter Kivy. The Hague: Martinus Nijhoff, 1973.

James, William. *Essays in Pragmatism.* Edited by Alburey Castell. New York: Hafner, 1951.

Kant, Immanuel. *Anthropology from a Pragmatic Point of View.* Translated by Mary J. Gregory. The Hague: Martinus Nijhoff, 1974.

Critique of Aesthetic Judgement. Translated by James Creed Meredith. Oxford: Clarendon Press, 1911.

Critique of Judgement. Translated by J. H. Bernard. New York: Hafner, 1961.

Critique of Judgment. Translated by Werner S. Pluhar. Indianapolis: Hackett, 1987.

Kivy, Peter. *The Fine Art of Repetition: Essays in the Philosophy of Music.* Cambridge University Press, 1993.

Music Alone: Philosophical Reflections on the Purely Musical Experience. Ithaca, N.Y.: Cornell University Press, 1990.

Osmin's Rage: Philosophical Reflections on Opera, Drama and Text. Princeton, N.J.: Princeton University Press, 1988.

The Seventh Sense: A Study of Francis Hutcheson's Aesthetics and Its Place in Eighteenth-Century Britain. New York: Burt Franklin, 1976.

Kivy, Peter, ed. *Essays on the History of Aesthetics.* Rochester, N.Y.: University of Rochester Press, 1992.

Kuhns, Richard. "Music as a Representational Art." *British Journal of Aesthetics* 18 (1978): 120–5.

Lamarque, Peter, and Stein Haugom Olsen. *Truth, Fiction, and Literature: A Philosophical Perspective.* Oxford: Clarendon Press, 1994.

Levinson, Jerrold. *Music, Art and Metaphysics: Essays in Philosophical Aesthetics.* Ithaca, N.Y.: Cornell University Press, 1990.

"Musical Profundity Misplaced." *Journal of Aesthetics and Art Criticism* 50 (1992): 58–60.

Lucretius. *De rerum natura.* Translated by W. H. D. Rouse and M. F. Smith. Cambridge, Mass.: Harvard University Press; London: William Heinemann, The Loeb Classical Library, 1975.

Margolis, Joseph, ed. *Philosophy Looks at the Arts.* 3d ed. Philadelphia: Temple University Press, 1987.

McEwin, Indra Kagis. *Socrates' Ancestor: An Essay on Architectural Beginnings.* Cambridge, Mass.: MIT Press, 1993.

Miller, Thomas. "On Listening to Music." *Journal of Aesthetics and Art Criticism* 52 (1994): 215–23.

Moyer, Ann E. *Musica Sacra: Musical Scholarship in the Italian Renaissance.* Ithaca, N.Y.: Cornell University Press, 1992.

Neil, Alex, and Aaron, Ridley, eds. *Arguing about Art: Contemporary Philosophical Debates.* New York: McGraw-Hill, 1995.

Pater, Walter. *The Renaissance: Studies in Art and Poetry.* Edited by Donald L. Hill. Berkeley: University of California Press, 1980.

Plato. *Ion.* Translated by W. R. M. Lamb. Cambridge, Mass.: Harvard University Press; London: William Heinemann, The Loeb Classical Library, 1962.

Enthyphro, Apology, Crito, Phaido, Phaedrus. Translated by H. N. Fowler. Cambridge, Mass.: Harvard University Press; London, William Heinemann, The Loeb Classical Library, 1966.

The Republic. Translated by John Llewelyn Davies and David James Vaughan. London: Macmillan Press, 1950.

Price, Kingsley, ed. *On Criticizing Music: Five Philosophical Perspectives.* Baltimore: Johns Hopkins University Press, 1981.

Reid, Thomas. *The Works of Thomas Reid.* Edited by Sir William Hamilton. 8th ed. 2 vols. Edinburgh: James Thin, 1895.

Reti, Rudolph. *The Thematic Process in Music.* London: Faber & Faber, 1961.

Schopenhauer, Arthur. *The World as Will and Representation.* Translated by E. F. J. Payne. 2 vols. Indian Hills, Colo.: Falcon's Wing Press, 1958.

Bibliography

Schroeder, David P. *Haydn and the Enlightenment: The Late Symphonies and Their Audience.* Oxford: Clarendon Press, 1990.

Scruton, Roger. *The Aesthetic Understanding.* London: Methuen, 1983.

Spingarn, J. E., ed. *Critical Essays of the Seventeenth Century.* 3 vols. Oxford: Oxford University Press, 1957.

Stewart, Dugald. *Works.* 7 vols. Cambridge: Hilliard & Brown, 1829.

Stolnitz, Jerome. "On the Origins of Aesthetic Disinterestedness." *Journal of Aesthetics and Art Criticism* 20 (1961): 131–44.

Strunk, Oliver, ed. *Source Readings in Music History.* New York: Norton, 1950.

Summers, David. *The Judgment of Taste: Renaissance Naturalism and the Rise of Aesthetics.* Cambridge University Press, 1987.

Thom, Paul. *For an Audience: A Philosophy of Performance.* Philadelphia: Temple University Press, 1993.

Tovey, Donald Francis. *Essays in Musical Analysis: Chamber Music.* Edited by Humbert J. Foss. Oxford: Oxford University Press, 1944.

Treitler, Leo. "Postmodern Signs in Musical Studies." *Journal of Musicology* 13 (1995): 3–17.

Uehling, Theodore E., Jr. *The Notion of Form in Kant's "Critique of Aesthetic Judgment."* The Hague: Mouton, 1971.

Vivas, Eliseo, and Murray Krieger, eds. *The Problems of Aesthetics: A Book of Readings.* New York: Holt, Rinehart, & Winston, 1960.

Walton, Kendall. "Listening with Imagination: Is Music Representational?" *Journal of Aesthetics and Art Criticism* 52 (1994): 47–62.

Mimesis as Make Believe: On the Foundations of the Representational Arts. Cambridge, Mass.: Harvard University Press, 1990.

White, David A. "Toward a Theory of Musical Profundity." *Journal of Aesthetics and Art Criticism* 50 (1992): 23–34.

Wittkower, Rudolf. *Architectural Principles in the Age of Humanism.* London: Alec Tiranti, 1962.

Ziff, Paul. "The Task of Defining a Work of Art." *Philosophical Review* 62 (1953): 58–78.

Zuckerkandl, Victor. *Sound and Symbol: Music and the External World.* Translated by Willard R. Trask. New York: Pantheon Books, 1956.

Index

Index

harmony, 10–11
Hart, Lorenz, 179
Hart, Moss, 206
Haydn, Joseph, 7, 22–3, 168, 177, 184, 194–202, 210–11
Hegel, Georg William Friedrich, 17, 19–24, 53, 222n, 227n
Henry, Patrick, 155
Hilton, James, 209, 231n
Hobbes, Thomas, 202
Homer, 65, 67, 69, 93
Hotho, G. H., 222n
Hume, David, 127, 199
Hutcheson, Francis, ix, 4, 10–11, 221n
hypothesis verification, in literature, 135–6, 138–9

Ibsen, Henrik, 67
imagination: constructive, 47–9; fictional, 47–9; and music, 47–9
ineffable content, 113–14
instrumental music, *see* absolute music

James, William, 126, 135, 229n
Janko, Richard, 225n
Jefferson, Thomas, 198
Josquin Des Prez, 151
Joyce, James, 173

Kant, Immanuel, 2, 12–17, 23, 47, 91–6, 111, 128, 144, 147, 177, 199, 221n, 222n, 225n, 227n; on free play, 16, 94–6; on genius, 91–3; rational ideas in, 91; spirit in, 91–2
Kaufmann, George, 206
Kivy, Peter, 140, 143–6, 157–8, 160–2, 220n, 221n, 222n, 223n, 226n, 230n, 231n
Knox, T. M., 21–3, 222n
Krieger, Murray, 223n, 226n

Kristeller, Paul Oskar, 2–5, 41, 220n
Kuhns, Richard, 49–52, 225n

Lamarque, Peter, 120–39, 228n, 229n
Lamb, W. R. M., 220n
Lattimore, Richmond, 105
Levinson, Jerrold, x–xi, 43–4, 146, 162–76, 184, 224n, 230n
liberation of music, 204–5, 209–17
Liszt, Franz, 167
literary criticism, 122–6
literature: appreciation of, 124–6, 128–35; content of, 201; general thematic statements in, 121–2; hypothesis verification in, 135–6, 138–9; and music, 142–3; perennial themes in, 136–7; propositional theory of, 121; value of, 179–80
live hypotheses, 126–7
Locke, John, 58–60, 196
Lucretius, 87–90, 107, 114–15, 227n

Mahler, Gustav, 167
Mandelbaum, Maurice, 38
Manet, Edouard, 24
Manns, James, 221n
Margolis, Joseph, 224n
mathematics, 210
Maudlin, Tim, 225n
McCarthy, Senator Joseph, 190
McEwin, Indra Kagis, 220n
Melville, Herman, 61
Mendelssohn, Felix, 167
Meredith, James Creed, 13, 221n, 222n
Meyer, Leonard, 195
Michelangelo, 206
Miller, Arthur, 67
Miller, Thomas, 225n
Milton, John, 129